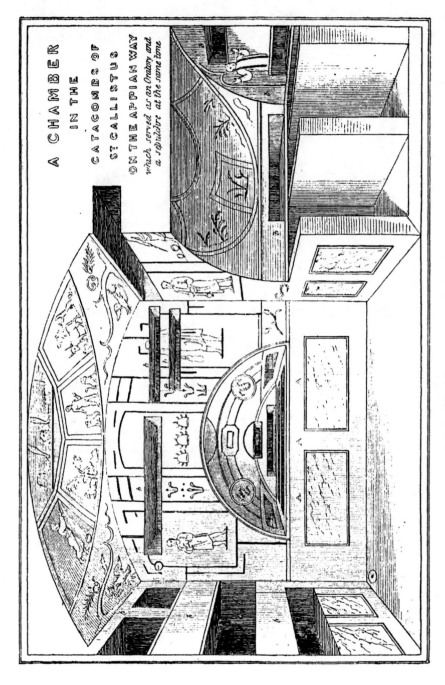

A CHAMBER

IN THE

CATACOMBS OF

ST. CALLISTUS

ON THE APPIAN WAY

which served as an Oratory and
a sepulchre at the same time

A.A.A. *The Altar over the tomb of a Martyr.*

b. b. b. *Niches pierced in the walls through the fresco-paintings to receive the bodies of the Martyrs.*

HIERURGIA;

OR,

THE HOLY SACRIFICE OF THE MASS.

WITH NOTES AND DISSERTATIONS

ELUCIDATING

ITS DOCTRINES AND CEREMONIES,

AND NUMEROUS ILLUSTRATIONS.

By DANIEL ROCK, D.D.

Third Edition, Revised

By W. H. JAMES WEALE.

VOLUME II.

JOHN HODGES,

AGAR STREET, CHARING CROSS, LONDON.

1892.

CONTENTS OF VOL. II.

———◆———

CHAPTER VIII.

ON CEREMONIES.

CHAPTER IX.

ON THE CROSS.

CHAPTER XIII.

OF BLESSED OR HOLY WATER.

CHAPTER XIV.

ON THE CREED.

APPENDIX I.

APPENDIX II.

APPENDIX III.

APPENDIX IV.

LIST OF ILLUSTRATIONS.

VOL. II.

PART II.

CHAPTER VI.

ON RELICS.

FROM ascertaining the doctrine of the Church as to the invocation of saints, we are led, by a natural transition, to enquire what she teaches concerning their relics—that is to say, those existing portions of the mortal remains, clothing, and personal belongings of those amongst the followers of Jesus who were saints whilst dwelling amid men, and are now in heaven in a state of glory.

I.—THE CATHOLIC CHURCH PAYS A RELIGIOUS RESPECT TO RELICS.

The Catholic believes that God alone is the object of his worship and adoration; yet he conceives that, without detracting anything from that supreme homage due to the Divinity, he may manifest a becoming reverence towards the relics of the saints; and he observes, in the language of the Council of Trent, 'that the bodies of holy martyrs, and of others now living with Christ, which were the members of Christ, and the temple of the Holy Spirit, and which shall be raised by Him to eternal life, and be glorified, are to be venerated by the faithful.'[1]

II.—RESPECT FOR RELICS AUTHORISED BY SCRIPTURE.

The proofs for such a doctrine are easily collected from Holy Scripture. That God has oftentimes imparted a virtue to the relics of His faithful servants is certain.

III.—VIRTUE POSSESSED BY SAINTS' RELICS.

It is recorded in the fourth book of Kings,[2] that when Eliseus struck the waters of Jordan with the mantle of Elias, they parted and the prophet passed over; and again, when a dead man was let down into the sepulchre of Eliseus, no sooner did he touch the bones of the prophet than he came to life, and stood upon his feet.[3]

---

[1] Mandat sancta Synodus omnibus episcopis, et caeteris docendi munus curamque sustinentibus, ut . . . fideles diligenter instruant, . . . sanctorum martyrum, et aliorum cum Christo viventium sancta corpora, quae viva membra fuerunt Christi (1 *Cor.* III, 16, et VI, 19), et templum Spiritus Sancti, ab Ipso ad aeternam vitam suscitanda et glorificanda, a fidelibus (S. HIERONYMUS *adversus Vigilantium*), veneranda esse.—*Concilium Tridentinum*, Sessio XXV.

[2] 4 *Kings*, II, 14.   [3] *Ibid.*, XIII, 21.

The healing virtues possessed by the garments of our Blessed Redeemer are particularly noticed: 'And, behold, a woman, who was troubled with an issue of blood twelve years, came behind Him, and touched the hem of His garment. For she said within herself: If I shall touch only His garment, I shall be healed. But Jesus turning and seeing her, said: Be of good heart, daughter, thy faith hath made thee whole. And the woman was made whole from that hour.' [1] The Almighty was pleased to allow a similar efficacy not only to the garments, but even to the shadows of His delegated ministers, the Apostles, for we read that, 'the multitude of men and women who believed in the Lord, was more increased, insomuch that they brought forth the sick into the streets, and laid them on beds and couches, that when Peter came, his shadow, at the least, might overshadow any of them, and they might be delivered from their infirmities . . . who were all healed.' [2] 'And God wrought by the hand of Paul more than common miracles; so that even there were brought from his body to the sick handkerchiefs and aprons, and the diseases departed from them, and the wicked spirits went out of them.' [3]

---

[1] *S. Matthew*, IX, 20–22. [2] *Acts*, V, 14–16.
[3] *Ibid.*, XIX, 11, 12.

IV.—A REVERENCE FOR THEM EXEMPLIFIED BY SCRIPTURE.

The veneration which has invariably been exhibited, from the earliest ages up to the present moment, by the Church to the remains or relics of the martyrs and the saints, is warranted by a variety of examples recorded in the Bible. On going out of Egypt, Moses was careful to comply with the dying request of holy Joseph, and took along with him that venerable patriarch's bones, to secure for them honourable sepulture in the land of promise.[1] Josias, who did that which was 'right in the sight of the Lord,' though he demolished the high places erected to Astaroth, the idol of the Sidonians, and to Chamos, the scandal of Moab; though he broke in pieces the statues, cut down the groves, and overturned the altars of idolatry; though, when he 'saw the sepulchres that were in the mount, he sent and took the bones out of the sepulchres, and burned them;' yet, amid all this, we observe this zealous and religious king making the following enquiry, and issuing the following orders: 'What is that monument which I see? And the men of the city answered: It is the sepulchre of the man of God, who came from Juda. . . . And he said: Let him alone, let no man move his

---

[1] *Exodus*, XIII, 19.

bones. So his bones were left untouched with the bones of the prophet that came out of Samaria.'[1]

V.—SHOWN BY THE FIRST CHRISTIANS.

That these examples were not thrown away upon the primitive Christians is evidenced by numerous and highly interesting proofs.

VI.—BY CARRYING OFF THE REMAINS OF THE MARTYRS.

The pious solicitude manifested in the times of persecution by the faithful, to rescue the mutilated bodies of their martyred brethren from the insults and contumely of the Pagans, is attested by a crowd of ancient and venerable authorities.

In the History of the Church by Eusebius is a letter from the Church of Smyrna, in which, after giving an account of the martyrdom of S. Polycarp, their bishop, the Smyrnians observe: ' Our subtle enemy, the devil, did his utmost that we should not take away the body, as many of us anxiously wished. It was suggested that we should desert our crucified Master, and begin to worship Polycarp. Foolish men ! who know not that we can never desert Christ, who died for the salvation of all men, nor worship any other. Him we adore as the Son of God ; but we show deserved respect

---

[1] 4 *Kings,* XXIII, 17, 18.

to the martyrs, as His disciples and followers. The centurion, therefore, caused the body to be burnt. We then gathered his bones, more precious than pearls, and more tried than gold, and buried them. In this place, God willing, we will meet, and celebrate with joy and gladness the birthday of His martyr, as well in memory of those who have been crowned before, as, by his example, to prepare and strengthen others for the combat.'[1]

VII.—BY COLLECTING EVERYTHING STAINED WITH THEIR BLOOD.

Such was the zeal of the early Christians in this regard, that they frequently purchased, by a bribe, the connivance of the guards to collect and carry off the scattered members of the Christian champions; and obtained, at considerable sums of money, those several instruments[2] which had

---

[1] EUSEBII *Hist. Eccl.*, lib. IV, cap. XV, pp. 170, 171. See BERINGTON and KIRK, *The Faith of Catholics.* London, 1830, p. 413.

[2] Several of those instruments, employed by the Gentile persecutors of the infant Christian Church for the laceration and torture of the martyrs' bodies, have come down to us, and are still preserved with particular respect in the churches and cabinets of Christian antiquities at Rome. They are made either of bronze or iron, and are variously fashioned in the shape of gloves, claws, hooks, combs, and whips. To these may be added certain large orbicular stones having rings fastened in them; all of which are accurately delineated after the originals in the accompanying plate. No. 1 exhibits an iron glove, which was discovered in that part of the Roman catacombs denominated the cemetery of Calepodius. (See ARINGHI, *Roma Subterranea*, tom. II, p. 687.) Its fingers are curved inwards and sharp at the extremities. No. 2 represents an iron hook, which

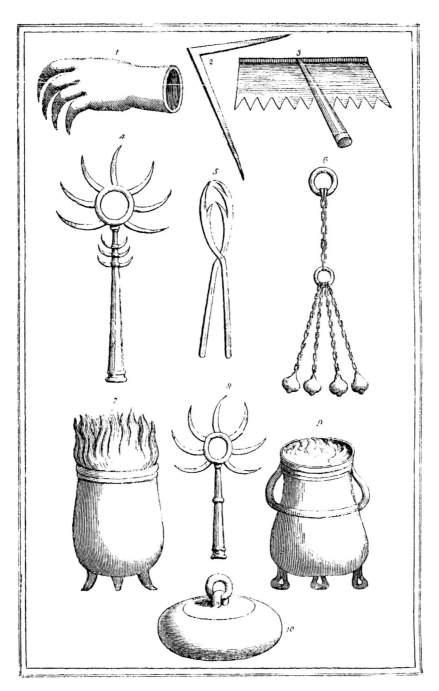

*Instruments of Martyrdom found at Rome in the Catacombs most of
them preserved at S. Peters and in the Vatican Library.*

been used by the public executioner for the purpose of inflicting death or torture on any of the

---

was found inserted in a martyr's head in the cemetery of S. Agnes. (See MAMACHI, *Origines et Antiquitates Christianae*, tom. III, p. 205.) No. 3 describes an iron comb which is now preserved in the convent of S. Mary Magdalene on the Quirinal Hill, belonging to the Dominican nuns. Boldetti (p. 319) and Mamachi (tom. III, p. 205) severally speak of it. Nos. 4 and 8 represent two instruments of martyrdom at present in the Museum of Christian Antiquities at the Vatican library, and bear a resemblance to the talons of a bird of prey. No. 5 is a figure of the double claws which were found during the pontificate of Paul III., and are now kept amongst the relics at S. Peter's. Similar claws, though smaller, are preserved at the church of S. Cecilia in Trastevere. They are a species of forceps or pincers, and were known by the name of 'ungulae bisulcae,' under which appellation they are designated by Prudentius (Περὶ Στεφάνων liber, Hymnus I, v. 87-90) when he says—

> Illa (*fides*) virgas, et secures,
>   et bisulcas ungulas
> ultro fortis expetebat,
>   Christi amore interrita.

And in another place where that poet beautifully observes, in describing the same ardour of the primitive Christians to undergo the pains of martyrdom—

> Amor coronae pene praevenit trucem
> lictoris artem, sponte nudas offerens
> costas, bisulcis exsecandas ungulis.
>   Περὶ Στεφάνων liber, Hymnus X, v. 71-73.

No. 6 represents a whip made of iron-wire chains, loaded at the ends with knobs of bronze, now preserved in the Christian Museum at the Vatican library. Sometimes this instrument of punishment was made of thongs on which were knotted leaden pellets, and is thus referred to by Prudentius:

> Tundatur, inquit, tergum crebris ictibus,
> plumboque cervix verberata extuberet:
>
> . . . . . .
>
> Pulsatus ergo martyr illa grandine,
> postquam inter ictus dixit hymnum plumbeos.
>   Περὶ Στεφάνων liber, Hymnus X, v. 115-121.

Nos. 7 and 9 represent two cauldrons which are frequently sculptured on the sepulchres of the martyrs, and are enumerated by Mamachi

faithful.[1] Pious females used to mingle in the crowd of spectators, in order to tinge their hand-kerchiefs in the holy victims' blood, and employ sponges to imbibe from the ground as much of it as possible. The blood so collected was after-wards pressed into small vitreous or earthen vases, and deposited, together with the body of the Christian hero, in the catacombs. This is

---

and others writers amongst the instruments of torture. No. 7 is copied from the one inscribed on the marble slab over the tomb of S. Victorina in the cemetery of Cyriaca, and is accompanied by this inscription—

BICTORINA IN PACE ET IN ☧

No. 9 is taken from another sepulchral marble, which closes up the niche in which reposes the body of S. Exsuperantius in the cemetery of Callistus, and has on one side of it EXVPERANTIVS IN PACE. These cauldrons were filled with boiling oil, pitch, or wax, into which the martyr was immersed. (BOLDETTI, p. 318, and MAMACHI, tom. III, p. 213.) No. 10 is an orbicular stone, with a ring fastened in the centre; many of these have been discovered in the catacombs, and some are shown in the churches at Rome. That such stones served the double purpose of weights for traffic and instruments of punishment would seem evident from the remarks of Boldetti. He asserts that several have been found with figures indicative of their respective value, and he proves that the lictors and public executioners at Rome were allowed, by the laws of the twelve tables, to punish culprits by hanging such weights to them. 'Vincito, aut nervo, aut compedibus quindecim pondo non minore, aut si volet maiore, maiore vincito.' (*Lib. XII Tabular.*, quoted by BOLDETTI, p. 520.) The martyrs were frequently left hanging by the arms, with weights attached to their feet; when drowning was their punishment they were precipitated into the Tiber with one of these stones suspended about the neck or fastened to their feet.

[1] The public executioner was frequently invited to sell even his own garments that had been stained with the blood of the martyrs. —*Acta S. Adriani et sociorum Martyrum,* quoted by BOLDETTI, p. 131.

attested in part by Prudentius, who makes the following allusions to this office of religious veneration :[1]

> Those crimson dews, from martyr's heart that ran,
> are rescued from th' unhallow'd tread of man

---

[1] Περὶ Στεφάνων *liber*, *Hymnus XI*, v. 141–144. The document from which Prudentius drew his information on this subject is as curious as it is valuable and interesting. It was no other than a fresco which adorned the walls of the chapel in the Roman catacombs in which the body of S. Hippolytus was deposited. This painting was quite perfect in the days of the poet, and he has furnished us with a most minute description of it in the hymn which he composed in honour of that martyr, who was put to death by being torn to pieces by wild horses. The name of this saint suggested this sentence to the Roman prefect, who, on learning it, exclaimed, 'Then like Hippolytus let him be dragged by wild horses!' The reader will recollect the story related by Ovid (*Metam.* lib. xv, fab. 14) concerning the fabulous son of Theseus, Hippolytus, who, falling over his chariot, and getting entangled in the harness of his own affrighted horses, was dragged along by them until he was dashed to pieces. The furious horses bounded off with the body of the saint trailing behind them. They dashed through brooks and over rocks and briars, they beat down hedges and everything they encountered on the road. The stones, the thorns were besprinkled with his blood, the ground was strewn with fragments of his mutilated body : these the faithful afterwards reverently gathered up, collecting what drops of blood they could with sponges. With weeping eyes they most carefully scrutinised the ground, picking up every portion of the martyr's remains, which they deposited in the catacombs. Such was the scene that formed the subject of the picture thus described by Prudentius :—

> Picta super tumulum species liquidis viget umbris,
>   effigians tracti membra cruenta viri.
> Rorantes saxorum apices vidi, optime Papa,
>   purpureasque notas vepribus impositas.
> Docta manus virides imitando effingere dumos,
>   luserat, e minio roseolam saniem.
> Cernere erat, ruptis compagibus, ordine nullo
>   membra per incertos sparsa iacere situs.
> Addiderat charos, gressu, lachrymisque sequentes,
>   devia qua fractum semita monstrat iter.

By pious brethren, who with linen band
wipe up the gore that stains the thirsty strand.
What blood that, reeking, on the club may stay,
a sponge impress'd will gently sip away.

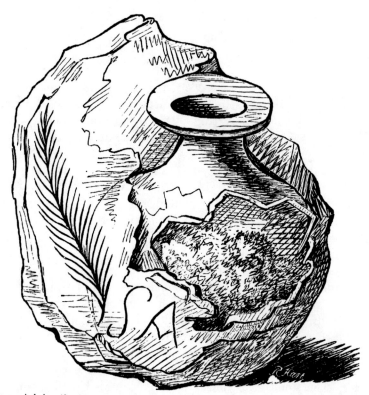

Vase containing the blood of a martyr, and the sponge by which it had been imbibed from the ground. See BOLDETTI, pp. 186, 187. The vase was imbedded in mortar, on which was scratched a palm-branch, with SA, the contraction of the word *sanguis* (blood).

Moerore attoniti, atque oculis rimantibus ibant,
    implebantque sinus visceribus laceris.
Ille caput niveum complectitur, ac reverendam
    canitiem molli confovet in gremio.
Hic humeros, truncasque manus, et brachia, et ulnas,
    et genua, et crurum fragmina nuda legit.
Palliolis etiam bibulae siccantur arenae,
    ne quis in infecto pulvere ros maneat
si quis et in sudibus recalenti aspergine sanguis
    insidet, hunc omnem spongia pressa rapit.

And again, while describing the martyrdom of S. Vincent, the poet says :

> Plerique vestem linteam
> stillante tingunt sanguine,
> tutamen ut sacrum suis
> domi reservent posteris.[1]

> Crowds haste the linen vest to stain
> with gore distilled from martyr's vein,
> and, thus, a holy safeguard place
> at home, to shield their future race.

In the catacombs [2] of Rome are daily discovered the tombs of the ancient martyrs, distinguished from the sepulchres of their brethren around them by a palm-branch,[3] or some other Christian

---

If other proofs were wanting, such a pious anxiety, depicted by the pencil of the painter and the pen of the poet, as manifested by the early Christians to collect the remains of S. Hippolytus, would alone be sufficient to demonstrate their religious veneration for the relics of martyrs.

[1] Περὶ Στεφάνων liber, *Hymnus V*, v. 341-344.

[2] Among the most celebrated of these catacombs were those belonging to SS. Praxedes and Pudentiana, daughters of Pudens the Roman senator, who, with his whole family, was converted to the faith by the apostles SS. Peter and Paul. These ladies, sisters in faith and holiness, as well as according to the flesh, expended their patrimony in yielding succour to the martyrs while in chains—in employing persons to rescue their remains from profanation—in giving them an honourable interment in those catacombs under their estate upon the Salarian Way, where they themselves were afterwards buried, and upon the enlarging and arranging of which they had expended much money. For some observations on the Roman catacombs in general the reader may consult Appendix IV.

[3] The multitude, which no man could number, that S. John saw standing before the throne of the Lamb, clothed in white, held palms in their hands. *Apocalypse*, VII, 9. For some other observations on the palm-branch, see the note on p. 328 of volume I. The dove,

hieroglyphic, inscribed on the tablet that seals
them up; but more particularly by the vase of
blood, which was usually inserted in the wall

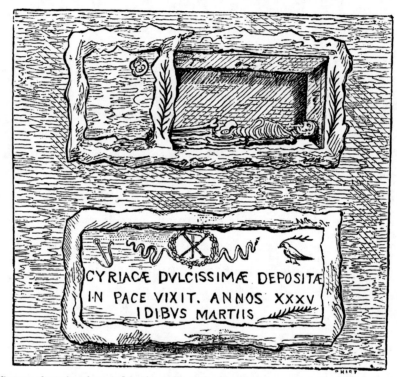

Graves of martyrs inserted in the walls of the Roman catacombs.—BOLDETTI, p. 213.

outside the horizontal excavation in which was
deposited the body of the martyr.[1]   The reason

---

another Christian emblem, will be noticed in chap. VII (see p. 82,
note 2); and the monogram ☧ is explained in chap. IX (see p. 129,
note 1).   These three symbols, together with the anchor, which
interprets itself as indicative of pious hope, are all discernible on
the lower of the two sepulchres exhibited in the woodcut.

[1] The graves in the catacombs of Rome were not, like ours, in the
ground, and liable to be trodden on, but were horizontal niches,
pierced in regular rows, like shelves, one above the other, in the
sides of the passages and subterranean labyrinths resorted to by the

assigned for such a custom is, that the primitive Christians, admonished by S. John in his book of the Apocalypse, regarded the martyrs as those 'who are come out of great tribulation, and have washed their robes, and have made them white in the blood of the Lamb;'[1] and who are, in fine, those blessed spirits of whom the same Evangelist observes: 'I saw under the altar the souls of them that were slain for the word of God, and for the testimony which they held. And they cried with a loud voice, saying: How long, O Lord (holy and true), dost Thou not judge and revenge our blood?'[2] Those ardent believers, therefore, zealously strove to procure some relic of the martyrs, which should be to them and to their household—to use the expression of Prudentius—'Tutamen sacrum,' a hallowed safe-guard and a visible pledge that those happy souls were making intercession, through the merits of the Saviour, for them and their families. So ardent was this fervour that it influenced many to attend at the execution of the martyrs, and to spread out their garments to catch, if possible, some drops of that blood belonging to those

---

primitive Christians in the time of persecution, for the triple purpose of concealment, of burying the bodies of the faithful, and of solemnising the Eucharistic sacrifice. The present and the following chapter, but especially the works of Aringhi, Boldetti, Seroux d'Agincourt, Bottari, Rossi, and Northcote and Brownlow, exhibit several engravings representing the catacombs as they now exist.

[1] *Apocalypse*, VII, 14.   [2] *Ibid.*, VI, 9, 10.

heroes of Christianity; and illustrious matrons were known to exchange the most costly jewels for a garment which had been sprinkled with it. But such zeal must have exposed a number of Christians to detection, and subjected them to the self-same tortures as had been inflicted on those for whose remains they exhibited so much veneration. To prevent all unnecessary exposure, and at the same time to encourage and gratify this laudable respect towards the combatants of Christ, it was recommended by the ecclesiastical authorities, that whatever blood of the martyrs was or might be collected by individual courage or address, should be deposited in vases affixed to their tombs, for the common benefit, in such a manner that the faithful might in security tinge their handkerchiefs with the precious gore, and carry it home as a glorious and invaluable relic.[1]

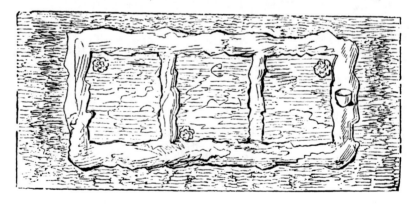

A grave in the wall of the catacombs with a vase containing the martyr's blood attached outside of it.—BOLDETTI, p. 213.

[1] See the observations of the learned prelate Bianchini, in his annotations to ANASTASIUS Bibliothecarius, *De Vitis Rom. Pont,* tom. II, p. 244. Romae, 1723.

VIII.—BY THE CUSTOM OF USING THE MARTYRS'
TOMBS AS ALTARS.

There is another and most important custom,
introduced amongst the faithful in the very first
ages of Christianity and practised ever since,
that clearly demonstrates the religious reverence
which, from the earliest antiquity to the present
time, has been unceasingly exhibited by the
Church to the relics of the saints. That the
primitive Christians were accustomed to erect
their altars, for the celebration of the unbloody
sacrifice of the Mass, upon the tombs of the
martyrs, is certain. This is demonstrated not only
by the descriptions of the Christian cemeteries
which we have in ancient authors, but by the
ocular proofs that are obvious to the world in
many of those very altars still extant in the Roman
catacombs, and accessible to the traveller.[1]

---

[1] Engravings of these altars may be seen in any of the authors on
the Roman catacombs: Bosio, Aringhi, Boldetti, Bottari, etc. One
of these altars, copied from the *Roma Sotterrnaea* of Bottari, is given
in Plate on opposite page. Seroux d'Agincourt has published one,
which he found in 1780, in the cemetery of S. Hermes situated just
outside the walls of Rome, on the Salarian Way. After enumerating
the paintings around this sepulchre, and noticing how it was excavated in the tufa, like a niche, in the shape of a segment of a
circle, and hence denominated by ecclesiastical writers, 'monu-
mentum arcuatum,' this profound antiquary observes: 'In the
midst of those venerable symbols, on a large slab of marble which
completely covered the sarcophagus of S. Hermes, prefect of Rome,
martyred in the second century, the first ministers of the Christian
worship celebrated the mysteries of our faith in the time of per-

Whether S. John, in his Apocalypse (vi, 9) —where he thus details his vision of the mystic sacrifice in heaven : 'I saw under the altar the souls of them that were slain for the word of God, and for the testimony which they held'—referred to the custom as already established, of making the tombs of the martyrs serve for altars, or whether those words suggested to the first believers the propriety of introducing such an observance, this passage in the writings of the beloved disciple is equally precious and well adapted to elucidate the practice. In one instance it will show its antiquity ; in the other, its scriptural origin. Amongst the early Christian writers there are two, S. Paulinus of Nola and Prudentius,[1] whose testimony on this point is of intrinsic value, not only from its being curiously interesting, but because it is so full and unequivocal ; and the monuments which these authors

---

secution. Seroux d'Agincourt, *Histoire de l'Art par les Monumens.* Paris, 1823, tom. I, p. 25, and pl. XII.

Most of the entrances into the Roman catacombs have been, for some years past, closed up to the public, on account of several persons, who would stray from their guides, having lost themselves and perished in these inextricable windings. Anyone, however, may readily procure an admittance into almost every one of the cemeteries, by applying to the proper quarter. Many of the most ancient and celebrated churches owe their origin to these altars on the martyrs' tombs in the catacombs. Instead of translating the bodies of S. Peter, S. Laurence, and several other distinguished martyrs, their respective churches were erected, and still remain, just over the spot in which they were first deposited in the cemeteries.

[1] Concerning the period when they flourished, and the different works they wrote, consult the notes at p. 321 of vol. I.

describe were perfectly entire at the epoch when they noticed them. In one of his letters addressed to Severus, S. Paulinus encloses some verses of his own composition, which were to be inscribed over the altar under which was deposited the body of S. Clare, of whom the venerable prelate says :

Sancta sub aeternis altaribus ossa quiescunt.[1]

Epist. XXXII, ad Severum.

His holy bones 'neath lasting altars rest.

After describing the Basilica of Nola, the saint proceeds to give a sketch of another but smaller church, which he had just erected in the town of Fondi,[2] and says that 'sacred ashes—some of the blessed relics of the apostles and martyrs—shall consecrate this little basilica also in the name of Christ, the Saint of saints, the Martyr of martyrs, and the Lord of lords.[3] For Christ has testified

---

[1] S. Paulinus, in several other verses, mentions the fact of S. Clare's body having been entombed under the altar.

Digna pio domus est altaria, sub quibus artus
conditur examinos ; nam spiritus aethere gaudet.

. . . .

Clare fide, praeclare actu, clarissime fructu,
 qui meritis titulum nominis aequiparas,
casta tuum digne velant altaria corpus
 ut templum Christi contegat ara Dei.

Epist. XXXII, ad Severum.

[2] A very old city, still bearing the same name, and situated on the Appian Way, between Terracina and Naples.

[3] Verum hanc quoque basiliculam, de benedictis apostolorum et martyrum reliquiis sacri cineres, in nomine Christi, sanctorum Sancti, et martyrum Martyris, et dominorum Domini, consecrabunt. —*Epist. XXXII, ad Severum.*

that He will reciprocally become the Confessor of His own confessors.'[1]   For this church two inscriptions were composed by Paulinus: one to accompany the painting with which he had adorned the apse; the other, to announce that portions of the relics of the apostle S. Andrew, the evangelist S. Luke, and S. Nazarius and other martyrs,[2] were deposited under the altar; of which he sings:

> Ecce sub accensis altaribus ossa piorum
>   regia purpureo marmore crusta tegit.
> Hic et apostolicas praesentat gratia vires
>   magnis in parvo pulvere pignoribus.
> Hic pater Andreas, et magno nomine Lucas,
>   martyr et illustris sanguine Nazarius,
> quosque suo Deus Ambrosio post longa revelat
>   saecula, Protasium cum pare Gervasio.
> Hic simul una pium complectitur arcula coetum,
>   et capit exiguo nomina tanta sinu.

> In regal shrines, with purple marble graced,
> their bones are 'neath illumined altars placed.
>
> .   .   .   .   .   .
>
> This pious band's contained in one small chest,
> that holds such mighty names within its tiny breast.

Prudentius visited not only the more celebrated sanctuaries in Spain, of which country he was a

---

[1] Ipse enim testatus est, Se vicissim confessorum Suorum Confessorem futurum (*Ep. XXXII, ad Severum*).   This is an allusion to those words of our Redeemer, when He said : 'Everyone, therefore, that shall confess Me before men, I will also confess him before My Father who is in heaven.'—*S. Matthew*, x, 32.

[2] *Epist. XXXII, ad Severum.*

native, but also those of Italy, on his road to
Rome, whither he travelled about the year 405.
During his residence in that capital of Christianity
the poet was a devout frequenter of the catacombs ;
he has bequeathed to posterity a valuable record
of his pious pilgrimages, in some beautiful hymns
which not only attest his own and his contemporary fellow-Christians' devotion towards the
relics of the saints and martyrs, but certify the
religious respect with which they were honoured
by the Church in different countries many years
anterior to the period in which he wrote.   In his
hymn in honour of S. Hippolytus he tells us that
he visited the crypt, or sepulchral chapel,[1] in
which the holy martyr's remains were deposited ;
and after having described the entrance into the
cemetery, and noticed with accurate minuteness
the different groups in the fresco which ornamented its walls, and to which we have already
had occasion to refer, he makes the following
remark :

> Talibus Hippolyti corpus mandatur opertis,
> propter ubi apposita est ara dicata Deo.

---

[1] This chapel was in the cemetery of Cyriaca, on the Tiburtine
Way, and in what is called the Ager Veranus, near the basilica
of S. Laurence outside the walls, in a vineyard, close to which
there are still some ruins supposed to belong to an ancient church
dedicated to S. Hippolytus, and built over his subterranean
chapel in the catacombs. The account of this holy martyr's death
has been given, and reference made to a fresco which depicted it, in
a note on p. 11 of this volume.

Illa sacramenti donatrix mensa, eademque
  custos fida sui martyris apposita,
servat ad aeterni spem Iudicis ossa sepulcro,
  pascit item sanctis Tibricolas dapibus.[1]

To such deep caves, in dark profounds that wind,
Hippolytus's corse is now consigned,
and with a holy sepulture is graced,
just where to God a sacred altar's placed
to guard with zealous care its martyred dead,
and yield the sacrament ; this table spread
those bones is keeping in its hallowed tomb,
to wait th' eternal Judge's gracious boon,
and nourishes with sacred food all those
who bow the knee to Christ where Tiber flows.

In his other hymns Prudentius bears the most
unequivocal testimony to the practice, even then
long in use, of depositing the relics of the saints
immediately under the altar. The hymn which
he composed in honour of S. Eulalia[2] concludes
with the following lines :

Sic venerarier ossa libet,
  ossibus altar et impositum :
  illa Dei sita sub pedibus
  prospicit haec, populosque suos
  carmine propitiata fovet.[3]

'Tis meet her bones with rev'rence should be graced,
and altar honoured o'er those bones that's placed.

---

[1] Περὶ Στεφάνων *liber*, *Hymnus XI*, v. 169-174.

[2] Eulalia was a Spanish young lady, a native of Merida, now a
poor town in Estramadura, and interwove the crown of virginity
with the palm of martyrdom. She suffered in the reign of
Diocletian.

[3] Περὶ Στεφάνων *liber*, *Hymnus III*, v. 211-215.

Eulalia, seated at her Saviour's feet,[1]
beholds those rites that thus her ashes greet.
Won by the hymns that God's own people wake,
she prays the prayer of mercy for their sake.

And in those verses on the celebrated Spanish martyr, S. Vincent,[2] he again recalls our attention to this practice.

Altar quietem debitam
praestat beatis ossibus :
subiecta nam sacrario,[3]
imamque ad aram condita
caelestis auram muneris
perfusa subtus hauriunt.

The altar opes its place of rest,
and holds the martyr's bones so blessed :
Beneath that altar now reposing,[4]
that sacred table o'er them closing,

---

[1] As the sacrifice of the Mass was continually offered upon the tomb of S. Eulalia, the saint is very appropriately said by Prudentius to be 'Dei sita sub pedibus,' seated at the feet of God, Jesus Christ, who is really and corporeally present in the Blessed Eucharist in a sacramental manner.

[2] Περὶ Στεφάνων liber, Hymnus V, v. 515–520.

[3] The poet no doubt intended to signify by the term 'sacrario' the table of the altar on which was consecrated the Blessed Eucharist ; and hence, as it became the seat on which were throned the Body and Blood of Christ, he describes the bones of S. Vincent, reposing underneath it, as imbued with the flood of grace which issued from the altar on account of the real and corporeal presence of Jesus there. He has embodied the same idea of the real presence of Christ in the Eucharist in that part of his hymn to S. Eulalia just now quoted.

[4] The assertion of ancient writers on this point has been several times verified by fact. The bodies of the martyrs have often been discovered under the high-altar in the churches dedicated to God in their memory. The body of S. Martina, together with those of two other martyrs, SS. Concordius and Epiphanius, was found in 1634,

enshrined within such hallowed bound,
suffused with heav'n-born gift profound,
those bones drink in that grace-infusing air
that's sweetly streaming all around them there.

---

under the high-altar of the ancient church near the Roman Forum (BOLDETTI, *op. cit.*, p. 701) which bears the name of that saint. The body of S. Agnes, and that of S. Emerentiana, were also ascertained in 1605 to be under the high-altar of the church of S. Agnes nella Via Nomentana (BOLDETTI, p. 684). The bodies of many other saints have been discovered both in and out of Rome, under the high-altar of their respective churches. The traveller who has visited that centre of Christianity will remember how he was admonished of this fact with respect to S. Cecilia by the beautiful recumbent statue of the saint, which lies so gracefully but modestly distended, with the head dissevered, and the greater part enveloped with a veil, exactly representing the body of S. Cecilia in the vesture and position in which it was discovered under the high-altar of her church in 1599, by Cardinal Sfrondati.

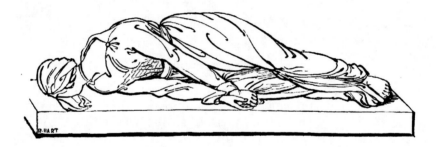

This beautiful statue, the production of Stefano Maderno (1599) before he had attained the age of twenty-three, is a masterpiece of modern art. Like a solitary star, it arose to irradiate the darkness of that eclipse which, at the decline of the sixteenth century, had overcast the Arts, and into which more especially sculpture had been thrown by the bold but tasteless handiworks of Bernini and his extravagant and meretricious school. This graceful figure represents the saint's body as if it had just fallen gently to the ground. Its extremities are as ably executed as they are well disposed. The draping does not smother the form which it veils, and is arranged with all decorous propriety. The undulating bendings of the body, though easy and very soft, are perfectly free from the slightest affectation. The consequence is that this figure may be regarded as a model of guileless, native gracefulness, tempered

IX.—BY THE PRACTICE OF ENCLOSING RELICS IN ALTARS AT THEIR CONSECRATION.

The profound respect of the primitive Church for the bodies of those who sealed their faith with their life-blood led her to esteem the tomb which held their remains as the most appropriate altar on which to offer the unbloody sacrifice of the new law. Hence is derived the ancient rite, still observed, of enclosing a small portion at least of relics in the altar at its consecration whenever the entire body of a saint cannot be procured to be placed beneath it. For the antiquity of this rite we possess the clearest testimony in the writings of the Fathers.

S. Ambrose, in a letter to his sister,[1] relates that when he had purposed to dedicate the new basilican church at Milan,[2] many persons, as with one voice, began to ask him if he would consecrate it with the same ceremonies as he had previously the Roman Basilica (another church at Milan near the Roman gate). To this inter-

---

with feminine dignity. While contemplating it, the beholder imagines that he is gazing on the type of original modesty and innocence. The Italian sculptor doubtless owed his success in great part to the restrictions imposed upon him by his patron, who bade him represent in marble the body of the saint exactly as it was discovered, without even varying one fold of the garments in which the virgin-martyr was arrayed.

[1] *Epist. XXII.*

[2] This church is still standing, and is called, from this illustrious bishop, the Ambrosian Basilica.

rogation he replied : 'I will, if I can discover any martyr's relics.'[1]   The saint's solicitude on this subject was gratified.   On excavating near the sepulchre of SS. Nabor and Felix, he discovered the bodies of SS. Gervasius and Protasius,[2] and thus speaks of the circumstance : 'Let these triumphant sufferers succeed to that place where Christ is the victim.   But He who suffered for all men is upon the altar; they who have been redeemed by His passion are under it.'[3]

S. Paulinus of Nola, on learning the ardent desire of his particular friend Severus to obtain some relics for the consecration of the church which he was then engaged in building, addressed a letter to him on the subject, and assured him that if he had but the smallest fragment of relics more than was necessary for the consecration of his own church, at that very moment on the point of being finished, he would have gladly sent it to him : as it was beyond his power to present

---

[1] Cum ego basilicam dedicassem, multi tamquam uno ore interpellare coeperunt, dicentes : Sic ut Romanam basilicam dedices? Respondi : Faciam, si Martyrum reliquias invenero.

[2] At the translation of these martyrs' bones, a man named Severus, well known throughout the city of Milan as being blind for many years, regained his sight by applying to his eyes a handkerchief that had been placed on the bier on which the relics lay. A prodigious multitude of people witnessed the miracle ; and the great S. Augustine, who was at Milan at the very time, more than once vouches for its veracity.   (S. AUGUSTINI *Conf.*, lib. IX, cap. VII ; *De Civitate Dei*, lib. XXII, cap. 8 ; *Serm.* 286, § 5.)

[3] Succedant victimae triumphales in locum ubi Christus hostia est. Sed Ille super altare, qui pro omnibus passus est : isti sub altari, qui Illius redempti sunt passione. *Epist. XXII.*

him with any remains of the martyrs, he would, however, send him some of the true Cross, a particle of which he had procured as a present from the Bishop of Jerusalem. Though but an atom of a tiny morsel, yet, S. Paulinus tells Severus, it will be to him a present safeguard and the pledge of his eternal safety.[1]

In another letter addressed to the same pious personage, Paulinus, under the supposition that by the kindness of Providence Severus has been able to obtain some relics belonging to the Apostles and martyrs, submits to him some verses to be inscribed near the altar, the purport of which is to announce not only that martyrs' relics, as well as a part of the true Cross which he had sent him, were enclosed in the altar, but that it was hallowed by the union of everything belonging to the

---

[1] Frater Victor inter alias operum tuorum et votorum narrationes retulit nobis, desiderare te ad basilicam, quam modo apud Primuliacum nostram maiorem priore condideris, de sacris sanctorum reliquiis benedictionem, qua adornetur domestica tua ecclesia, ut fide et gratia tua dignum est. Testis est autem Dominus, quod si vel scrypulum sacri cineris habuissemus, supra quam nobis ad basilicam, quae proxime in nomine Domini consummabitur, dedicandam necessarium erat, misissemus unanimitati tuae: sed quia nos non habuimus huius muneris copiam, et ille se spem eiusdem gratiae copiosam habere dixit a sancta Silvia, quae illi de multorum ex Oriente martyrum reliquiis spopondisset, invenimus quod digne et ad basilicae sanctificationem vobis, et ad sanctorum cinerum cumulandam benedictionem mitteremus partem particulae de ligno divinae Crucis. Quod nobis bonum benedicta Melanius ab Hierusalem munere sancti inde episcopi Ioannis attulit. . . . Accipite magnum in modico munus; et in segmento pene atomo astulae brevis, sumite munimentum praesentis, et pignus aeternae salutis.—PAULINI *Epist. XXXI, ad Severum.*

Passion of Christ. For His Cross, His Body and His Blood, He Himself the God of martyrs— were all assembled there.[1]

While these writers, whose works we have just been citing, attested what were the practice and religious feelings of Europe, the Church of Africa exhibited equally strong proofs of a similar devotion, and proclaimed that she used corresponding rites in regard to the relics of the saints. In the decree which was promulgated in 398 by the fifth Council of Carthage, it was ordained that the altars scattered over the country and by the way-sides, that were constituted just like the memorials of the martyrs,[2] in which neither the body nor

---

[1] Quod si Dominus desiderium animae vestrae fecerit secundum fidem vestram, adiiciens ornatui et sanctificationi operum vestrorum, ut sacros cineres de sanctis gloriosorum Apostolorum aut martyrum reliquiis adipiscamini . . . dignum opere fidei vestrae et operis fideliter elaborati dedicatione procul dubio celeberrima, sanctorum quoque reliquiis decens arbitramur, ut hoc etiam quod de Cruce missimus, pariter depositum sacratumque veneremini. Quod si ita placuerit, placitum vestrum hi, si videbitur, versiculi nuntiabunt.

Divinum veneranda tegunt altaria foedus,
  compositis sacra cum Cruce martyribus.
Cuncta salutiferi coëunt martyria Christi,
  Crux, Corpus, Sanguis, martyris Ipse Deus.
              PAULINI *Epist. XII, ad Severum.*

[2] The oratory or altar erected over the tomb of a martyr was anciently denominated either a Martyry, from the Greek Μαρτύριον, Confession, from the equivalent term in Latin, *confessio*,—or Memorial, because built to do honour to his memory. S. Optatus, bishop of Milevis, who wrote about the year 365, designates the churches built over the tombs of S. Peter and of S. Paul by the appellation of Memoria, as he thus interrogates the Donatist Macrobius: 'Ibi Romae sunt duorum memoriae apostolorum. Dicite si ad has ingredi potuit, ita ut obtulerit illic; ubi sanctorum memorias esse constat. *De Schismate Donatistarum*, lib. II.

any relics of the martyrs could be proved to be deposited, should, if it were possible, be overturned by the bishops who presided over those districts.[1] The honour and respect which the Greek Church rendered to the martyrs' relics are abundantly testified by two of its most eminent saints and writers, S. Chrysostom and S. Cyril of Jerusalem. The eloquent bishop of Constantinople frequently proclaims the reverence in which the relics of the saints were held amongst the Greeks. He asserts that whole cities might be witnessed hurrying to the tombs of the martyrs.[2] The venerable catechist of Jerusalem thus addressed his catechumens: 'In order that not only the souls of the just should be honoured, but that it might also be

---

[1] Placuit, ut altaria quae passim per agros aut vias, tamquam memoriae martyrum constituuntur, in quibus nullum corpus aut reliquiae martyrum conditae probantur, ab episcopis, qui eisdem locis praesunt, si fieri potest, evertantur. *Can. XIV Concil. Carthaginen. V, apud* LABBEUM, *Concil Gen.*, tom. III, col. 971.

[2] Σκόπει καὶ πρὸς τῶν μαρτύρων τοὺς τάφους τὰς πόλεις συντρεχούσας. *Expositio in Psal. CXV.*

'We depart not,' Οὐκ ἀναχωροῦμεν τῶν τάφων αὐτῶι, etc. (*Hom. I in Psal. XLVIII*) he affirms, 'from their sepulchres; it is here that kings put aside their diadems, and remain praying to be rescued from impending dangers, and to achieve a victory over their enemies.' He triumphantly remarks, in reference both to Jew and Gentile, that 'the Apostles after their deaths became more honoured than the greatest sovereigns upon earth, for at Rome itself, the imperial metropolis, emperors and consuls and generals abandoned everything, and hastened to the sepulchres of the fisherman and tent-maker; and at Constantinople those who wore the diadem earnestly desired to be buried, not along with the Apostles, but before their porches; so that the emperors themselves became the fisherman's portal-keepers.' S. CHRYSOSTOMI *Demonstratio Quod Christus sit Deus*, § v, p. 839.

credited that there was a virtue infused into their bodies, the dead man who was thrown into the monument of Eliseus, on touching the corpse of the prophet, was again restored to life. The dead body of the prophet discharged an office which appeared peculiar to the soul, and what was itself lying dead imparted life to the defunct, and what gave animation remained as before amongst the departed. For what reason? That lest if Eliseus had arisen, such an event might have been attributed to his soul alone; and that it might be shown that in the absence of the soul there still resided a certain virtue and power in the body of each saint on account of the just soul which during so many years inhabited that body and employed its agency. Let us not withhold our belief in such a thing as if it were not so, for if the handkerchiefs and aprons which exteriorly adhere, when applied to the bodies of the sick, raised up the infirm, how much more did the body itself of the prophet raise the dead to life again.'[1]

---

[1] Ἵνα δὲ μὴ μόνον τιμηθῶσι τῶν δικαίων αἱ ψυχαί, πιστευθῇ δέ, ὅτι καὶ ἔγκειται ἐν τοῖς τῶν δικαίων σώμασι δύναμις, ὁ ῥιφεὶς ἐν τῷ μνημείῳ τοῦ Ἐλισσαίου νεκρὸς, τοῦ νεκροῦ σώματος τοῦ προφήτου ἐφαψάμενος, ἐζωοποιήθη. Καὶ τὸ σῶμα τοῦ προφήτου τὸ νεκρὸν, ἀπετέλεσε ψυχῆς ἔργον· καὶ τὸ τελευτῆσαν καὶ κείμενον, ζωὴν παρέσχε τῷ τελευτήσαντι· καὶ παρασχὸν τὴν ζωὴν, αὐτὸ ὁμοίως ἔμεινεν ἐν νεκροῖς. Διὰ τι; Ἵνα μὴ ἐξαναστάντος Ἐλισσαίου, τῇ ψυχῇ μόνῃ προσγραφῇ τὸ πρᾶγμα· δειχθῇ δὲ, ὅτι καὶ ψυχῆς μὴ παρούσης, ἔγκειταί τις δύναμις τῷ τῶν ἁγίων σώματι, διὰ τὴν ἐν τοσούτοις ἔτεσιν ἐνοικήσασαν ἐν αὐτῷ δικαίαν ψυχην, ἧς ὑπηρέτημα γέγονε. Καὶ μὴ ἀπιστῶμεν, νήπιοι, ὡς μὴ γεγενημένου τούτου. Εἰ γὰρ σουδάρια καὶ σημικίνθια, τὰ ἔξωθεν ὄντα, τῶν σωμάτων ἁπτόμενα τῶν νοσούντων, ἤγειρε τοὺς ἀσθενεῖς· πόσῳ μᾶλλον

X.—RESPECT ANCIENTLY PAID TO RELICS PROVED FROM THE CALUMNIES OF THE HEATHEN.

From the furious invectives and calumnies launched against the Christian faith by the sophist Eunapius, who lived about the year 389, may be accurately collected various facts which testify what religious veneration the Church at that epoch exhibited towards the relics of the saints.[1] The virulent declamations of that assailant of Christianity assure us: 1. That at the period in

---

αὐτὸ τὸ σῶμα τοῦ προφήτου ἤγειρε τὸν νεκρόν.—S. CYRILLI *Catech. Myst.* XVIII, p. 293.

Another ancient Father has embodied the substance of the same remarks in some very elegant ideas. After noticing, from Sacred Scripture, that the earthly tabernacle of the righteous man becomes the temple of the Holy Ghost, S. Germanus of Constantinople institutes a comparison between the body of the saint departed and a vessel once employed to hold some precious perfume, but now empty of the fragrant liquid; and observes that as the vase continues redolent of the delicious aroma of the balm it once contained after every drop of it has evaporated, so the relics of the saint—the vase that once was hallowed and replenished with the Holy Ghost—remain imbued with its sanctifying sweets, and exhale its odour though the spirit be departed. This elegant comparison of the venerable Patriarch may be happily expressed by employing, with a very little variation, the beautiful language of Moore :—

> Long, long *shall saints' relics with virtue be* filled,
> like the vase, in which roses have once been distilled—
> you may break, you may shatter the vase, if you will,
> but the scent of the roses will hang round it still.

[1] Ii (Christiani) namque condita et salita eorum (Martyrum) capita, qui ob scelerum multitudinem a iudicibus extremo supplicio fuerant affecti, pro divis ostentabant ; iis genua submittebant, eos in deorum numerum receptabant, ad illorum sepulcra pulvere sordibusque conspurcati : in iis nonnulli martyres, diaconi alii, et legati, arbitrique precum petitionumque apud eos nominabantur.—EUNAPIUS, *apud* BARONIUM, *anno* 389, *num.* LXXXI, tom. VI, p. 59.

which he wrote (anno 389) whenever a temple of some heathen deity became appropriated to the service of the One true living God, or when a new edifice was erected for the purpose of religion, it was the universal custom to deposit in it relics of the martyrs; 2. That these mortal remains of the saints enshrined beneath the altars were, on certain days, exposed to the public veneration of the faithful, who were sedulous in rendering them a respectful homage; 3. That such was the reverence which the ancient Church displayed towards the bodies of the martyrs, that the unbelievers, judging from mere exterior appearances, erroneously asserted that the Christians looked upon the saints as gods, and worshipped them with divine honours; 4. That the saints were regarded by the faithful as patrons who could assist them by their prayers and friendly intercession.

XI.—FROM THE OBJECTIONS OF HERETICS.

In the following century (anno 404) S. Jerome triumphantly defended the practice of venerating the relics of the saints against the attacks and contumely of Vigilantius and others. That heretic and his partisans denounced all those who rendered this pious homage as idolaters, and Cinerarians or worshippers of ashes. To that acrimonious objurgation S. Jerome answered: 'We do not adore the relics of the martyrs . . . but we honour them that we may adore Him whose martyrs they are ; we honour the servants that the respect which is paid to them may be reflected back upon the Lord.'[1] Vigilantius feigned to be indignant that their relics were folded up in costly silks and precious stuffs. S. Jerome asks him if Constantine had perpetrated a sacrilege by translating to Constantinople, in most splendid shrines, the relics of SS. Andrew, Luke, and Timothy? Or if the Roman pontiffs acted wrongly when they offered up sacrifice to God over the bones of the deceased Peter and Paul, which the true believer considered to be venerable, but Vigilantius contemned as vile dust; or when they, as well as every other bishop throughout the earth, looked upon the tombs of the martyrs as the altars of Christ? Vigilantius tauntingly noticed a usage which then prevailed of illuminating the martyrs' sepulchres; S. Jerome vindicated this manifestation of religious homage from the strictures of his adversary by the following reply : 'The Apostles also murmured that the ointment was squandered, but the voice of Chris-

---

[1] Honoramus reliquias martyrum, ut Eum, cuius sunt martyres, adoremus. Honoramus servos, ut honor servorum redundet ad Dominum.—S. HIERONYMI *Epist.* CX, *ad Riparium presbyterum.*

Male facit ergo Romanus episcopus, qui super mortuorum hominum Petri et Pauli, secundum nos ossa veneranda, secundum te vilem pulvisculum, offert Domino sacrificia, et tumulos corum Christi arbitratur altaria ?—S. HIERONYMI *contra Vigilantium liber.*

Himself rebuked them, for neither did Jesus stand in need of the ointment, nor are wax-lights necessary for the martyrs.'[1]

XII.—VENERATION OF RELICS IN THE ANGLO-SAXON CHURCH.

If we consult the annals of our native history, we shall discover that in the veneration which they exhibited towards the relics of the saints our Anglo-Saxon forefathers emulated the piety of their Roman and Oriental brethren in the faith. 'The veneration of relics was diffused as far as the knowledge of the Gospel, and their presence was universally deemed requisite for the canonical dedication of a church or an altar. With this view, Gregory the Great, as soon as he heard of the success of the missionaries, was careful to send them a supply of relics;[2] and scarce a pilgrim returned from Gaul or Italy who had not procured, by entreaty or purchase, a portion of the remains of some saint or martyr. But the poverty of the Saxon Church was quickly relieved by the virtues of her children, and

---

[1] *Liber contra Vigilantium.*

[2] Hence we are informed by Carte that the veneration of relics was introduced into England by the Roman missionaries, but was unknown to the Scottish bishops Aidan, Finan, and Colman (*History of England,* vol. I, p. 241). Yet Finan ordered the bones of his holy predecessor to be taken out of his tomb and placed on the right side of the altar, '*iuxta venerationem tanto pontifice dignam*' (BEDAE *Hist. eccl. gentis Anglorum,* lib. III, c. 17), and Colman, at his departure, carried with him into Scotland a part of the relics of the same saint (*Ibid.,* lib. III, c. 26). See also lib. III, c. 11, 12.

England became a soil fertile in saints. Scarcely was there a monastery that did not possess one or more of these favourites of heaven: their bodies lay richly entombed in the vicinity of the principal altar, and around were suspended the votive offerings of the multitudes who had experienced the efficacy of their intercession. In the hour of distress or danger the afflicted votary threw himself at the foot of the shrine with an avowal of his unworthiness, but expressed an humble confidence that the Almighty would not refuse to the merits of the patron what He might justly deny to the demerit of the suppliant. Success often attended these petitions: the clergy of each community could appeal to a long list of preternatural cures, owing to the intercession of the saints whose bodies reposed in their church; and the crowds of visitants whom these miracles attracted added to their reputation and importance.'[1]

XIII.—MIRACLES WROUGHT THROUGH RELICS ATTESTED BY PROTESTANTS.

That the same Almighty God, who wrought such miracles by the bones of Eliseus,[2] by S. Peter's shadow,[3] and by the handkerchiefs which had touched the body of S. Paul,[4] has also con-

---

[1] LINGARD, *The Antiquities of the Anglo-Saxon Church*, pp. 282, 283.
[2] *4 Kings*, II, 14.   [3] *Acts*, V, 15.   [4] *Ibid.*, XIX, 12.

descended to impart, on various occasions, a wonder-working efficacy to the relics of those saints who adorned the Church at more recent periods, is acknowledged by Protestants themselves. Chemnitz admits[1] that the great S. Augustine mentions the fact of a blind woman having recovered her sight at the translation of S. Stephen's relics. In the observations of Sir Wm. Hamilton on the terrible eruption of Mount Vesuvius in the year 1767 is the following curious paragraph: 'In the midst of these horrors, the mob, growing tumultuous and impatient, obliged the Cardinal to bring out the head of S. Januarius, and go with it in procession to the Ponte Maddalena, at the extremity of Naples, towards Vesuvius; and it is well attested here that the eruption ceased the moment the Saint came in sight of the mountain; it is true, the noise ceased about that time, after having lasted about five hours, as it had done the preceding days.'[2] Talking of the withered elm in the Piazza del Duomo at Florence, which was instantly restored to vegetation by the shrine in which was enclosed S. Zenobia's body resting on its trunk during the ceremony of translation, Forsyth makes the following remark: 'This elm puzzles me more than any of their (the Catholics') miracles. The event happened at a time when

---

[1] *Examen Decretorum Concilii Tridentini,* pars IV, p. 10.
[2] *Observations on Mount Vesuvius.* London, 1772, p. 35.

Florence was more populous than at present, and the most enlightened city in Europe — it happened in the most public place in the whole town—on an object familiar to every inhabitant —and in the presence of many thousands, who were then attending the solemn removal of the saint from San Lorenzo to the cathedral. The event is recorded by contemporary historians, and is inscribed on a marble column now standing where the tree stood—a column erected in the face of those very persons who saw the miracle performed, and who certainly, if the inscription were false, would not have suffered so impudent a forgery to insult them.' [1]

XIV.—RELICS COLLECTED BY PROTESTANTS.

That the Catholic custom of venerating the relics of the saints should be censured by English Protestants is inconsistent, or, rather, inexplicable. An Englishman will manifest a devotion occasionally enthusiastic towards every memorial appertaining to the great and glorious personages of the olden times. Whenever he visits those places that have been signalised by their sufferings, ennobled by their virtues and achievements, or have served as their residence, he labours to discover and carry away with him a particle of

---

[1] J. FORSYTH, *Remarks on Antiquities, Arts, and Letters, during an Excursion in Italy in the years* 1802 *and* 1803. London, 1835, p. 372.

something in any way connected with their story;[1] and so far has the mania for gleaning such curiosities prevailed amongst us, that many persons have been known to expend large sums of money to possess themselves not only of articles that were at some time or other used by public and remarkable individuals,[2] but even of those

---

[1] At Hardwick in Derbyshire is preserved a coverlet, said to have been wrought by the needle of the unfortunate Mary Queen of Scots while a captive there ; but it suffered such mutilations from relic-stealing visitants to that interesting pile, that it was withdrawn from public inspection.

[2] The chair in which Wickliffe expired, together with the pulpit from which he was accustomed to preach, a piece of his cloak, and an oak table which belonged to him are still preserved in Lutterworth church.

A recent author, talking of the crowds of classic travellers who go to pay their homage to the tomb of Vergil, as a small grotto near Naples is denominated, observes : 'The English pilgrims are the most numerous. A bay-tree did grow out of the top of it, but the keeper told me that the English had pulled off the leaves as long as any remained ; in the same spirit, I suppose, which induced the ladies in England to pull the hairs out of the tail of Platoff's horse.' —H. MATTHEWS, *The Diary of an Invalid.* London, 1820, p. 202.

Not only cuttings from the weeping willow, but blades of grass that grew over the tomb of Napoleon have been regarded as valuable gifts. The tree under which the Duke of Wellington stood during part of the day at Waterloo has entirely disappeared through the avidity of travellers to secure a chip of it. The uniform which was worn by the gallant Nelson when he fell at Trafalgar is carefully preserved in Westminster Abbey. King Edward's staff and crown are looked upon with so much veneration that they are most conspicuously employed at the coronation of our sovereigns. A coat that once belonged to Charles XII. of Sweden was lately sold in London for a large sum of money. At Eisenach in Germany there stands the ancient Castle of Wartburg, in which Martin Luther resided some time ; the room is still shown which that innovator occupied, and in which the discussion between himself and the devil, as Luther himself relates, took place (*Opera*, tom. VII, *Wittembergae*, 1588, fol. 443, and tom. VI, *Germ.* fol. 28). On the table, which has

objects that once belonged to the most flagitious characters.[1]

Whatever the Protestant can adduce in favour of this custom of honouring and preserving the memorials of the illustrious or infamous dead, whether orator or poet, general or statesman, will be advanced with double energy by the Catholic in his defence of the veneration which he exhibits to the relics of the saints.

If the classic scholar may innocently indulge his raptures as he gazes on the Formian cenotaph of Cicero, the tomb of Vergil, and the sarcophagus of Scipio, or exultingly gathers up a fragment of the tessellated pavement trodden on by Horace in his Sabine villa; if without the slightest imputation of superstition he may make a poet-pilgrimage to the grave of Petrarch at Arquà—to Ariosto's chair and inkstand—to the prison-cell of Tasso at Ferrara—to the birth and burial place of his own Shakespeare at Stratford-upon-Avon, and join there in celebrating the festival of the English bard;—surely the Catholic may as harmlessly in-

---

been despoiled of many a splinter, there are two logs of wood regularly supplied by the servant who shows the house, and are purposely left to satisfy the cravings felt by the admirers of Luther for some relic of their hero; and when the writer of this note saw them, they were closely pared.

[1] It not unfrequently happens that the very instruments which some wicked wretch employed in the murder of his neighbour are in great request. The very rope in which the notorious Thurtell was executed, and his famous air-gun, were contended for by purchasers of such wares.

dulge his religious feelings while, standing by the shrines of S. Peter and S. Paul, S. Matthew and S. Bartholomew,[1] he offers his homage to the dust of those venerable lips by which Jesus Christ has spoken to us, and from which came forth a 'light more resplendent than lightning,'[2] whose bodies in this life were the temples of the Holy Ghost— whose pens were guided by the same celestial Spirit—who have bequeathed to the world not only specimens of the most sublime and stirring eloquence—not only examples of the most exalted heroism,[3] but the word of God—the Gospel truths of Jesus, in place of a love-sick sonnet and a tale of ribaldry that, instead of elevating and purifying, corrupt and enervate the human heart. Nor can it be criminal in him to yield a fitting reverence to Christian heroes and the propagators of the Gospel, and a harmless action in his fellow-countryman to pay a similar respect to heathen

---

[1] The bodies of those apostles are preserved at Rome, S. Matthew's excepted, which is at Salerno.

[2] S. CHRYSOSTOMI *Hom. XXXII.*

[3] 'To abstract the mind from all local emotion would be impossible, if it were endeavoured, and would be foolish, if it were possible. Whatever withdraws us from the power of our senses, whatever makes the past, the distant, or the future predominate over the present, advances us in the dignity of thinking beings. Far from me and from my friends be such frigid philosophy as may conduct us indifferent and unmoved over any ground which has been dignified by wisdom, bravery, or virtue. That man is little to be envied whose patriotism would not gain force upon the plain of Marathon, or whose piety would not grow warmer among the ruins of Iona.' S. JOHNSON, *A Journey to the Western Islands of Scotland.* London, 1775, p. 346.

worthies, or modern writers of splendid though oftentimes perverted talents.

We may conclude this portion of our subject in the language of S. Ambrose: 'We honour the memory of that virtue which shall never die; we honour those ashes which the confession of faith has consecrated; we honour in them the seeds of eternity; we honour that body which has shown us how to love the Lord, which has taught us not to fear death for His sake. And why should not the faithful honour the body which even devils venerate? which they tormented indeed in death, but which they glorify in the sepulchre? We honour then the body which Christ Himself honoured in the sword, and which will reign with Him in heaven.'[1]

---

[1] *Sermo S. Ambrosio ascriptus LV, in Natali SS. martyrum Nazarii et Celsi.*

CHAPTER VII.

ON PURGATORY.

AFTER having vindicated the doctrine of the Church concerning the honour which she invites us to manifest towards such amongst her members as are already triumphing along with Christ in the heavenly Jerusalem, we will now proceed to the elucidation of that dogma of her creed respecting those others of her children who have left this life with souls too stained with sin to find an immediate entrance into heaven, but whose transgressions were not of such enormity as to merit the eternal torments of hell, and are therefore dwelling in a middle state, and going through a purgation preparatory to their admittance into heaven.

I.—DEFINITION OF PURGATORY.

This middle state, between hell and heaven, is denominated Purgatory, which we define to be a place or state wherein are purified, before their admittance into heaven, 'where nought defiled can enter,'[1] such souls as leave this life with the pardon of their sins, as far as regards the GUILT and ETERNAL punishment, but are yet subject to some temporal pain still remaining due, or are not perfectly cleansed from the blemish of those defects and imperfections which we designate venial sins.

II.—BELIEF OF THE CHURCH ON THIS POINT.

Concerning this article of faith, the Church, in the Council of Trent, has expressed herself in the following manner: 'The Catholic Church, instructed by the Holy Spirit, has taught in her councils, from the sacred writings, and the ancient tradition of the Fathers, and this synod has now recently declared, that there is a Purgatory, and that the souls therein detained are helped by the suffrages of the faithful, but principally by the acceptable sacrifice of the altar[2]': and, by a particular canon of that Council, she pronounces a formal condemnation on those who shall maintain, 'That after receiving the grace of justifica-

---

[1] *Apocalypse,* XXI, 27.

[2] Cum Catholica Ecclesia, Spiritu Sancto edocta, ex sacris litteris, et antiqua patrum traditione, in sacris conciliis, et novissime in hac oecumenica synodo docuerit, Purgatorium esse ; animasque ibi detentas, fidelium suffragiis, potissimum vero acceptabili altaris sacrificio, iuvari ; praecipit sancta Synodus episcopis, ut sanam de Purgatorio doctrinam a sanctis patribus et sacris conciliis traditam, a Christi fidelibus, credi, teneri, doceri, et ubique praedicari diligenter studeant.—Sessio XXV, *Decretum de Purgatorio.*

tion, the guilt and eternal punishment are remitted to every repentant sinner, in such a way
that no temporal pain remains to be endured
either in this or in the world to come, in Purgatory, before an entrance into heaven can be
obtained.'[1]

The Catholic, therefore, believes that there is
a middle state for souls who depart this life in
God's grace, yet not without some smaller stains
and guilt of punishment, which retard their
entrance into heaven; and that the souls of the
faithful, although they be detained in this purgatory, continue to be the living members of that
body of which Christ Jesus is the head, and are,
in consequence, alleviated by the prayers and suffrages of their fellow-members living upon earth.
The situation of this place—the quality and nature
of its punishments—the period of time during
which the captive souls may be confined there—
the mode in which the prayers, the alms-deeds,
and the fastings offered up to Heaven in their
behalf are rendered available to their refreshment,
whether by way of intercession or satisfaction—
the appellation of this place, whether it should be
purgatory, limbo, or a middle state, we consider

---

[1] Si quis post acceptam iustificationis gratiam, cuilibet peccatori
poenitenti ita culpam remitti, et reatum aeternae poenae deleri
dixerit, ut nullus remaneat reatus poenae temporalis exsolvendae, vel
in hoc saeculo, vel in futuro in Purgatorio, antequam ad regna
caelorum aditus patere possit; anathema sit.—Sessio vi, *Canon* 30.

as questions impertinent to faith, and, indeed, as altogether idle and superfluous.[1]

III.—TRUTHS INCLUDED IN THE DOCTRINE OF PURGATORY.

The definition of the Church comprehends four articles of doctrine, which we should be careful to discriminate.

The first is, that after the guilt of sin and its *eternal* punishment have been forgiven in the sacraments, still there may remain a temporal pain to be endured by the offender; the second is, that when this punishment is not completed in this life, it may be inflicted, after death, upon the soul; the third is, that the prayers and good works of the living are serviceable to the dead; the fourth, that the Mass has the virtue of satisfying the Divine justice for the transgressions of the living and the dead.

IV.—TEMPORAL PUNISHMENT TO BE ENDURED FOR SIN, THOUGH ITS ETERNAL PUNISHMENT BE PARDONED.

That after the guilt of sin and its eternal punishment have been forgiven there still may remain some temporal pain to be endured, is a truth that can be easily established by various proofs presented to us in the Holy Scriptures. Death, we

---

[1] BELLARMINUS, *De Purgatorio,* lib. II. VERON, *Regula Fidei Catholicae,* cap. II, § v.

are assured by S. Paul, is one of the punishments inflicted on the human race in consequence of original sin: 'Wherefore as by one man sin entered into this world, and by sin death; and so death passed upon all men;'[1] and the book of Genesis contains this sentence pronounced upon Adam and his race: 'Because thou hast eaten of the tree, whereof I commanded thee that thou shouldst not eat, cursed is the earth in thy work; with labour and toil shalt thou eat thereof all the days of thy life. In the sweat of thy face shalt thou eat bread till thou return to the earth.'[2] Now, though we be cleansed from the stain of original sin in the sacrament of baptism, yet death, the hardships, the trouble and afflictions of this world infallibly await us, and constitute the temporal pain inflicted upon us on account of our original transgression committed in the sin of Adam. David being admonished of his crimes by the prophet's parable, exclaimed to Nathan: 'I have sinned against the Lord. And Nathan said to David: The Lord also hath taken away thy sin: thou shalt not die. Nevertheless, because thou hast given occasion to the enemies of the Lord to blaspheme, for this thing the child that is born to thee shall surely die.'[3] This temporal punishment was rigorously inflicted, although a prophet's mouth assured the royal penitent that

---

[1] *Romans*, v, 12.   [2] *Genesis*, III, 17–19.
[3] 2 *Kings*, XII, 13, 14.

the Lord had taken away the sin, and consequently obliterated its guilt and remitted its *eternal* chastisement. The instances of Moses, of Aaron, and of the people of Israel—who sinned against the Lord, and, though forgiven, were visited with punishment—are equally pertinent.[1]

The people of God, under the Old Law, most explicitly believed in this infliction of temporal chastisement for sin, even after the remission of its eternal punishment; and being persuaded that in the event of the transgressor's departing out of this life before he had gone through the whole of it, he must endure the remainder in a future world, they offered up special sacrifices for the repose and comfort of the dead.[2] Prayer for their departed brethren is a practice still observed most scrupulously amongst the Jews.

This religious belief of the Jews must necessarily include the doctrine of a middle state, an article of faith equally comprised in the symbol of genuine Christianity, and which we shall now proceed to notice.

V.—THE BELIEF IN A MIDDLE STATE HELD BY THE PATRIARCHS, ETC.

The most conspicuous traces of a belief in a third or middle state are obviously discernible

---

[1] *Numbers*, XIV, 20.
[2] 2 *Machabees*, XII, 43–46. Concerning the canonicity of this part of Scripture, the reader is referred to Appendix III.

throughout the whole of the Old Testament. It
was thus that Jacob, while weeping for his son
Joseph, under the impression that a wild beast
had devoured him, exclaimed: 'I will go down
to my son into HELL, mourning.'[1] The Royal
Psalmist is continually making an allusion to
such a belief. In one of his canticles he sings:
'Thou wilt not leave my soul in HELL;'[2] in
another he exclaims: 'Thou hast delivered (O
Lord) my soul out of the LOWER HELL;'[3] and
again he asks: 'Who is the man that shall deliver his soul from the hand of HELL?'[4] That
the hell which is so positively mentioned in
these passages is not the abode of Satan and his
fallen angels is certain, since it is incredible
that Jacob should have presumed that the soul
of his youthful, almost infant Joseph was condemned to a place of such eternal punishment;
and David would neither have said that his soul
was not to be left there if he wished to speak
of that region from which there is no returning;
nor would he have signified his soul's deliverance
from the 'lower hell,' unless he knew there was a
lowest one.

These, and similar portions of the ancient Scriptures, were such powerful auxiliaries in supporting
the dogma of purgatory, by the demonstration

---

[1] *Genesis*, XXXVII, 35.   [2] *Psalm* XV, 10.   [3] *Ibid.*, LXXXV, 13.
[4] *Ibid.*, LXXXVIII, 49.

which they furnished of the existence of a middle state, that they offered considerable annoyance to the innovators of the sixteenth century, who, to weaken, if not annihilate their strength, did not hesitate to corrupt them by incorrect translations. Hence in those English versions of the Scripture which were severally made in the years 1562, 1577, and 1579, whenever the Hebrew שְׁאוֹל *sheol*, the Greek ᾅδης of the Septuagint, and the 'Infernus' of the Latin Vulgate, seemed to favour the doctrine of Purgatory, these words were rendered into English by '*grave*,' without caring in the least about the violent distortion which was inflicted on the passage, or the absurdity it was condemned to assume by such a translation. Thus it is that in the Protestant Bible Jacob is made to say: 'I will go down into the *grave* unto my son,'[1]—as if the patriarch imagined that his son Joseph had been buried in a *grave*, when on the contrary he had just before exclaimed: 'It is my son's coat; an evil wild beast hath *eaten* him, a beast hath *devoured* Joseph.'[2] The Catholic Bible maintains the reverence of the sacred volume by rendering the passage in a proper manner, thus: 'I will go down to my son into *hell*.'

---

[1] *Genesis*, XXXVII, 33.   [2] *Ibid.*, 35.

VI.—A MIDDLE STATE BELIEVED IN BY THE HEATHEN.

That the existence of a middle state constituted a part of that revelation communicated by
Almighty God to the first inhabitants of the earth
and the early patriarchs, is a truth which may be
demonstrated from other sources than those of
the inspired volumes. The belief in such a doctrine forms a most prominent article in the theology of all the nations of the ancient world,
amongst whom the uniformity of credence on
this point cannot be ascribed to any other
incident than the one and universal tradition
originating from the same promulgation, and
afterwards regularly handed down through each
successive generation amid the various nations
of the earth. Though much deformed by the
ridiculous errors and the superstitions with which
Gentilism and idolatry had connected this dogma,
still it is eminently conspicuous in the religious
systems of ancient Egypt, India, Greece, and
Rome. Vestiges of such a primitive doctrine may
be easily recognised in many of their religious
ceremonials; but nowhere do we discover it so
strikingly as in the writings of some of their
poets, who principally contributed to disfigure
the native simplicity of this truth with such a
superstructure of frivolous though elegant fable.[1]

---

[1] According to the Egyptian mythology, the ‘Amenti’ was
supposed to be the region of the dead, and the same place as that
which the Greeks denominated ‘Hades,’ and the Latins ‘Tartarus.’

VII.—THE EXISTENCE OF A MIDDLE STATE BETWEEN
HEAVEN AND HELL FORMALLY ATTESTED BY THE
JEWS.

That the whole nation of the Jews openly professed a formal belief in a middle state is incon-

---

Thoth was the perpetual companion of Osiris, and after him the first
personage in the Amenti, where he had fixed his residence and his
tribunal to regulate the destinies of the souls of each in their trans-
migrations from the body of one man into another. The Egyptians
divided the whole world into three zones. 'The first was the earth,
or the zone of trial; the second was the zone of the air, perpetually
agitated by winds and storms, and was considered as the zone of
temporal punishment; and the third was the zone of rest and
tranquillity, which was above the other two. . . . It was supposed
that some souls after having parted from the body were thrown
into the second zone, to be whirled about by the winds through the
regions of the air till they were called upon either to return to the
first zone, to animate a new body, and to undergo fresh trials, in
expiation of their former sins, or to be removed into the third, where
the air was perpetually pure and tranquil.' (SPINETO, *Lectures on
the Elements of Hieroglyphics and Egyptian Antiquities.* London,
1829, p. 142.) At Table 5 at the end of the Lectures may be seen
a curious picture representing the trial and judgement which the
Egyptians supposed the soul of man to undergo before it was
allowed to enter the region of rest and happiness. It is taken
from a valuable MS. existing in the Vatican library, and has been
accurately described by that learned Italian prelate, Monsignor
Angelo Mai, in a work of his entitled *Catalogo de' Papiri Egiziani
della Biblioteca Vaticana con riflessioni,* Roma, 1825. The doctrine
of the transmigration of souls was not only held by the ancient
Brahmins, but is still retained amongst the present Banians (F.
BERNIER, *Lettre touchant les Superstitions des Gentils de l'Hin-
doustan.* Paris, 1671, p. 73), and many others in India and China
(S. DE LA LOUBÈRE, *Du Royaume de Siam.* Paris, 1619, tom. I), and
constitutes the principal foundation of their religion. The Mahome-
tans admit the existence of a purgatory, and offer up prayers for
their dead. (See ALLATIUS, *De utriusque Ecclesiae de Purgatorio
consensione,* p. 276.) Pythagoras, in ancient times, was the strenuous
advocate of the same opinion amongst the Greeks and their colonies

testable; for whether we admit, with the Catholic
Church, the book of Machabees to be divinely in-

---

in Italy and Sicily, and taught his followers to believe by his
metempsychosis that after death men's souls passed into other
bodies of this or that kind, according to the manner of life they
had led. If they had been vicious, they were imprisoned in the
bodies of miserable beasts, there to do penance for several ages, at
the expiration of which they returned again to animate the bodies of
men. The whole ceremonial observed by the ancient Greeks in
celebrating the funeral obsequies of their departed relatives and
the expiatory sacrifices they offered to the infernal gods—θεοῖς
καταχθονίοις—in their behalf, sufficiently attest their belief in a middle
state. The authority of Vergil puts the question beyond a doubt
with regard to the Romans. In his descent into hell Æneas meets
the shade of Palinurus wandering upon the wrong bank of the Styx,
and in the company of those other spirits of the dead who are thus
described (lib. vi, v. 325) by the Latin poet :—

> Haec omnis, quam cernis, inops inhumataque turba est ;
> portitor ille, Charon ; hi, quos vehit unda, sepulti.
> Nec ripas datur horrendas et rauca fluenta
> transportare prius, quam sedibus ossa quierunt.
> Centum errant annos volitantque haec litora circum
> tum demum admissi stagna exoptata revisunt.

> The ghosts rejected are th' unhappy crew
> depriv'd of sepulchres and fun'ral due :
> the boatman, Charon : those, the buried host,
> he ferries over to the farther coast ;
> nor dares his transport vessel cross the waves
> with such whose bones are not compos'd in graves.
> A hundred years they wander on the shore ;
> at length, their penance done, are wafted o'er.
>
> DRYDEN.

Continuing his progress, the Trojan chief afterwards encounters the
shade of his own father Anchises, from whom he receives (v. 735)
the following description :—

> Quin et supremo cum lumine vita reliquit,
> non tamen omne malum miseris nec funditus omnes
> corporeae excedunt pestes ; penitusque necesse est,
> multa diu concreta modis inolescere miris.
> Ergo exercentur poenis, veterumque malorum
> supplicia expendunt : aliae panduntur inanis

spired scripture, or, erroneously, like Protestants,
attach no more importance to it than to any other

suspensae ad ventos ; aliis sub gurgite vasto
infectum eluitur scelus, aut exuritur igni.
Quisque suos patimur Manis ; exinde per amplum
mittimur Elysium, et pauci laeta arva tenemus,
donec longa dies, perfecto temporis orbe,
concretam exemit labem, purumque relinquit
aetherium sensum atque aurai simplicis ignem.
Has omnis, ubi mille rotam volvere per annos,
Lethaeum ad fluvium deus evocat agmine magno,
scilicet inmemores supera ut convexa revisant
rursus et incipiant in corpora velle reverti.

Nor death itself can wholly wash their stains ;
but long contracted filth ev'n in the soul remains.
The relics of invet'rate vice they wear ;
and spots of sin obscene in ev'ry face appear.
For this are various penances enjoin'd ;
and some are hung to bleach upon the wind,
some plung'd in waters, others purg'd in fires,
till all the dregs are drain'd, and all the rust expires.
All have their manes, and those manes bear :
the few, so cleans'd, to these abodes repair,
and breathe, in ample fields, the soft Elysian air.
Then are they happy, when by length of time
the scurf is worn away of each committed crime ;
no speck is left of their habitual stains ;
but the pure ether of the soul remains.
But, when a thousand rolling years are past,
(so long their punishments and penance last)
whole droves of minds are, by the driving god,
compell'd to drink the deep Lethean flood,
in large forgetful draughts to steep the cares
of their past labours and their irksome years,
that, unrememb'ring of its former pain,
the soul may suffer mortal flesh again.

S. Justin Martyr, in the second part of his *Exhortation to the Greeks*,
demonstrates that many of the Greek authors had borrowed from
the Jewish writings those few correct ideas they possessed concerning divine subjects ; and that both Homer and Plato had drawn
copiously from the same fountain ; and how greatly the Greeks in
general were indebted to the Hebrew people for much of their
wisdom and information, is exposed, in an able manner, by S.

historical narration, this fact in either case is irre-fragably established by its authority.[1]

VIII.—EVIDENCED BY THE NEW TESTAMENT.

But this truth is copiously attested by the New Testament. Our Divine Redeemer raised to life the daughter of Jairus,[2] as well as the son of the widow of Naim;[3] and called Lazarus, though four days buried, from the sepulchre: and when He Himself yielded up the ghost, many bodies of the saints that had slept arose, and coming 'out of the tombs after His resurrection, came into the holy city and appeared to many.'[4]

Now it is positively certain that no one had ever entered heaven previously to the ascension of our blessed Redeemer, who told Nicodemus: 'No man hath ascended into heaven, but He

---

Clement of Alexandria (A.D. 194), in that valuable work of his, entitled *Stromata* (lib. I et v). We must, therefore, admit it was originally from the chosen people of God that the Greeks, and the Romans who borrowed their theogony and religion from Greece, came to the knowledge of this divinely revealed doctrine of a middle state after death, which they, however, corrupted by amalgamating with it their own ridiculous fables and superstitions. That the Druids taught the doctrine of a transmigration of souls appears from the remarks of Cæsar (*De Bello Gallico*, lib. VI) and of Diodorus (lib. v, c. 28), and from the authority of other ancient writers it would seem that they believed in the existence of a species of middle state (STRABO, lib. IV; MELA, lib. III, c. 2; VALERIUS MAXIMUS).

[1] This argument, furnished by the second book of Machabees, will be more amply developed in two succeeding paragraphs.

[2] *S. Matthew*, IX, 18–25.   [3] *S. Luke*, VII, 12–15.

[4] *S. Matthew*, XXVII, 52, 53.

that descended from heaven, the Son of man, who is in heaven.'[1] Where, then, had been dwelling the souls of these individuals from the moment of their departure from the flesh until they were recalled to animate and tenant it again? In what place had been the sojourn where Moses and Elias had enjoyed repose until they were summoned to appear to Peter, James, and John, talking to our Saviour Jesus as He was transfigured before those favourite disciples on the mountain?[2] Certainly not in the hell of the damned, for from that empire of Satan there is no redemption; its sentence is irrevocable, as its torments are eternal;—most certainly not in heaven, since before His ascension Christ Himself assures us that no one had ever entered there.

But in the supposition that the souls of the just *could* have entered heaven before the gates, which Adam's sin had closed against the human race, had been thrown open by our Divine Redeemer, it would have been a punishment instead of a kindness to have called them from that happy region. We are, therefore, warranted to conclude that the soul of Lazarus, for example, had not been conveyed to heaven, nor had lingered in hell; for the justice of God would have prevented Him from reversing the final sentence of punishment in one instance, and in the other His

---

[1] *S. John*, III, 13.　　　　[2] *S. Matthew*, XVII, 3.

mercy would have forbidden Him to have recalled a soul from perfect bliss to involve it again in this world's miseries.

Some amongst the parables employed by Christ necessarily presuppose that a belief in a middle state was unexceptionably admitted by the Jews, to whom they were directed.

It was thus that the voice of Truth itself addressed the multitude upon the Mount : ' Be at agreement with thy adversary betimes, whilst thou art in the way with him : lest perhaps the adversary deliver thee to the judge, and the judge deliver thee to the officer, and thou be cast into prison. Amen I say to thee, thou shalt not go out from thence till thou repay the last farthing ; ' [1] a passage which the ancient Fathers of the Church [2] interpret concerning purgatory, the prison of those souls defiled with sin, and which are there detained until they have been purified through the blood of Jesus from the very smallest stain. The parable of the rich man and Lazarus clearly establishes the ancient belief in a middle state : ' And it came to pass, that the beggar died, and was carried by the angels into Abraham's bosom. And the rich man also died ; and he was buried in hell. And lifting up his eyes when he was in torments, he saw Abraham afar off, and Lazarus

---

[1] *S. Matthew*, v, 25, 26.
[2] TERTULLIANUS, *de Anima*, c. 17 ; CYPRIANUS, lib. IV, *Epist. II ;* ORIGENES, *Hom. XXXV in Lucam ;* HIERONYMUS, *in cap. V Matt.*

in his bosom. And he cried, and said : Father Abraham, have mercy on me, and send Lazarus, that he may dip the tip of his finger in water, to cool my tongue : for I am tormented in this flame. And Abraham said to him : Son, remember that thou didst receive good things in thy lifetime, and likewise Lazarus evil things, but now he is comforted, and thou art tormented. And besides all this, between us and you, there is fixed a great chaos : so that they who would pass from hence to you, cannot, nor from thence come hither.'[1] Lazarus does not repose on the breast of an angel in heaven, but on the bosom of Abraham, who had not as yet entered into that celestial kingdom, but was resting in a place so near the hell of the damned that, though there is a great chaos fixed between them, the rich man may be discerned, and his prayer is capable of being heard by Abraham. But what is the purport of this rich man's supplication? Not that he himself be sent, for that was impossible, but Lazarus, to his father's house, to warn his brethren against the flames of hell. This belief amongst God's ancient people in a middle state is still further corroborated by the words addressed by the thief upon the cross to our Divine Redeemer, and also by the answer given to them by those lips of truth. It was thus the repentant

---

[1] *S. Luke*, XVI, 22-26.

malefactor prayed : 'Lord, remember me when Thou shalt come into Thy kingdom.'[1] This sup- pliant was just about to expire, so was Jesus ; yet he does not say, Grant me to go along with Thee into Thy kingdom ; no, his petition is, to follow our Lord, at some future period, into that blessed country : 'Remember me,' he cries, 'when Thou shalt come into Thy kingdom.' The good thief consequently believed that, while death would convey our blessed Saviour to the glory of His kingdom, it must carry a sinner like him- self not to such beatitude, but to some other place—not heaven, and yet not hell : not heaven, because although he awaited a place different from the kingdom of his Lord, yet it was to be a place of such a nature that his Lord, when enthroned in glory, might have compassion on him ; but the souls in heaven cannot be com- miserated, they do not stand in need of mercy ; not hell, because neither hope, nor grace, nor pity can ever enter there. Our Divine Redeemer answered this petition by this assurance to the thief : 'This day thou shalt be with Me in paradise.'[2] But where is this paradise into which the thief is to have an entrance together with his Saviour ? Is it heaven ? No ; for neither that day, nor three days later, had Jesus ascended into heaven ; for the reason which He assigned to Mary Magdalene why she should not touch Him

---

[1] *S. Luke*, XXIII, 42.   [2] *Ibid.*, 43.

when she saw Him, after His resurrection, in the garden, was: 'Do not touch Me, for I am not *as yet* ascended to My Father.'[1] That the place to which the thief was transported along with Christ was not hell is certain, for hell is not a paradise, a place of pleasure.

S. Peter, however, informs us where this place was to which the good thief accompanied our Saviour. 'Christ,' writes that Prince of the Apostles, 'Christ . . . being put to death indeed in the flesh, but enlivened in the spirit. In which also coming, He preached to those spirits that were in prison; which had been some time incredulous, when they waited for the patience of God in the days of Noe.'[2] An admirable elucidation of this point is furnished by the Catechism of the Council of Trent, which observes: 'That the Son of God descended into hell; that, clothed with the spoils of the arch-enemy, He might conduct into heaven those holy Fathers, and the other just souls, whose liberation from prison He had already purchased. This He accomplished in an admirable and glorious manner, for His august presence at once shed a celestial lustre upon the captives, filled them with inconceivable joy, and imparted to them that supreme happiness which consists in the vision of God; thus verifying His promise to the thief on the cross: "Amen, I say to thee,

[1] *S. John*, xx, 17.   [2] 1 *S. Peter*, iii, 18-20.

this day thou shalt be with Me in paradise." This deliverance of the just was long before predicted by Osee in these words: "O death! I will be thy death; O hell! I will be thy bite;"[1] and also by the prophet Zacharias: "Thou also by the blood of thy testament hast sent forth thy prisoners out of the pit, wherein is no water;"[2] and, lastly, the same is expressed by the Apostle in these words: "Despoiling the principalities and powers, He hath exposed them confidently in open show, triumphing over them in Himself."[3]

'However, to comprehend still more clearly the efficacy of this mystery, we should frequently call to mind that not only those who were born after the coming of the Saviour, but also those who preceded that event from the days of Adam, or shall succeed it to the consummation of time, are included in the redemption purchased by the death of Christ. Before His death and resurrection heaven was closed against every child of Adam: the souls of the just, on their departure from this life, were borne to the bosom of Abraham; or, as is still the case with those who require to be freed from the stains of sin, or die indebted to the Divine justice, were purified in the fire of purgatory.'[4]

---

[1] *Osee*, XIII, 14.   [2] *Zacharias*, IX, 11.   [3] *Colossians*, II, 15.
[4] J. DONOVAN, *The Catechism of the Council of Trent*. Dublin, 1829, p. 60.

SECTION II.

IX.—THIS MIDDLE STATE PROVED TO BE A PLACE OF PUNISHMENT, OR PURGATORY.

So far, a belief in a middle state between heaven and hell has been contended for and clearly demonstrated. That this middle state was not merely the abode into which the souls of the just who died before Christ were received, and where, without experiencing any sort of pain, they enjoyed peaceful repose, but that it still continues to exist, and is a place of punishment where the souls of those who die before they have discharged the debt of temporal pain to be inflicted on them for sins which were either venial, or of which the eternal chastisement had been remitted, is a doctrine corroborated by Holy Scripture and attested by the Church in every age of her existence.

Our blessed Saviour most significantly points to such a dogma on several occasions.

The passage in the sermon on the Mount: 'Be at agreement with thy adversary betimes, whilst thou art in the way with him: lest perhaps the adversary deliver thee to the judge, and the judge deliver thee to the officer, and thou be cast into prison. Amen I say to thee, thou shalt not go out from thence till thou repay the last farthing,'[1] — which, we have already mentioned, is most naturally construed as affirmative of Purgatory, that prison of the soul, in which she is detained a captive by the angel-ministers of justice, by order of the judge Christ Jesus, until she shall have repaid the last farthing; that is, made atonement for the very smallest sin, to the anger of a violated gospel, so irritated by her transgressions as to become her adversary; and whom she had neglected to propitiate through the merits of her Saviour whilst she was still in the way upon her earthly pilgrimage.

But the words of our Redeemer, whilst reprehending the malice of the stubborn Pharisees, who so obstinately withstood His preaching, are much less exposed to an ambiguous interpretation. They announce that: 'Whosoever shall speak a word against the Son of man, it shall be forgiven him : but he that shall speak against the Holy Ghost, it shall not be forgiven him neither in this world, nor in the world to come.'[2] From such a declaration we conclude that there are *some* sins forgiven in the world to come, otherwise the expression of our Saviour would

---

[1] *S. Matthew*, v, 25, 26.

[2] *S. Matthew*, xii, 32.   From these words S. Augustine (*De Civitate Dei*, lib. xxi, cap. 13) and S. Gregory (*Dialog.*, lib. iv, cap. 39) gather that some sins may be remitted in the world to come, and consequently that there is a purgatory or middle place.

be devoid of meaning, and His denunciation superfluous and impotent. As, however, the guilt and eternal punishment of sin cannot be pardoned in a future life, it is its temporal punishment only that can be forgiven there. This sentence of our Saviour, therefore, not only triumphantly evinces the existence of a middle state, but proves that there are souls abiding there defiled with sin, and in consequence liable to punishment which can be and is remitted by a just but clement judge.

It was thus that S. Peter, immediately after being filled with the Holy Ghost, addressed the citizens of Jerusalem: 'Ye men of Israel, hear these words: Jesus of Nazareth . . . whom God hath raised up, having loosed the sorrows of hell, as it was impossible that He should be holden by it. For David saith concerning Him: . . . *Because Thou wilt not leave my soul in hell,* nor suffer Thy holy one to see corruption.'[1] In the Protestant version it is: 'having loosed the pains of death.' But it should be observed that the 'Infernus,' or hell of the Vulgate, not only is authorised by several Greek manuscripts, which read ᾅδης instead of θανάτος, but that such a reading is more accordant with the citation which the apostle afterwards produces from the psalmist. The sorrows or pains to which S. Peter here refers

---

[1] *Acts,* II, 22-27.

cannot be those of death, properly so understood, since Christ had endured those pains in
all their most excruciating rigour on the cross;
nor those of the grave, since the body of Jesus,
deposited in the sepulchre and separated from
His soul, was incapable of suffering; nor those
of the damned, since Jesus Christ never merited
them, and it would be ridiculous to say that
God had ever delivered or preserved Him from
those tortures. We are, therefore, compelled to
understand by these sorrows the pains which are
endured by souls neither in heaven nor in hell,
but in an intermediate state between those places.
Our Redeemer did not endure these afflictions;
on the contrary, He afforded, by His Divine
presence, consolation to the souls of those who
were detained or suffering in this hell of purgation, and He assured them of their approaching
deliverance.

The doctrine of Purgatory, though incidentally
noticed by S. Paul in his first Epistle to the
Corinthians, is, nevertheless, insisted on by that
apostle of the Gentiles in the most explicit
manner in the following words: 'For other
foundation no man can lay, but that which is
laid; which is Christ Jesus. Now if any man
build upon this foundation, gold, silver, precious
stones, wood, hay, stubble: every man's work
shall be manifest; for the day of the Lord shall
declare it, because it shall be revealed in fire;

AND THE FIRE SHALL TRY EVERY MAN'S WORK, of
what sort it is. If any man's work abide, which
he hath built thereupon, he shall receive a reward.
If any man's work burn, he shall suffer loss; but
HE HIMSELF SHALL BE SAVED, YET SO AS BY FIRE.'[1]

It would be impossible to offer a more satisfactory or more lucid comment on this passage of
S. Paul than that which is furnished by two
illustrious fathers of the Church, Origen and S.
Augustine. It is now more than sixteen hundred
years since the learned Catechist of Alexandria[2]
thus observed: 'Sin, in its nature, is like to
that matter which fire consumes, and which the
apostle says is built up by sinners, who upon
the foundation of Christ build wood, hay, and
stubble, which words manifestly show that there
are some sins so light as to be compared to
stubble, in which when fire is set, it cannot
dwell long; that there are others like to hay,
which the fire easily consumes, but a little more
slowly, than it does stubble; and others resemble wood, in which, according to the degree
of criminality, the fire finds an abundant substance on which to feed. Thus each crime, in
proportion to its character, experiences a just
degree of punishment.'[3]

---

[1] I *Corinthians*, III, 11-15.

[2] Origen succeeded S. Clement of Alexandria as Catechist in
that celebrated city, and died in the year 253.

[3] *Homil. XIV in Levit.*

'When we depart this life, if we take with us virtues or vices, shall we receive rewards for our virtues, and those trespasses be forgiven to us which we knowingly committed; or shall we be punished for our faults, and not receive the rewards of our virtue? Neither is true; because we shall suffer for our sins, and receive the rewards of our good actions. For if on the foundation of Christ you shall have built, not only gold and silver and precious stones, but also wood and hay and stubble, what do you expect when the soul shall be separated from the body? Would you enter into heaven with your wood and hay and stubble, to defile the kingdom of God; or, on account of these encumbrances, remain without, and receive no reward for your gold and silver and precious stones? Neither is this just. It remains, then, that you be committed to the fire, which shall consume the light materials; for our God, to those who can comprehend heavenly things, is called a CONSUMING FIRE. But this fire consumes not the creature, but what the creature has himself built, wood and hay and stubble. It is manifest that, in the first place, the fire destroys the wood of our transgressions, and then returns to us the reward of our good works.'[1]

Two centuries later the illustrious S. Augustine

---

[1] *Homil. XVI ad XII in Ierem.*

thus exclaimed: 'Cleanse me so, O Lord, in this life, make me such that I may not stand in need of that purifying fire designed for those who shall *be saved, yet so as by fire.* And why, but because (as the apostle says) they have built upon the *foundation wood, hay, and stubble?* If they had built *gold and silver and precious stones,* they would be secured from both fires; not only from that in which the wicked shall be punished for ever, but likewise from that fire which will purify those who shall be saved by fire.[1] But because it is said, *he shall be saved,* that fire is thought lightly of; though the suffering will be more grievous than anything man can undergo in this life.'[2]

The reader's attention must be again directed to a passage in the epistles of S. Peter which has been already cited. The prince of the apostles thus remarks of Christ: 'Being put to death indeed in the flesh, but enlivened in the spirit. In which also coming He preached to those spirits that were in prison; which had been sometime incredulous, when they waited for the patience of God in the days of Noe, when the ark was a-building, wherein a few, that is, eight souls, were saved by water.'[3] From this text it appears certain:—I. That even *after* Christ had

---

[1] Sed etiam de illo qui emendabit eos qui per ignem salvi erunt.
[2] *Enarratio in Psal. XXXVII.*   [3] 1 *Peter,* III, 18-20.

suffered for sins, and had already paid the price of His precious blood for the ransom of all mankind, still there were some souls to whom the merits of their Redeemer's all-sufficient sacrifice upon the cross had not as yet been applied, and who were in an actual state of suffering in prison in the other world. II. That such souls were neither in heaven nor in hell, because heaven is not a prison—a place of punishment, where those who are held in captivity can be corrected and improved by *preaching;* and because it is absurd to imagine that Christ's soul would have gone down amongst those wicked spirits who are damned for all eternity, or that He would have *preached* to Satan and his demons, since the object of preaching is reformation and improvement, neither of which can ever be effected amongst devils.

Another argument in attestation of the Catholic dogma of a middle state of punishment may be deduced from the second book of Machabees:—'The valiant Judas, making a gathering, sent twelve thousand drachms of silver to Jerusalem for sacrifice to be offered for the sins of the dead, thinking well and religiously concerning the resurrection. . . . It is therefore a holy and wholesome thought to pray for the dead, that they may be loosed from sins.'[1]

---

[1] 2 *Machabees,* XII, 43–46. The canonicity of this book is shown in Appendix III.

From this passage we gather: First, that more than a century and a half before the coming of our Saviour, the custom of praying for the dead prevailed amongst the Jews. Secondly, that such a custom was not peculiar to an individual sect amongst the Jews, but was practised by the whole nation, since it was observed by the priesthood as well as by the people; a particular sacrifice was appointed for the purpose, and the Temple at Jerusalem was often made to witness its solemnisation. Thirdly, that this sacrifice, and these supplications for the departed, were expiatory; since the purport of them was that *the dead might be loosed from their sins;*[1] and, therefore, the souls of those individuals for whom they were offered were regarded by the Jewish people not to be in Abraham's bosom, where nothing defiled could be admitted: much less in hell, which was irrevocably barred against hope and pardon: but to be in a state of painful suffering.

X.—NEGATIVE PROOF OF PURGATORY.

Hitherto we have considered the positive proofs only, which establish with such precision the dogma of Purgatory; we should, however, notice a negative one which is equally conclusive. Our Saviour and His apostles frequently censured, in the most energetic and unmeasured language,

---

[1] 2 *Machabees*, XII, 46.

many practices of the Jews which they knew to be erroneous or deemed particularly worthy of reproof. Now, considering the books of Machabees not as inspired Scripture, but as mere history, we must believe that public prayer and sacrifice for the dead were acts of piety in constant use amongst the Hebrew people.[1]

If, therefore, these practices had not been orthodox, but blameworthy, our Lord would have denounced them as an innovation of the Jewish priesthood, whose disorders He reproved with so much freedom and indignant eloquence; and would have stigmatised the ministers of the Temple for inventing them to gratify their avarice, and the apostles would have been sedulous in exhorting each proselyte from the synagogue to abandon their usage; instead of this, however, our Lord and His apostles permit the Jews to follow their ancient devotion of praying for the dead, and thus authorised the practice by affording it their tacit approbation.

XI.—PURGATORY CONSONANT WITH SEVERAL EXPRESSIONS OF SCRIPTURE.

Several indirect arguments may be produced in favour of the Catholic doctrine of Purgatory.

---

[1] Josephus vouches for the belief, which was held at his day by the Jews, who, as he assures us (*Wars of the Jews*, chap. 91), would not pray for those amongst their brethren who committed suicide. The exception proves that they prayed for those who had died by any other kind of death.

Our Lord assures us that 'every idle word that men shall speak, they shall render an account for it in the day of judgement.'[1]

Every idle word, however, cannot subject men to *everlasting* punishment: Christ himself has distinguished the various degrees of culpability contained in certain expressions, and apportioned the corresponding intensity of punishment to be inflicted upon those who utter any of them. 'Whosoever,' says our Saviour, 'is angry with his brother shall be in danger of the judgement. And whosoever shall say to his brother, Raca, shall be in danger of the council. And whosoever shall say, Thou fool, shall be in danger of hell-fire.'[2] There must, consequently, be some smaller pain to suffer after the particular judgement which takes place immediately after death.[3]

S. Paul assures us that every man shall receive reward according to his own labour; and he warns us not to be 'deceived, for God is not mocked. For what things a man shall sow, those also shall he reap.'[4] But we are told by Scripture that no one lives without some kind of sinfulness

---

[1] *S. Matthew*, XII, 36. [2] *Ibid.*, V, 22.

[3] Immediately after death, the damned are buried in hell, as appears from the example of the rich glutton in *S. Luke*, XVI ; and to the just is awarded future happiness, as we see in the good thief, to whom it was said, 'This day thou shalt be with Me in Paradise " (*S. Luke*, XXIII, 43). It is impossible to conceive how rewards and punishments can be assigned without judgement.

[4] *Galatians*, VI, 7, 8.

either of omission or commission, for there is no man who sinneth not;[1] and 'if we say that we have no sin, we deceive ourselves, and the truth is not in us.'[2] While, therefore, it is certain that no one lives without sin, at the same time it cannot possibly be doubted that many, even of the most faithful servants of God, depart this life before they have cleansed away all their sins of thought, word, and deed in the blood of the Lamb. How often does Death go wandering through the world to snatch his prey, with such a silent tread, and casting before him no shadow of his approach, that he sometimes steals upon his unsuspecting victims, and without one notice or a moment's preparation beckons them away from amid the feast and sound of mirth and revelry. Now, let us suppose that some practically good man is surprised, by apoplexy for instance, and that he dies with some little stain of sin upon his soul—guilty of some idle word, some trifling unrepented fault; his soul must be purified from such a speck, however faint and trivial, *before* it can be admitted into heaven, since 'there shall not enter into it anything defiled.'[3] But where? Not in hell certainly; therefore, in some place *between* heaven and hell. This place in which sin is cleansed away,

---

[1] 3 *Kings*, VIII, 46.   [2] I *S. John*, I, 8.
[3] *Apocalypse*, XXI, 27.

this state in which the soul is purified from this world's dross, and rendered fit for heaven, is what Catholics properly denominate PURGATORY.

XII.—PURGATORY TAUGHT BY THE APOSTLES' CREED.

The substance of this doctrine, so conspicuously contained in Holy Scripture, is likewise embodied in that epitome of Christianity which was drawn up by the Apostles, and attests by its appellation that it was their creed. This document of apostolic faith expressly calls upon us to believe that our Saviour 'descended into hell.' Can what is here denominated 'hell' be interpreted the 'grave'? No, certainly; for, just before, we are taught that our Redeemer died and was *buried*—that is, put into the grave; something different from the grave is therefore signified by this expression. It cannot be the hell of the damned which is here indicated; for while our reverence for Christ prohibits us from thinking that His spotless soul would take up its abode with Satan and his accursed spirits, our piety, instructed by the words of S. Peter,[1] will bid us consider the 'hell' of which the Apostles speak here as the prison of the spirits who had been sometime incredulous, and to whom Christ went in order to improve such as were in a state of

---

[1] 1 *Peter*, III, 18 20.

purification by His preaching, and to comfort those others who were waiting for Him to carry them to heaven, but, in the interim, were enjoying the repose of Abraham's bosom. This 'hell' mentioned by the Apostles was, at the same time, a purgatory for some and a paradise for others, and for the good thief amongst the rest, Christ not having as yet ascended into heaven.

XIII.—THE DOCTRINE OF PURGATORY ATTESTED BY THE CHURCH IN EVERY AGE.

A more definite exposition of the doctrine delivered by the Apostles on this article of faith may be readily procured by consulting the records of those Churches which they founded, and by interrogating those venerable pastors who succeeded those Apostles as depositaries of the faith of Jesus and in the office of publicly explaining it. The ancient liturgies are so many faithful registers of the doctrine taught by those who framed them. But it is universally admitted by the learned that, though the present may vary in some unimportant points from the original form of the liturgies, the substance and materials out of which they are constructed are identically the same as those furnished by the Apostles. Now all the ancient liturgies, as well as that which is used at this day by the Church of Rome, unanimously attest the doctrine of Purgatory, since in each of them a particular remembrance is made for the souls of departed brethren.[1]

The limits of this work are too narrow to admit of the insertion of those numerous citations which might be extracted from the writings of the Fathers in support of Purgatory, and the reader who may be desirous of further information on this subject is referred to a work designedly composed to exhibit a well-connected series of ancient testimonies in confirmation of the various points of Catholic doctrine.[2]

---

[1] Extracts from the liturgies of the Greek and Oriental Churches are given in chapter xv on the Diptychs, no. 6. The actual accordance of the Greeks, whether schismatical or orthodox, with the Latins on this point of faith is demonstrated in the most lucid manner by Leone Allacci, in his very able work : *De utriusque Ecclesiae Occidentalis atque Orientalis perpetua in dogmate de Purgatorio consensione.* Romae, 1655.

[2] See J. BERINGTON and J. KIRK, *The Faith of Catholics.* 3rd edition, revised and enlarged by James Waterworth. 1846.

SECTION III.

XIV.—THE PRAYERS OF THE LIVING ARE SERVICEABLE TO THE DEAD.

HAVING established the existence of Purgatory, that is, the existence of a third place or state in which the souls of those who are guilty of smaller sins, called venial, or remaining under the sentence of some temporal punishment unatoned for, are detained in order to be purified for heaven, it will be admitted as a necessary consequence by every reasonable man that it is lawful, nay, as far as charity can bind us, an obligation, to offer up our prayers for the souls of the departed. The Apostle of the Gentiles tells us that, 'We being many, are one body in Christ, and every one members one of another;'[1] and that 'God hath tempered the body together . . . that the members might be mutually careful one for another.'[2] The figure which S. Paul employs is as beautiful as it is expressive. He paints to us the Church under the semblance of a body, the head of which is Christ, and its members all the faithful. These members are finally united to their head and linked among themselves by the Holy Spirit, by

---

[1] *Romans*, XII, 5. [2] I *Corinthians*, XII, 24, 25.

faith, by the sacraments, by prayer, and by the holy ministry, which, like the joints and arteries of the human frame, serve to connect them with Christ and with one another, as well as to convey nourishment and influence from the head to every individual member of this spiritual and mystic body. But we, who are still in this life, as well as those who are detained in purgatory, continue to be fellow-members of one same body, the Church, since we both adhere to Christ, the head of that mystic body, and are united through Him by a common link of charity. This union requires that we render one another mutual assistance when necessary. Such a duty, however, can never be more binding than in the case of those who are lingering in purgatory, and breathe such ardent sighs to gain the beatific presence of the Godhead. After this argument deduced from the words of S. Paul it will be unnecessary to insist upon the performance of an office which is so expressly recommended, at the same time that it is taught by the Apostles in that portion of the Creed which instructs us to believe in the 'Communion of saints.'

XV.—ANTIQUITY OF PRAYER FOR THE DEAD.

The antiquity of the custom of praying for the dead is sufficiently attested by the passage in the second book of Machabees to which we have more than once referred, and from which we gather that the 'valiant Judas, making a gathering, sent twelve thousand drachms of silver to Jerusalem, for sacrifice to be *offered for the sins* of the dead;' concluding that 'it is a holy and wholesome thought to pray for the dead, that they may be loosed from sins.'[1]

XVI.—STILL PRACTISED AMONGST THE JEWS.

This act of religious piety, which was exercised amongst the Jews two thousand years ago, is still practised by them, as may be ascertained by examining their manuals of prayer, in which they are instructed to offer up supplications for the repose of their departed brethren.

In the Hebrew-Spanish ritual, which is in more general use in the synagogues, and holds amongst the Jews the same rank as the Roman ritual does amongst Catholics, it is appointed that at funerals there shall be recited for the deceased a particular form of prayer, part of which is as follows : 'Have pity on him, O Lord, living God, master of the world, with whom there is the source of life, that he may always walk in the way of life, and that his soul may repose amongst those elected unto life eternal. May the merciful God, according to the extent of His mercy, pardon him his iniquities; may his good works be before His eyes, and may he be admitted into His presence amongst the

---

[1] 2 *Machabees*, XII, 43–46.

number of the faithful; may he walk in His presence in the regions of life.' To this succeeds another supplication in behalf of the departed, who is thus feelingly addressed: 'May the gates of heaven be thrown open to you; may you be given to behold the city of peace, and the tabernacles of security; may the angels of peace hasten with joy unto you; may the high-priest receive and conduct you; may your soul go to the double cave of Abraham, and hence upon the cherubim, and hence to Eden's garden; may the angel Michael open to you the gates of the sanctuary; may he present your soul as an oblation unto God; and may the angel-redeemer accompany you to the portals of the delightful places where dwell the Israelites.' All the other prayers which compose the office of interment, and which the Jews denominate ' *Seder Abelut*,' or the 'order of mourning,' abound with similar expressions.[1]

---

[1] In the Talmudical treatise on Benedictions, chap., III, purgatory or a middle state of purification is especially mentioned by the rabbins, who say that: 'The soul does not immediately go to heaven on its separation from the body, but remains wandering about this world during the space of twelve months, at the expiration of which it returns to the grave. It endures, however, much torment in purgatory; at length, at the end of twelve months, it enters into heaven, where it enjoys repose.'

Although the Jews, like the Catholics, admit, first, that there is a middle state for souls after this life; secondly, that the spirits there undergo a temporary punishment for sins committed in this world, are, in fine, purified for heaven; and thirdly, that the prayers of the living may be offered for the dead: still the ideas of the Hebrews concerning minor particulars belonging to this middle state are fanciful, and differ very widely from the more received

XVII.—PRAYERS FOR THE DEAD IN USE IN THE PRIMITIVE CHURCH PROVED FROM ANCIENT INSCRIPTIONS.

From this short notice on the ancient, as well as modern custom amongst the Jews, of making prayer for the dead, we will now proceed to a review of certain monuments of Christian antiquity which exhibit in such a convincing manner the pious solicitude displayed by the true believers in Jesus, from the earliest ages of the faith, to comply with that Divine precept of extending our fraternal charity beyond the grave, and of praying for the souls of our departed brethren.

---

opinions of the Christian Church. The Jews believe that almost every Israelite must go to purgatory, and pass at least a year there ; that when this period has transpired, the soul, and, in the estimation of some, together with the body also, is conveyed through subterraneous channels to the land of Israel, whence it takes its flight to the paradise of Eden. It was asserted by the rabbi Eliezer, whose opinion is put down in the Talmud, that every Israelite had a part in the world to come ; only the excommunicated and such as die burdened with crime are excluded. As the Jews believe that all who depart this life in communion with the synagogue are saved, many individuals are thus supposed to pass through purgatory. A tradition prevails amongst them of a certain pain inflicted after death by an angel, who comes to the tomb and lashes the deceased three several times with a bright-red iron chain. To be spared the infliction of this punishment forms a specific petition in their mortuary prayers. (BOSSUET, *Œuvres*, tom. XLII, p. 615. Versailles, 1819.)

Leone Allacci observes that the Jews pray and give alms for the dead, not only on the day of the funeral and the Sabbaths, but more particularly on the tenth moon of September, when a solemn service is performed, and much is bestowed in charity in suffrage for the souls of the departed. The same author produces copious extracts, in the original Hebrew, of the prayers used on these occasions. *De utriusque Ecclesiae Occidentalis atque Orientalis perpetua in dogmate de Purgatorio consensione*, p. 913.

In excavating the Roman catacombs many very interesting Christian inscriptions have been discovered. Amongst them are several in which peace and rest and benediction are beautifully implored, in a pious prayer of few but touching words, on the soul of him or her over whose sepulchre it was inscribed.[1]

From a great number of the sepulchral inscriptions traced by the hands of the Christians in the first ages a few only have been presented to the reader's notice. They will, however, abundantly suffice to convince him that the Church of Christ, at the epoch of her very infancy, taught her members, as she teaches them at present, to offer up their prayers for the dead.

---

[1] Strolling round the Certosa or public cemetery of Bologna, Byron read and was sensibly affected by the following sepulchral inscriptions : 'Martini Luigi implora pace ;' 'Lucrezia Picini implora eterna quiete.' 'These two and three words,' says the poet, 'comprise and compress all that can be said on the subject. . . . They contain doubt, hope, and humility ; nothing can be more pathetic than the "implora" and the modesty of the request. . . . There is all the helplessness, and humble hope, and death-like prayer, that can arise from the grave—"implora pace."'—MOORE, *Letters and Journals of Lord Byron.* London, 1833, vol. II, pp. 472, 476.

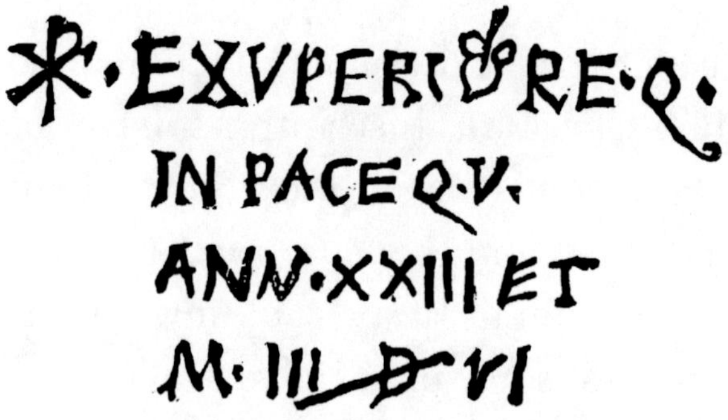

�֍·EXVPERI✶RE·Q·
IN PACE Q·V·
ANN·XXIII ET
M·IIL⊅·VI

EXVPERI REQ*uiescas*
IN PACE Q*ui* V*ixit,*
ANNOS XXIII. ET
M*enses* III. D*ies* VI.

Mayst thou rest in peace, O Exuperius! who lived XXIII *years,*
III *months, and* VI *days.*[1]

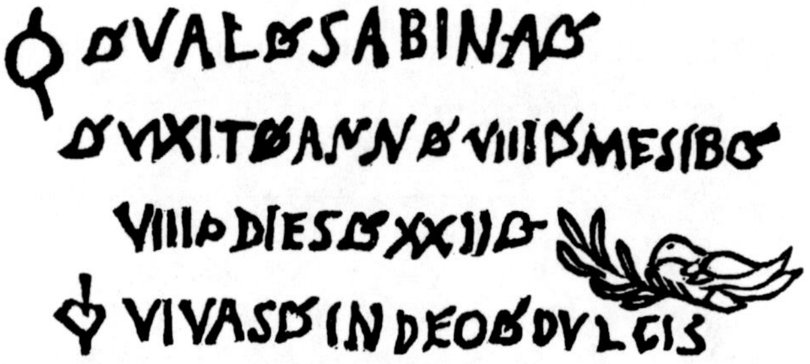

Q ⊘VAL⊘SABINA⊘
⊘VIXIT⊘ANN⊘VIII⊘MESIB⊘
VIIII⊅DIES⊘XXII⊘
⊹ VIVAS⊘IN DEO⊘DVLCIS

VA*le* SABINA
V*i*XIT ANN*os* VIII. M*ens*I*bus* VIII.
DIES XXII.
VIVAS IN DEO DULCIS.

Farewell, O Sabina! she lived VIII *years,* VIII *months,* XXII *days.*
Mayst thou live sweet in God.[2]

---

[1] This inscription was extracted from that part of the catacombs
denominated the cemetery of Callistus, and may be seen in F.
BUONARRUOTI, *Osservazioni sopra alcuni frammenti di Vasi antichi di
Vetro,* p. 165.

[2] This was found in the cemetery of Callistus; see BUONARRUOTI,
p. 166. The dove was a favourite symbol with the primitive be-

IN PACE ET BENEDICTIONE
SVFSVA TE VIXIT ANIS XXX PLVSMINVС
REDDIDIT XÀL ⋅ FEBR ⋅

Mayst thou be in peace and benediction, O Sufsuatus! He lived thirty years more or less. He departed on the Kalends of February.[1]

DOMITI
IN PACE
LEA FECIT

DOMITI

IN PACE

LEA FECIT.

O Domitius! mayst thou be in peace. Lea made this.[2]

ΑΦΘΟΝΑ ΕΝ ΘΕΩ ΖΗ
CHC

Aphthona! mayst thou live in God.[3]

---

lievers. It perpetually occurs in the paintings, inscriptions, and other graphic monuments of Christian antiquity. The early Fathers, Tertullian, S. Clement, and S. Cyprian, constantly refer to it; and no hieroglyphic was considered more appropriate for the Christian's sepulchre than the emblematic dove with its olive-bough of peace. An inspection of the learned works of Aringhi, Boldetti, Buonarruoti, Bottari, and Northcote and Brownlow will richly repay the reader who may feel any curiosity on this subject.

[1] From the same cemetery; BUONARRUOTI, p. 165.

[2] *Ibid.*, p. 164. The above was inscribed in red letters, and is copied from the original, found in the cemetery of Callistus.

[3] *Ibid.*, p. 166. On the word Ζησης the learned reader may consult Buonarruoti (pp. 203 *et seq.*) for some interesting observations on this Greek formula of wishing happiness.

ROXANE   ROXANE

D. B. QVES   *Dulcis. Bene* QUIES

QVAS   QUAS.

O sweet Roxanus ! mayst thou rest well.[1]

LEA BENE CESQVAS.   LEA BENE *Quiescas.*

O Lea ! mayst thou rest in peace.[2]

The following are some other sepulchral inscriptions that contain a prayer for the dead :—

---

[1] This inscription was engraved on a cornelian ring. To those who have studied Greek and Roman antiquities it is well known that anciently it was the custom to bury with the deceased a variety of ornaments. This ring was no doubt one of those funeral objects consigned to the sepulchre together with the corpse of some Roman Christian, that it might not only announce him to have been a member of the faith, but at the same time exhibit a proof that his surviving friends cherished the remembrance of him by their prayers for his departed soul. To what was an unmeaning Gentile custom was thus imparted a Christian and an edifying meaning. S. Clement of Alexandria, who flourished towards the decline of the second century (A.D. 194), in one of his works, called "The Instructor" (*Paedagogus*, lib. III, c. 11), recommends the Christians of his day to have the rings they wore 'engraved, not with the images of idols, nor of utensils which contribute to sin or intemperance, but with a dove, a fish, a ship scudding before the wind, a musical lyre, or a ship's anchor.' All these were Christian hieroglyphics—symbols of Jesus Christ and His Gospel, and of a future life in happiness. Rings bearing these various emblems have been found in the graves of the catacombs, and may be seen engraved in BOLDETTI (p. 502). Aringhi has dedicated the greater part of the sixth book of his *Roma Subterranea* to the elucidation of these and other symbolical figures introduced into fresco-paintings and other works of art by the ancient Christians.

[2] From the cemetery of Calepodius ; BOLDETTI, p. 432.

DOMINA DVLCISSIMA
STERCORIA FILIA QVI
BIXIT AN. II. MENS. IIII. IN
PACE DOMINI DORMIAS.

> BOLDETTI, p. 418.

OLIMPIODORE VIVAS IN
DEO

> *Ibid.*, p. 340.

GENSANE PAX ISPIRITO
TVO.

> *Ibid.*, p. 418.

VLPIA VIVA SIS CVM FRA
TRIBVS TVIS.

> *Ibid.*, p. 419.

IANVARIA. VIVAS IN PACE. DEP. XIIII.
KAL. DEC. VICTOR. PATER. ET SPORTVLA
MATER. FECIT.

> *Ibid.*, p. 420.

These exclamations, by expressing such an anxious tender wish that those departed friends for whom they are ejaculated may repose in bliss, in reality betray some doubts about their enjoyment of that happiness; and thus exhibit proof that the pious Christians who uttered them believed that the soul of the deceased might be in an intermediate state, where the efficacy of such aspirations could reach him, and his spirit could be refreshed and benefited by the supplications of his surviving brethren.

SECTION IV.

XVIII.—THE SACRIFICE OF THE MASS OFFERED FOR THE DEAD.

THE principal amongst those offerings which the Catholic Church presents to heaven in behalf of the souls in purgatory is the holy sacrifice of the Mass. There is no Catholic who doubts that Christ, in dying, most perfectly satisfied for the sins of the whole world without exception; and what the Holy Scripture teaches we are careful to recite at Mass by saying: 'Behold the Lamb of God, behold Him who taketh away the sin of the world;[1] have mercy on us.' But we believe that, by the sacrifice of the Mass, the merits of Christ's death and passion are applied to us; Protestants consider that these same merits are applied to the soul by faith. When the Church teaches that the Mass is a propitiatory sacrifice, she maintains that Jesus Christ, actually present on the altar in the state of a victim, demands pardon for sinners as He did upon the cross; that He satisfies the justice of His Father, and appeases His anger, while He averts those chastisements which our sins have merited. It

---

[1] *S. John*, I, 29.

has already been proved [1] that the Mass is a true sacrifice, in which Jesus Christ is both priest and victim. He it is, therefore, who offers up Himself to His Father by the hands of His ministers in the new covenant. The motive of this unbloody oblation is the same as that which prompted Him to make an offering of Himself in a bloody manner on the cross: therefore He daily makes this self-same oblation in the Mass, in order to obtain mercy for all men by applying the merits of His passion, once suffered in a bloody manner, to their souls, and thus efface the transgressions of the living and the dead.

This dogma implies another, which has been demonstrated when, by the authority of Scripture, it was proved that after the remission of the guilt of sin and its eternal punishment the sinner is yet obliged to make atonement, either in this or in a future world, to the Divine justice for those temporal pains which still remain to be expiated.

Such is the solid foundation which upholds the doctrine of praying, and of offering up the propitiatory sacrifice of the Mass for the faithful departed. Such are the reasons which induce the Church to make a pious remembrance of the dead each time the Mass is celebrated. As it is her infallible belief that those amongst her children who leave this world without having sufficiently

---

[1] Chap. i.

expiated their offences are obliged to endure a temporary chastisement in the world to come, she, with the feelings of the tenderest of mothers, supplicates Almighty God to have compassion on them, and remit to them this temporary pain through the merits and the blood of Jesus.

XIX.—ANTIQUITY OF THIS CUSTOM.

Were it requisite, it would be easy to establish, by a number of venerable and well authenticated monuments, the antiquity of this practice of offering up Mass for the departed. But the fact is so notorious, that the Protestant Bingham, with all his dislike for the Catholic dogma of Purgatory, is compelled, though with most evident reluctance, to make the following admissions, which to the Protestant reader must be so satisfactory as to render any other citation quite superfluous: 'Possidius tells us,[1] S. Austin was buried with the oblation of the SACRIFICE to God for the commendation of his body to the ground. And so S. Austin himself tells us,[2] his mother Monica was buried with the offering of the SACRIFICE of our redemption, according to custom, before her body was laid in the ground. . . . In like manner

---

[1] POSSIDII *Vita Augustini*, cap. 13. Pro eius commendanda corporis depositione sacrificium Deo oblatum est, et sepultus est.

[2] S. AUGUSTINI *Confess.*, lib. IX, cap. 12. Cum offerretur pro ea sacrificium pretii nostri, iam iuxta sepulchrum posito cadavere, priusquam deponeretur, sicut fieri solet, etc.

Eusebius describes the funeral of Constantine.[1] He says the clergy performed the Divine service with prayers; and lest we should take this for prayers only, he adds: They honoured him with the mystical liturgy, or service of the EUCHARIST, and the communion of the holy prayers. So S. Ambrose gives us to understand it was in the funeral of Valentinian, by those words in his oration upon his death: Bring me the holy mysteries; let us pray for his rest with a pious affection.'[2] Concerning particular prayers for the dead, Bingham goes on to say: 'Now this was the rather done, because in the Communion Service, according to the custom of those times, a solemn commemoration was made of the dead in general, and prayers offered to God for them; some eucharistical by way of thanksgiving for their deliverance out of this world's afflictions; and others by way of intercession, that God would receive their souls to the place of rest and happiness; that He would pardon their human failures, and not impute to them the sins of daily incursion, which in the best of men are remainders of natural frailty and corruption.'[3]

---

[1] EUSEBII *Vita Const.*, cap. 71.

[2] S. AMBROSII *de Obitu Valentiniani Consolatio.* Date manibus sancta mysteria? Pio requiem eius poscamus affectu.

[3] J. BINGHAM, *The Antiquities of the Christian Church*, book XXIII, c. iii, sect. 12, 13. Milles, who was afterwards elevated to the Protestant bishopric of Waterford, in the edition of S. Cyril's works which he printed at Oxford in 1703, candidly acknowledges that

XX.—BELIEF OF THE ANGLO-SAXON CHURCH IN PURGATORY.

Of the belief in Purgatory maintained by all our Catholic ancestors, as far back as the Anglo-Saxon times, we possess magnificent and interesting monuments.[1] We will not stop to enumerate the many splendid piles that were erected, or the numerous religious houses and charitable establishments that were endowed by their founders for the especial purpose of having prayers and masses daily offered for them after death. History attests what treasures were expended, through this pious motive, by the kings, the nobles, and the clergy of Britain, during those ages which elapsed from the conversion of England to Christianity until the period when the old was exchanged for a new religion, at the commencement of the sixteenth century. It is sufficient for our present purpose to glance merely at those various religious customs observed a thousand years ago amongst the Anglo-Saxon inhabitants of this

'The custom of praying and offering up sacrifice for the faithful departed, though not supported by any express testimony of Sacred Scripture, most evidently appears to have prevailed in the Church even from the very times of the Apostles.' (S. CYRILLI *Opera*, ed. THO. MILLES, p. 297.) An admission that this article of Christian faith was warranted by Holy Writ would have been too great a concession to be expected from a Protestant divine and a member of the University of Oxford.

[1] Not a few of our more celebrated ecclesiastical monuments, such as churches, chantries, etc., owe their origin to this belief.

island, and placed on record by the writers of
that nation. That the practice of praying for the
dead exerted a powerful and extensive influence
on the manners of that people is evident from
their anxious endeavours to secure the prayers of
the faithful after their decease, and from the
religious ceremonies they employed in the interment of their dead. 'To secure,' says Dr.
Lingard, in his elegant and learned history of
the Anglo-Saxon Church, 'to secure the future
exertions of his friends was, in the eyes of the
devout Saxon, an object of high importance : and,
with this view, numerous associations were formed,
in which each individual bound himself to pray
for the souls of the deceased members.[1]

'Gilds were an institution of great antiquity
among the Anglo-Saxons. . . . They were of
different descriptions. Some were restricted to
the performance of religious duties. . . . As a
specimen of their engagements, I may be allowed
to translate a part of the laws established in the
gild at Abbotsbury. " If," says the legislator,
" anyone belonging to our association chance to
die, each member shall pay one penny for the
good of the soul before the body be laid in the

---

[1] 'See HICKS, *Dissert. Epis.*, p. 18 ; WANLEY, MSS., p. 280. With
the history of S. Cuthbert, which he had composed, Bede sent the
following petition to the monks of Lindisfarne : " Sed et me de-
functo, pro redemptione animae meae quasi familiaris et vernaculi
vestri orare, et missas facere, et nomen meum inter vestra scribere
dignemini." BEDAE *Vita S. Cuthberti*, p. 228.'

grave. If he neglect it, he shall be fined in a triple sum. If any of us fall sick within sixty miles, we engage to find fifteen men, who may bring him home: but if he die first, we will send thirty to convey him to the place in which he desired to be buried. If he die in the neighbourhood, the steward shall enquire where he is to be interred, and shall summon as many members as he can, to assemble, attend the corpse in an honourable manner, carry it to the minster, and pray devoutly for the soul." . . . With the same view, the Anglo-Saxons were anxious to obtain a place of sepulture in the most frequented and celebrated churches. The monuments raised over their ashes would, they fondly expected, recall them to the memory, and solicit in their behalf the charity of the faithful.[1] . . . But the more opulent were not content to rest their hopes of future assistance on the casual benevolence of others. They were careful to erect or endow monasteries, with the express obligation, that their inhabitants should pray for their benefactors. Of these an exact catalogue was preserved in the library of each church; the days on which they died were carefully noticed; and on their anni-

---

[1] That such was their expectation is clearly expressed by Bede : 'Postulavit eum possessionem terrae aliquam a se ad construendum monasterium accipere, in quo ipse rex defunctus sepeliri deberet : nam et seipsum fideliter credidit multum iuvari eorum orationibus, qui illo in loco Domino servirent.'—BEDAE *Hist.*, lib. III, c. 23; lib. IV, c. 5.

versaries, prayers and masses were performed for the welfare of their souls.[1] . . . The assistance, which was usually given to the dead, consisted in works of charity and exercises of devotion. To the money which the deceased had bequeathed for the relief of the indigent, his friends were accustomed to add their voluntary donations, with a liberal present to the church in which the obsequies were performed.[2]

'The devotions performed in behalf of the dead, consisted in the frequent repetition of the Lord's Prayer, which was generally termed a belt of Paternosters: in the chaunting of a certain number of psalms, at the close of which the congregation fell on their knees, and intoned the anthem "O Lord, according to Thy great mercy give rest to his soul, and, in consideration of Thy infinite goodness, grant that he may enjoy eternal light in the company of Thy saints;" and in the sacrifice of the Mass,

---

[1] 'In the Cotton Library (*Dom. A.* 7) is a manuscript of the reign of Athelstan, in which the names of the principal benefactors of the church of Lindisfarne are inscribed in letters of gold and silver. The list was afterwards continued, but with less elegance, till the Reformation. (WANLEY, p. 249.) In every monastery they also preserved the names of their deceased members, and were careful to pray for them on the anniversaries of their death.' BED. lib. IV, c. 14.

[2] 'In the gild at London, when any of the members died, each of the survivors gave to the poor a loaf for the good of his soul (*Leg. Sax.*, p. 68). This was the origin of doles, of which some instances still remain. Before the distribution, the following prayer was pronounced : "Precamur Te, Domine, clementissime Pater, ut eleemosyna ista fiat in misericordia Tua, ut acceptus sit cibus iste pro anima famuli Tui, ill. et ut sit benedictio Tua super omnia dona ista."—WANLEY, MSS., p. 83.'

which was always offered on the third day after
the decease, and afterwards repeated in proportion
to the solicitude of the friends of the dead.[1] . . .
The body of the deceased was placed on a bier,
or in a hearse. On it lay the book of the Gospels,
the code of his belief, and the Cross, the signal
of his hope. A pall of silk or linen was thrown
over it, till it reached the place of interment.
His friends were summoned; strangers deemed
it a duty to join the funeral procession. The
clergy walked before, or on each side, bearing
lighted tapers in their hands, and chaunting a
portion of the psalter. They entered the church.
If it were in the evening, the night was passed
in exercises of devotion. In the morning, the
sacrifice of the Mass was offered for the departed
soul; the body was deposited with solemnity in
the grave, the sawlshot paid, and a liberal dona-
tion distributed to the poor.'[2]

OBJECTIONS ANSWERED.

It will not require much labour to overthrow
the objections which are usually urged against
the doctrine of Purgatory. They may be classified

---

[1] *Poenit. Egb.* apud WILKIN, p. 122.

[2] LINGARD, *The History and Antiquities of the Anglo-Saxon Church*,
pp. 245–261. Though prayers for the dead were abolished at the
Reformation, the payment of Soul-scot continued to be enforced by
the clergy down to the middle of the present century.

under four heads. 1. Exception is sometimes made by Protestants to the dogma of a middle state, through an erroneous belief that from the beginning of the world those who departed this life were immediately consigned to Hell or admitted into Heaven. 2. Because it is asserted by the inspired writers that the faithful have nothing to fear, it is falsely argued there can be no Purgatory. 3. It is pretended that a belief in a temporary punishment after death does not coincide with those passages of Scripture which represent the dead as resting in peace. 4. It is erroneously concluded that the doctrine of Purgatory must lessen the perfection of God's mercy and the infinitude of Christ's merits.

XXI.—FIRST OBJECTION REFUTED.

One amongst the bold but unauthorised assertions advanced by the innovators in religion towards the commencement of the sixteenth century is—'That there never was from the beginning of the world any other place for souls after this life but two : Heaven for the blessed, and Hell for the damned.' In this novel doctrine are included several errors. It denies that all the venerable patriarchs, prophets, and other holy personages who lived previously to the Christian dispensation went into a third place denominated Abraham's bosom, or *Limbus Patrum*, but asserts them all to have been admitted immediately into heaven; a refutation of this is furnished in those proofs of a middle state which have been already noticed.[1] It maintains that these saints of the Old Law were in heaven before our blessed Saviour had discharged the price of our redemption; whence it would follow, in contradiction to the word of God, that Jesus Christ was not the first who ascended and entered into heaven. S. Paul, however, while instituting a comparison between the Jewish sanctuary and the sanctuary of heaven, observes that: 'Into the tabernacle after the second veil, which is called the Holy of Holies, the high priest alone entered once a year, the Holy Ghost signifying this, that the WAY INTO THE HOLIES WAS NOT YET MADE MANIFEST, whilst the former tabernacle was yet standing[2] . . . . for Jesus is not entered into the Holies made with hands, the patterns of the true : but into heaven itself:[3] having therefore, brethren, a confidence in the entering into the Holies by the blood of Christ; a NEW and living way which He hath dedicated for us through the veil.'[4] The same way in which Jacob laments the supposed death of his favourite Joseph[5] completely refutes the Protestant supposition that the saints of the Old Law were admitted into the joys of heaven

---

[1] See N^os. V to VIII of this chapter, pp. 47–60.
[2] *Hebrews*, IX, 3, 7, 8.   [3] *Ibid.*, 24.   [4] *Ibid.*, X, 19, 20.
[5] See N^o. V of this chapter, p. 48.

immediately they died. No one believes that Jacob on his departure from this world was to be consigned to the hell of the damned. According to the modern principles adopted by some Protestants, the patriarch was to be immediately conveyed to heaven, and not to go to any third place; he himself, however, did not expect such a happiness as the instantaneous enjoyment of the heavenly presence, but, on the contrary, declares that he is to go to a third place—hell (where our Saviour afterwards went), and there find his child. It will be of no service to adduce the examples of Henoch's translation or of Elias's ascent in a fiery chariot. Of Henoch the book of Genesis tells us, 'That he walked with God, and was seen no more: because God took him.'[1] S. Paul rehearses almost verbatim this passage from the Pentateuch.[2] But neither in the writings of Moses, nor in the letter of the Apostle, is there uttered a syllable which indicates that this holy man was introduced into the beatific vision—that is, heaven properly so called. With regard to the prophet who went up into *heaven* by a whirlwind,[3] it is to be observed that the word שָׁמַיִם (*shamaim*) in the Hebrew original, which is translated in the Bible by the term 'heaven,' also signifies the *celestial expanse*, and is not unfre-

---

[1] *Genesis*, v, 24.
[2] *Hebrews*, xi, 5.   [3] *4 Kings*, ii, 11.

quently rendered in Greek ἀήρ, and in English *air*.[1]

The inspired pages, therefore, merely inform us that Elias was removed from the earth and elevated into the air, but say nothing of his being transported into the unclouded presence of God. Indeed, so far were the sons of the prophets at Jericho from believing that Elias, though wafted in a fiery chariot, and borne by a whirlwind into *heaven* (the air), was admitted into the kingdom of Jehovah, that they said to Eliseus: 'Behold, there are with thy servants fifty strong men, that can go, and seek thy master, lest perhaps the Spirit of the Lord hath taken him up and cast him upon some mountain or into some valley.'[2]

---

[1] Aquila and Theodotion render שָׁמַיִם by ἀήρ in *Job*, XXXV, 11, and the Protestant translation frequently by *the air*. See *Genesis*, I, 30, and VII, 3; 2 *Samuel*, XXI, 10; *Proverbs*, XXX, 19; *Ecclesiastes*, X, 20.

[2] 4 *Kings*, II, 16. That death must be endured by all men is continually asserted in the Holy Scriptures, and is especially noticed by S. Paul in his Epistle to the Romans, whom he thus addresses: 'Wherefore as by one man sin entered into this world, and by sin death; and so death passed upon *all* men.' (*Romans*, V, 12.) It would seem, therefore, when the same Apostle, while writing to the Hebrews (XI, 5), says: 'By faith Henoch was translated, that he should not see death; and he was not found, because God had translated him,'—that his words are to be interpreted in a qualified sense, as expressive, not that a sentence common to ALL men was ultimately and absolutely annulled in favour of this holy patriarch; but that he should not have it passed upon him in the manner and according to the ordinary course of nature. The form of expression adopted by the inspired writer of the book of Kings while recording the departure of the prophet on the whirlwind, is not for-

In fine, this erroneous opinion of Protestants, that there are and ever were but two states— heaven and hell, is directly refuted by Holy Scripture and by the Creed of the Apostles.

The phrase perpetually made use of by the inspired writers of the Old Testament, even when they are treating of the most holy personages, is, that at their death they went down to hell;[1] or, in other words, they descended not into a grave which could receive their bodies only, but 'into hell,'—into that common receptacle wherein reposed the souls of the holy patriarchs and prophets, and of all those righteous men who lived before the time of the Messiah, whom they were expecting to unbar the gates of heaven, that had been closed against all the sons of Adam,—into that hell, whither our Divine Redeemer, after expiring on the cross, went and 'preached to those

---

tuitous ; but, as it perfectly resembles that employed by Moses in noticing the translation of Henoch, seems to have been designedly selected. This circumstance affords another motive to support a pious belief entertained by the Church, that Henoch and Elias were removed from the earth to some other place, where they are still living, and whence both of them will return to preach penance to the nations, and combat against Antichrist, by whom they are to be put to death. Many commentators on the Holy Scriptures refer to Henoch and Elias that passage of the Apocalypse in which it is promised : 'And I will give unto my two witnesses, and they shall prophesy a thousand two hundred sixty days, clothed in sackcloth. These are the two olive-trees, and the two candlesticks, that stand before the Lord of the earth.' *Apocalypse*, xi, 3, 4.

[1] In Hebrew, שְׁאוֹל, *sheol;* in Greek, ᾅδης ; in Latin, *ad inferos* or *ad infernum*.

spirits that were in *prison.*'[1] The doctrine of the Apostles' Creed is in perfect accordance with the Scriptures. That symbol of Christianity teaches us that after our Saviour was dead and BURIED, that is, put into the grave, 'He descended into hell,' according to His soul. S. Jerome, in reference to the Mosaic dispensation, observes: 'If Abraham, Isaac, and Jacob were in hell, who was in the kingdom of heaven?' and again: 'Before the coming of Christ, Abraham was in hell; after His coming, the thief was in paradise.'[2]

S. Jerome, however, was well aware that neither the hell in which abode the patriarchs, nor the paradise that received the soul of the repentant thief upon the cross, was heaven. The comment of S. Augustine on the Psalms is pertinent to the present subject. Of that passage,[3] 'Thou hast delivered my soul out of the lower hell,' the celebrated doctor of the Church observes that the *lower hell* is the place where the damned for all eternity are tortured; the *higher hell* is that in which the souls of the just found rest; and hence both abodes are denominated hell. To avoid this distinction of a lower and higher hell, the first Protestant translators of the Bible rendered it *lowest grave,* under the apprehension that by giving the true version of the words of the psalmist

---

[1] 1 *Peter,* III, 19. [2] *Epitaph. Nepot.,* cap. III.
[3] *Psalm* LXXXV, 13.

the clearest Scripture proof might be furnished to establish the belief of two hells, out of one of which there was a possibility of returning, and where, indeed, the spotless soul of Jesus Christ abode for part of three days, and whence it afterwards arose and was united to His body. In the new Protestant version of the Bible, made in 1683, this passage was partially amended. For 'grave' was substituted the proper word 'hell;' but the superlative 'lowest' was not changed for the comparative 'lower,' as it should have been. The translators were perfectly aware that the comparative 'lower' would have clearly indicated a distinction between the higher and a 'lower' hell, between a purgatory and a place of eternal reprobation; for so decisively is the text in favour of such a doctrine that Tertullian remarked: 'I know that the bosom of Abraham was no heavenly place, but only the higher part of hell.'[1]

XXII.—ARGUMENTS FROM SCRIPTURE ANSWERED.

Under this head may be arranged those objections which Protestants study to raise up against the existence of a third place, on the authority of the following passages in Holy Scripture. Because the wise man has declared that—'If the tree fall to the south, or to the north, in

---

[1] *Adversus Marcion*, lib. IV. Tertullian flourished about the year 194. Consult T. WARD, *Errata to the Protestant Bible*.

what place soever it shall fall, there shall it be;'[1]
—it is gratuitously assumed that after death
there are but two places open for us, whence
there is no returning; and that, in consequence,
there is no purgatory. That such a sentence of
the wise man does not, however, exclude the
existence of a purgatory, is evident. In the first
place, if the comparison between the soul of
man and a cut-down tree, supposed to be included in this passage of Ecclesiastes, be rigorously insisted on, it would go to deny the general
resurrection, and persuade us to conclude that
as the tree, once felled, will decay and moulder
away, and never more be animated with sap, nor
sprout, nor live again, so man, when once he
be overtaken by death, will crumble into dust,
from which he sprang, nor will he ever rise again,
but be annihilated. In the second place, though
these words be applied to indicate the future
destiny of the soul, and to express that if we
leave this world under the guilt of mortal sin
we shall be adjudged to suffer hell's perpetual
torments, but if, in God's favour, heaven is to
be our never-ending recompense, still they by no
means exclude the *passage* of the soul through
the cleansing fire of purgatory before it arrives
at its ultimate destination. It is true that immediately we die we are to receive our sentence of

---

[1] *Ecclesiastes*, XI, 3.

final pain or *final* happiness. While the deten-
tion of the soul in purgatory is but for a certain
period, the very fact of its being sent there
makes its *ultimate* destiny to be fixed—it is
decreed to go to heaven when purified in such
a manner that it may be admitted 'where nought
defiled can enter.'[1] According to S. Jerome,
the south is indicative of a region of light, the
north signifies a land of obscurity and darkness;
hence the first is a figure of heaven, the second
of the infernal dungeon. But he who dies in
the favour of God, yet not without some smaller
faults to make atonement for—some fainter
stains of sin upon his soul—has fallen to the
south; since his spirit is detained for a limited
period in purgatory, with the *certitude* of *final*
happiness—is bid to stand for a season at the
threshold of that kingdom of holiest, celestial
light, until it be pure enough to pass the beaming portals.

Again, it is argued, though falsely, that there
can be but two places, since S. Matthew informs
us[2] that, at the last day, Christ our judge will
indicate but two places, and mention nothing
about purgatory; for He will say to those on
His right hand: 'Come, ye blessed of My Father,
possess you the kingdom prepared for you from
the foundation of the world;' while He will turn

---

[1] *Apocalypse*, XXI, 27.   [2] *S. Matthew*, XXV, 34, 41.

to those who shall be on His left hand, and say to them: 'Depart from me, you cursed, into everlasting fire, which was prepared for the devil and his angels.' To this it may be replied, that after the day of general judgement, concerning which S. Matthew is here speaking, there will be two states only, for purgatory will then have an end. There will remain no other places but heaven for the righteous and hell for the wicked. Those, however, who advance these words of the evangelist in opposition to the doctrine of Purgatory should not neglect to consider the expression made use of by the Judge while pronouncing the sentence of eternal reprobation on the impious: 'Depart,' He will say to them, 'Depart, you cursed, into everlasting fire,'—not into flames which, on some day, shall cease to scorch you like those of the lower hell, that did exist till now—not into a place of *temporary* punishment, like that of ancient purgatory—but, go into EVERLASTING fire; yes, go, not into that fire that served to fit the saints of every era for heaven, that purified their souls from every smaller speck of earthly imperfection and of human frailty, and in whose regard the declaration of My servant Paul has been exemplified, since they have been SAVED, yet so as by FIRE;[1] but go, depart into that very fire which was prepared for the DEVIL

---

[1] *Corinthians*, III, 15.

and HIS ANGELS. To those who ponder well this passage of Scripture, it may ultimately appear that, instead of presenting any arguments against the dogma of Purgatory, it rather tends to corroborate that doctrine, by showing us how emphatically our Divine Redeemer, at the day of general judgement, will by inference distinguish, while pronouncing condemnation, between a temporal and an everlasting flame—a fire that was prepared for Satan and his angels, and some other fire not prepared for devils.

XXIII.—SECOND OBJECTION ANSWERED.

Because it is asserted by the inspired writers that the faithful have nothing to fear, it is falsely argued that there can be no purgatory. Such a conclusion is sometimes inferred from the words of S. Paul, in which he asserts that 'There is now no condemnation to them that are in Christ Jesus, who walk not according to the flesh, . . . but according to the Spirit.'[1] It should be remarked that in this passage, as well as in others that resemble it, is indicated everlasting punishment, which, accurately speaking, is alone to be denominated condemnation. With reference to the words of the Apostle just recited, it is evidently his intention to signify by them that Christians, 'being delivered from the law of sin

---

[1] *Romans*, VIII, 1, 4.

and death by the grace of Jesus,' have now, through the medium of that precious and spontaneous gift, no reason for apprehending condemnation at the final judgement, provided they continue incorporated 'in Christ Jesus' by the means of faith and charity, and do not yield assent to the concupiscence of the flesh. Nothing, therefore, can be extracted from this text either to support or to combat the doctrine of Purgatory.

XXIV.—THIRD OBJECTION.

The objection which it is attempted to deduce from those portions of the sacred volume that represent the souls of the departed as resting in peace, is not more weighty than the former one. What though S. John announces to us that 'Blessed are the dead who die in the Lord: from henceforth now, that they may rest from their labours; for their works follow them.'[1] Must we, therefore, conclude that the inspired writer who penned this sentence did not recognise a third place, a state between heaven and hell, in fact, a purgatory? May we assume that the belief of temporary punishments after death does not agree with those texts which represent the dead as resting in peace? We are by no means warranted to draw such inferences. Who are those of whom S. John speaks in the text we

---

[1] *Apocalypse*, XIV, 13.

have noticed? Those who *die in the Lord*—such as depart this life in the PERFECT love and favour of Almighty God, and are professors of His true and uncontaminated faith. As these die in the grace of God, they, as it were, fall asleep upon His bosom, and will repose there for eternity. It is to these the angel of the Lord announces that, from that moment, they are to enjoy the rest and bliss of heaven for endless ages. This, however, has not the slightest connection with the state after death of such amongst the faithful as have lived and died with certain blemishes upon their souls. It is for these *imperfect* Christians, and not for spotless *saints and martyrs*, that a state of purification is requisite. It is for such, and such only, that the Catholic Church puts up her prayers and offers the propitiatory sacrifice of the Mass; for she knows that those who have ordered all their ways according to the paths of righteousness, and those who seal the profession of their faith and testify their love of God with their life-blood by a cruel martyrdom, die in the Lord, and are wafted by angel-spirits to His beatific presence; where, instead of requiring our prayers in their behalf, they continually pray for us and offer our petitions to the throne of mercy.

XXV.—FOURTH OBJECTION ANSWERED.

But it is erroneously pretended that the doctrine of Purgatory must deteriorate the perfection of God's mercy, and diminish or detract from the infinite and all-atoning merits of Christ Jesus. The Catholic Church instructs us to believe that every pardon of our sins which we can possibly receive either in the present life, or in purgatory, proceeds from God's pure mercy, and that for the very smallest stain of sin the precious blood of Christ must be applied before it can be possibly effaced. She teaches, however, that God Himself has instituted certain channels for the conveyance of His grace into the souls of men, and requires certain conditions absolutely requisite before He will allow the all-sufficient and superabundant merits of Christ Jesus to be imparted to them: such are faith, repentance, and the sacraments for the living; to which is added purgatory for those who leave this world in God's favour, but still with some venial imperfections to be atoned for.

That the recognition of certain channels and particular conditions does not detract from the perfection of God's mercy is a truth that must be assented to by every rational and pious Christian, since such channels and such conditions constitute the medium of communication between the human race and the Divinity; and are, in fact, the instruments which God Himself has thought proper to select for the purpose of imparting His graces to the soul. This is a principle which in reality is admitted by everyone who bears the Christian name, however widely he may be separated from the Catholic Church, since there is not a sect which does not strenuously insist upon the necessity of some one condition or other indispensable for the application of Christ's merits to the soul for obtaining salvation. Whether that requisite be *faith alone*, or faith together with baptism and good works, is perfectly indifferent; the implied or explicit admission that something is demanded is an open recognition of the principle. Now it may be asked how the man who asserts that faith, which is a mental act, a motion of the will, and that the sacrament of Baptism, which is an outward sign and sacred ceremony, are necessary preparations to justification—are channels by which the grace of God is infused into the soul, can continue to be consistent with himself and reject the doctrine of Purgatory on the plea that it detracts from the merits of God's mercy? Faith —Baptism—the sacrament of the Lord's Supper— all the sacraments are so many means by which the mercy of heaven is applied to the soul; purgatory is nothing more. Now, as neither faith, nor Baptism, nor any sacrament detracts from the mercy of God, so neither does purgatory: whatever arguments can be produced against purgatory are available against the necessity of faith and the administration of the sacraments.

In the second place, it is to be observed that the doctrine of Purgatory, so far from diminishing the inexhaustible and superabundant merits of Christ's passion, multiplies those channels through which those precious merits are distributed and applied to man; and tends no more to undervalue their inestimable price and their efficacy than the doctrine of the necessity of faith, of baptism, of prayer, etc. The satisfaction which Jesus Christ made for man is of an *infinite* price, but He intended that it should be applied to us in a *finite* manner. Though Christ, by His *infinite* merits, procured for us the gifts of grace and life eternal, still it is His wish that *we co-operate* with those spiritual gifts in order to obtain eternal happiness. For what purpose did He himself teach us to pray thus : 'Thy kingdom come'—'Forgive us our trespasses,'—and to continue the recital of this petition even after the price of our redemption should have been paid and heaven unbarred for our reception? For no other purpose than to assure us that prayer was one amongst those mediums by which the merits of His passion might be applied to us. Our blessed Saviour did not conceive that a purgatory or a place of punishment in another world could diminish the value of that inestimable ransom He paid upon the Cross for man's redemption; since, even after He had actually suffered, He withheld the immediate application of it in the instance of those spirits who were still confined in prison, and to whom 'Christ *being put to death* indeed in the flesh, went *to preach*.'[1] Indeed, we have no stronger motives to assert that the doctrine of Purgatory diminishes the merits of the sacrifice upon the Cross, than we have to maintain that the apostle S. Paul derogated from its value when he taught 'That Christ ALWAYS liveth to make INTERCESSION for us;'[2] or when he said, 'I fill up those things that are wanting of the sufferings of Christ, in my flesh.'[3]

From investigating these several dogmas we will now proceed to illustrate the ritual observances comprehended in the Eucharistic sacrifice.

---

[1] I *Peter*, III, 18, 19.   [2] *Hebrews*, VII, 25.   [3] *Colossians*, I, 24.

CHAPTER VIII.

ON CEREMONIES.

I.—MAN'S NATURE PROVES THE NECESSITY OF RELIGIOUS CEREMONIES.

If man were a disembodied spirit like the angels he might worship with his soul only; but he superadds a body to his mortal existence: as long, therefore, as his spirit is the tenant of an earthly tabernacle, and animates a portion of the visible creation; as long as his spirit receives the impress of its ideas, and acquires its notions through the medium of the senses, and explains its own sensations by their instrumentality, so long must the use of some exterior ceremonial be necessary for man to exhibit a becoming religious reverence towards his Maker, who requires that all His creatures, both visible and invisible, should pay Him the homage of their adoration.

II.—EXEMPLIFIED BY THE EARLIEST HISTORY OF MAN.

So consonant is this with the sentiments of nature, that we discover her dictating to the human race, in the earliest period of its existtence, certain rites and ceremonies to be observed for the outward worship of Almighty God. Abel offered sacrifice ; Enoch invoked the name of the Lord ; and the patriarchs built up altars.

III.—CEREMONIES WARRANTED BY GOD IN THE OLD LAW.

God Himself was pleased to promulgate those ritual observances which were to be practised by the Jews.

IV.—BY CHRIST IN THE NEW.

Our Divine Redeemer, though He could have wrought His miracles with the same facility as He called the world out of nothing by a single word, still, however, condescended to employ certain ceremonies while He performed them. He mingled spittle in the clay[1] with which He restored sight to the man born blind ; He groaned in spirit and troubled Himself before He called forth Lazarus from the tomb ;[2] He blessed and broke the bread before He converted it into His body and gave it to His disciples to eat. The example which the Saviour has furnished was imitated by His disciples. We find S. Paul exhorting the Corinthians to 'do all things according to order' in the Church ;[3] and S. John,

---

[1] *S. John,* IX, 6.　　[2] *Ibid.,* XI, 33.　　[3] I *Corinthians,* XIV, 40.

to impress upon our minds the grandeur of the heavenly Jerusalem, describes in fervent language the splendour of the awful ritual to which he was a witness, as he saw in vision the throne of the Lamb in the celestial city; and particularly noticed the four-and-twenty elders, with their harps and fragrance-breathing vials, full of the prayers of the saints, as prostrate before the Lamb without spot, who was reclining upon the golden altar.

V.—CEREMONIES RECOMMENDED BY PROTESTANT WRITERS.

So efficacious, indeed, are the ceremonies of religion for arresting the vagrancy of thought during the season of prayer, so calculated are they for abstracting the heart of man from this world and for assisting him to stand in imagination at the throne of the Divinity in heaven, and pour out his soul in profound adoration before it, that many writers, though they differ from the Catholic Church in their religious credence, lend a willing testimony in favour of her ceremonial. 'If all men,' says Knox, 'were enlightened by education and philosophy, and at all hours actuated by the principles of reason, it would be unnecessary to have recourse to external objects in producing devout and virtuous affections. But as there must always be a great majority, who, from the want of opportunities or

capacities for improvement, are weak and ignorant; and as even among the wise and learned
there are none who are constantly exempted
from the common infirmities of human nature,
it becomes expedient to devise modes of operat-
ing on the soul through the medium of the
senses. It was for this reason that in all great
communities the officers and offices of religion
have been surrounded with whatever is calculated
to rouse the attention, to interest the heart, to
strike the eye, and to elevate the imagination.
I cannot help thinking, therefore, that those well-
meaning reformers, who wish to divest religion
of external splendour, are unacquainted with the
nature of man, or influenced by narrow motives,
. . . and that they who repudiate all ornament,
and all the modes of affecting the senses of the
vulgar in the offices of religion, as indecent, impious, or improper, do not recollect the temple
of Solomon, but suffer their good sense to be
overpowered in this instance by the zeal of a
barbarous fanaticism.'[1]

The author of the 'Principles of Taste' remarks: 'Every person, who has attended the
celebration of High Mass at any considerable
ecclesiastical establishment, must have felt how
much the splendour and magnificence of the

---

[1] VICESIMUS KNOX, *Essays Moral and Literary.* London, 1795,
n°. CLI, vol. II, p. 278.

Roman Catholic worship tends to exalt the spirit of devotion, and to inspire the soul with rapture and enthusiasm. Not only the impressive melody of the vocal and instrumental music, and the imposing solemnity of the ceremonies, but the pomp and brilliancy of the sacerdotal garments, and the rich and costly decorations of the altar, raise the character of religion, and give it an air of dignity and majesty unknown to any of the reformed Churches.' [1]

The rational opinion which good sense has induced these and many other reflecting Protestant writers to adopt and advocate, on the propriety and advantages of impressing the aid of ceremonies into the service of religion, is in perfect accordance with those principles which have at all times and in every place influenced the Church in the regulation of her economy and discipline throughout the widely extending household of the faith. This we gather from the solicitude with which she everywhere insists upon the exact observance of those ancient rites according to which we always behold her celebrating the liturgy and administering the sacraments, as well as from her recorded declarations on the subject. 'Such,' observes the Council of Trent, 'such being the nature of man that, without exterior

---

[1] R. P. KNIGHT, *An Analytical Enquiry into the Principles of Taste.* 2nd ed., London, 1805, part III, chap. I, sect. XLVIII, p. 363.

aids, he cannot be easily elevated to a meditation on divine subjects, on this account our pious mother, the Church, has instituted certain rites; for instance, that some parts of the Mass should be pronounced in an under-voice, other parts in an elevated tone. She has also employed ceremonies, such as mystic benedictions, lights, incense, vestments, and other things of this kind, in accordance with apostolic discipline and tradition, for the purport not only that the majesty of so great a sacrifice might appear in becoming splendour, but that the minds of the faithful might, by these visible signs of piety and religion, be excited to a contemplation of those sublime things which lie hid in this sacrifice.'[1]

Instead of blaming, therefore, we should rather applaud the Catholic Church for employing such various but appropriate ceremonies in her public service. They fix the attention; they throw a certain awe around the mysteries of religion; to the unlettered they are so many sources of the

---

[1] Cum natura hominum ea sit, ut non facile queat sine adminiculis exterioribus ad rerum divinarum meditationem sustolli; propterea pia mater Ecclesia ritus quosdam, ut scilicet quaedam submissa voce, alia vero elatiore, in Missa pronuntiarentur, instituit. Caeremonias item adhibuit, ut mysticas benedictiones, lumina, thymiamata, vestes, aliaque id genus multa, ex apostolica disciplina et traditione, quo et maiestas tanti sacrificii commendaretur, et mentes fidelium per haec visibilia religionis et pietatis signa ad rerum altissimarum, quae in hoc sacrificio latent, contemplationem excitarentur.—*Concil. Trident., Sessio* XXII, *De Sacrificio Missae*, c. v.

easiest instruction; and on every occasion, by teaching man to abstract himself from the common usages of ordinary life, they impart a becoming dignity to the minutest action which is performed in the service of Almighty God.

CHAPTER IX.

ON THE CROSS.

I.—SIGN OF THE CROSS REFERRED TO IN THE OLD TESTAMENT.

IN many passages of Holy Scripture the Cross is referred to with peculiar distinction. The earliest record of such a notice occurs in the book of Ezechiel, where the prophet narrates that, during the vision in which it was given him to behold the abominations perpetrated in Jerusalem, the Lord directed one of the six destroyers to mark TAU upon the foreheads of the men who sighed and mourned for all the abominations that were committed; but to the other five He said: 'Go ye after him through the city, and strike; . . . utterly destroy old and young, maidens, children and women : but upon whomsoever ye shall see Tau, kill him not.'[1] The letter Tau is the last in the Hebrew alphabet. According to its ancient manner of being written, it perfectly resembled a cross, as S. Jerome remarked[2] 1500 years ago,

---

[1] *Ezechiel*, IX, 4–6.
[2] Antiquis Hebraeorum litteris, quibus usque hodie utuntur Samaritani, extrema Thau, littera, Crucis habet similitudinem, quae

and as may be observed at the present day, by consulting the medals, manuscripts, inscriptions, and other ancient monuments of Hebrew antiquity in which this letter occurs.[i]

II.—IN THE NEW.

Our Lord Himself has been pleased to refer on more than one occasion to this instrument of His passion. For He says: 'He that taketh not up

---

in Christianorum frontibus pingitur, et frequenti manus inscriptione signatur.—S. HIERONYMI *Commentaria in Ezechielem*, cap. IX, v. 4.

[i] See B. WALTON, *Prolegomena*, edited by WRANGHAM, tom. II, at the beginning of which there is a plate with the presumed ancient Hebrew alphabet, in which the Tau is written exactly in the form of what is denominated a Greek Cross in one instance, and, in another, like that called S. Andrew's Cross, thus ✕, ✢.

Bernard's Tables by Morton, in the '*Alphabetum ante Christi* (1509) *a nummis Iudaicis, Africanisque et a Pentateucho Mosis*,' exhibit the Tau (*t. th.*) thus—ᚦ, ✕; and in J. SWINTON, '*Inscriptiones Citieae*' (Oxonii, 1750), among the '*Literae Alphabeti Samaritani et Phœnicii numismaticae*,' we find Tau written thus—†, ✕, ✢. In the Spanish translation of Sallust by the Infant Don Gabriel de Bourbon, published at Madrid in 1772, there is a curious dissertation by Father Perez Bayer on the resemblance between the ancient Hebrew and Phœnician alphabets, in which it is observed that the Hebrew Tau was written in pure Phœnician, †, ⵣ. The learned Friar collected the letters of his comparative Hebrew, pure Phœnician, Carthaginian, and Spanish-Phœnician alphabets from ancient coins and medals, as he himself informs us : ' Letras de los Fenices y de sus colonias que se hallen en las monedas de que se ha tratado en este Escrito, colejados con las del Alfabeto Hebreo.'

Not far from Mount Sinai there is a desert valley called the

his cross, and followeth Me, is not worthy of Me;'[1] and He observes to His disciples: 'If any man will come after Me, let him deny himself, and take up his cross, and follow Me;'[2] and the Evangelist, in his enumeration of those terrible prognostics which are to herald the coming of the day of final judgement, mentions the appearance of the Cross amid the heavens, where the sun shall then be darkened, and the moon shall not give her light, and whence the stars shall have fallen: 'And then shall appear the sign of the Son of man in heaven, and then shall all the tribes of the earth mourn; and they shall see the Son of man coming in the clouds of heaven with much power and majesty.'[3] All the most learned and ancient Fathers, as S. Chrysostom, S. Jerome, S. Hilary, Theophylactus, and our countryman the Venerable Bede, are unanimous in interpreting 'the sign of the Son of man' to signify the Cross; and the ablest among

---

Waady el Muketteb, or the Written Valley. Upon the surface of the red sandstone rocks that line this pass in the desert there are many inscriptions, several of which are written in an unknown character. Some scholars have conjectured that these latter inscriptions were traced by the children of Israel at the exodus from Egypt. However this may be, it is curious to behold in them letters perfectly resembling the figure of the Cross, as the reader may observe by consulting the ' *Transactions of the Royal Society of Literature*' (vol. II, part I), where these inscriptions are inserted after the copy which was taken of them, in the year 1820, by the Rev. G. F. Grey.

[1] *S. Matthew*, X, 38.   [2] *Ibid.*, XVI, 24.
[3] *S. Matthew*, XXIV, 30.

our Biblical scholars have applauded such an interpretation.

This instrument of our redemption through the blood of Jesus was perpetually before the eyes of S. Paul, who makes beautiful and appropriate allusions to it in almost every one of his epistles,[1] but more emphatically in the concluding part of his letter to the Galatians, where he exclaims: 'God forbid that I should glory, save in the cross of our Lord Jesus Christ.'

This reverence for the Cross was imparted by the Apostles to the new believers, who, from considering it with horror as the instrument of ignominy, after their initiation in the Christian faith regarded it as the most glorious of trophies and the emblem of their victorious Master. They oftentimes impressed their foreheads with this mystic sign, to manifest their own Christianity or to recognise that of an unknown brother in the faith. That such was the fact may be established by the most irrefragable authorities.

III.—ANTIQUITY OF THE CUSTOM OF MAKING THE SIGN OF THE CROSS.

Tertullian, writing about the year 202, observes: 'At every step and movement, whenever we come in or go out, when we dress

---

[1] 1 *Corinthians*, I, 17, 18. *Galatians*, V, 11; VI, 12–14. *Ephesians*, II, 16. *Philippians*, II, 8; III, 18. *Colossians*, I, 20; II, 14. *Hebrews*, XII, 2.

ourselves, or prepare to go abroad, at the bath,
at table, when lights are brought in, on lying, or
sitting down; whatever we be doing, we make
the sign of the Cross upon our foreheads.'[1]   S.
John Chrysostom, Archbishop of Constantinople
(398–407), thus addresses his auditors: 'Everywhere is the symbol of the Cross present to us.
On this account we paint and sculpture it on our
houses, our walls, and our windows, we trace it
on our brows, and we studiously imprint it on
our souls and minds.'[2]   A similar testimony con-

---

[1] Ad omnem progressum atque promotum, ad omnem aditum et
exitum, ad vestitum et calciatum, ad lavacra, ad mensas, ad lumina,
ad cubilia, ad sedilia, quaecumque nos conversatio exercet, frontem
Crucis signaculo terimus.—TERTULLIANI *liber de corona militis*, c. III.

[2] Πανταχοῦ τὸ τῆς νίκης ἡμῖν παρίσταται σύμβολον. Διὰ τοῦτο καὶ ἐν οἰκίαις,
καὶ ἐπὶ τῶν τοίχων, καὶ ἐπὶ τῶν θυρῶν, καὶ ἐπὶ τοῦ μετώπου, καὶ ἐπὶ τῆς διανοίας
μετὰ πολλῆς ἐπιγράφομεν αὐτὸν τῆς σπουδῆς.—S. CHRYSOSTOMI *Ecloga
de veneranda Cruce*. The figure of the Cross may be frequently
seen chiselled on the jambs of the doorways conducting to the
little oratories in the Roman catacombs, as may be observed in the
plates in BOLDETTI, *Osservazioni sopra i Cimiteri*, pp. 16, 35. A
curious passage illustrating the practice of the early Christians on
this point is here extracted from an interesting work by the Rev.
M. Russell, entitled, *A view of ancient and modern Egypt*. Noticing
the numerous sepulchral monuments which constitute the Necropolis, or cemetery in the great Oasis, Dr. Russell says: 'One, in
particular, is divided into aisles like our churches; and that it has
been used as such by the early Christians is clearly evinced by the
traces of saints painted on the walls. In all there is a Greek Cross,
and the celebrated Egyptian hieroglyphic, the *Crux ansata*, or Cross
with a handle, which, originally signifying life, would appear to
have been adopted as a Christian emblem, either from its similarity
to the shape of the Cross, or from its being considered the symbol
of a future existence' (chap. IX).

Socrates (A.D. 440), the ecclesiastical historian, mentions that on
demolishing at Alexandria a temple dedicated to Serapis, several
stones were observed sculptured with letters denominated hiero-

cerning the ancient custom of making the sign of the Cross is furnished by S. Jerome, who

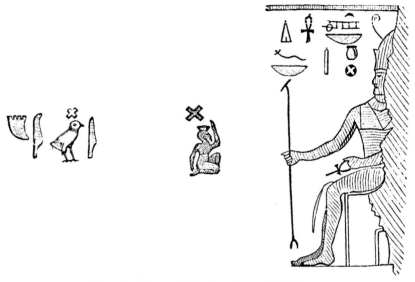

Hieroglyphics exhibiting the figure of the Cross.

delivers the following exhortation in one of his epistles to his friend: 'Frequently trace the

---

glyphics, which exhibited the figure of the Cross. Certain Gentile inhabitants of the city who had lately been converted to the Christian faith, initiated in the method of interpreting these enigmatic characters, declared that the figure of the Cross was considered as the symbol of future life. Ἐν τῷ ναῷ τοῦ Σαράπιδος λουομένου καὶ γυμνουμένου ηὕρητο γράμματα ἐγκεχαραγμένα τοῖς λίθοις, τῷ καλουμένῳ ἱερογλυφικῷ.—Τούτων δὲ ἀμφισβητουμένων, τινὲς τῶν Ἑλλήνων τῷ Χριστιανισμῷ προσελθόντες, τὰ ἱερογλυφικά τε γράμματα ἐπιστάμενοι, διερμηνεύοντες τὸν σταυροειδῆ χαρακτῆρα, ἔλεγον σημαίνειν ζωὴν ἐπερχομένην. SOCRATES, Hist. Eccles., lib. v, c. 17.

Rufinus had some years before (A.D. 399) recorded the same fact in almost similar expressions : 'Signum Dominicae Crucis inter illas quas dicunt ἱερατικὰς, id est, sacerdotales litteras, habere Aegyptii dicuntur, velut unum ex caeteris litterarum, quae apud illos sunt, elementis. Cuius litterae seu vocabuli hanc esse asserunt interpretationem : *vita ventura.*'—RUFINUS, *Hist. Eccles.*, lib. II, c. 29.

Not only the celebrated *Crux ansata,* but other hieroglyphic

sign of the Cross upon your forehead.'[1] The
Christian poet Prudentius, who wrote in the
second half of the fourth century, notices the

---

characters bearing an exact resemblance to a Cross, frequently recur
on Egyptian monuments of the highest antiquity, as well as on
those of comparatively recent erection.   Particular examples of this
fact may be instanced in the Lateran, Campensian, and Barberini
obelisks, as those monuments which now stand at Rome are denominated.   The first two are beautiful and very ancient specimens
of Egyptian art and grandeur; the third is of more modern date,
as the names of Hadrian, Cæsar, Sabina, and Antinous are inscribed
upon it.   The first of the accompanying woodcuts is copied from
the lower part of the Campensian, the second from the Barberini
obelisk, both of which are given in G. ZOEGA, *De origine et usu
Obeliscorum.*   Romae, 1797.

That the first believers in the doctrines of Jesus, whether in Egypt
or Nubia, regarded the Cross with religious veneration, and considered it, like Catholics of the present day, to be the most expressive symbol of Christianity, may be evidenced in many of the
ruins scattered through those interesting countries where the traveller frequently discovers the remains of ancient Pagan temples,
which he ascertains to have been once dedicated to the worship
of the true God by observing the figure of the Cross hallowing every
corner of them, and standing out conspicuously upon their walls and
columns, to announce its triumph over the fabled deities to whom
those fanes were originally erected.   The author of a valuable little
work on Egyptian Antiquities, published in the *Library of Enter-
taining Knowledge* (vol. XVII, part I), in speaking of the monuments
in Upper Nubia, observes : 'The few remains of Dongola Agusa,
on the east bank of the Nile, lat. 18° 15″, show that the Christian
worship was once established in this place.   These granite columns
and capitals, ornamented with crosses and lilies, mark the epoch to
which this edifice belonged, and express, with more certainty than
the evidence of books alone, a fact not without interest in the history
of this barbarous country' (*British Museum, Egyptian Antiq.*, vol.
I, p. 159).   When the day arrives that London shall be a lonely
wilderness, where shall the traveller who explores its ruins light
upon the fragments of a Cross to tell that Christ was ever known
and worshipped there?

[1] *Epist. ad Demetriadem*, t. I, p. 64.   We have, in a recent note,
given this father's words on the mystic Tau mentioned in Ezechiel.

Catholic practice of making the sign of the Cross in the following verses :—

> When sleep steals on, you go to rest,
> and the chaste couch you've scarcely prest,
> O ! let the Cross's figure sign
> that forehead, and that heart of thine.
> The Cross drives every harm away,
> darkness ne'er will bide its stay ;
> mark'd with this sacred sign, the mind
> to fluctuate you'll never find.[1]

Constantine the Great, the first Christian emperor, as well as his whole army, when encamped about a mile from Rome, on the day before the battle with the tyrant Maxentius, beheld at noon a Cross of brilliant light just above the sun, with these words in shining letters around it : Τούτῳ νίκα —'By this conquer.' This circumstance we gather from the life of Constantine written by the historian Eusebius,[2] who assures us that he was favoured with the narration of it by the emperor himself.[3]

---

[1] Fac, cum vocante somno
castum petis cubile,
frontem, locumque cordis
Crucis figura signet.
Crux pellit omne crimen ;
fugiunt Crucem tenebrae ;
tali dicata signo
mens fluctuare nescit.—*Cath. VI, ante somnum.*

[2] *Vita Constantini*, lib. I, cap. 28.

[3] In a letter addressed to the Emperor Constantine, S. Cyril of Jerusalem describes the miraculous appearance of a Cross in the heavens, which this holy bishop and all his flock witnessed on the

IV.—RESPECT OF THE ANCIENT CHRISTIANS
TOWARDS THE CROSS.

That the primitive Christians were exemplary in the reverence which they manifested towards the Cross may be gathered from a variety of sources. According to Tertullian, they were denominated by the Pagans, 'Crucis religiosi,' or, 'devout towards the Cross.' Among the fragments of early Christian antiquities which are still preserved we recognise splendid testimonials of this respect. In the Christian cemeteries scarcely one sepulchral monument has been discovered which does not bear the monogram of

---

7th of May in the year 351. From about nine o'clock in the morning until a late hour in the day was this Cross visible to all the inhabitants, whether Christian or Pagan, of Jerusalem. It extended through the heaven, from Mount Golgotha to the Mount of Olives, and shone with an effulgence more splendid than the rays of the sun. The people, including all ranks and ages, hastened in a crowd to the church and unanimously celebrated the praises of the only begotten Son of God, Christ Jesus, the worker of wonders.—S. CYRILLI *Opera, cura* ANT. TOUTTÉE, p. 351. The genuineness of this epistle has been ably vindicated against the futile objections of the Protestant Rivet by the Benedictine editor, who produces at the end of the letter the testimony of S. Jerome, Socrates, Idatius, and the Alexandrine Chronicle in corroboration of this miraculous event, the anniversary of which still continues to be celebrated all through the Greek Church as a solemn festival. (*Vide Menaeum Graecum, ad diem 7 Maii.*) Dr. Adam Clarke observes: 'If this letter be really the production of S. Cyril, the fact is a curious one, and the appearance might have been designed to accredit, in the sight of the heathen, that doctrine of *Christ crucified* which was the grand keystone in the Christian fabric.' *A Concise View of the Succession of Sacred Literature.* London, 1830, vol. I, p. 300.

Christ, arranged in the form of a cross.[1] The rings that have been found in these tombs display the same emblem, and the fresco-paintings perpetually exhibit the same holy sign.

---

[1] This monogram ☧ may almost invariably be discerned upon the greater part of the monuments of Christian antiquity which have descended to us. Its appearance upon the marbles, mortuary tiles, and lamps extracted from the catacombs, and exhibiting the sepulchral inscriptions of the martyrs and early believers in the Gospel who were buried there, must be familiar to everyone who is anywise conversant with Christian archæology. It is composed of the two Greek characters X and P, the two letters with which the name of Christ commences in Greek, Χριστός. It was inserted along with the palm-branch, in the inscription over the tomb of Pope S. Caius, who suffered martyrdom in the reign of Diocletian (BOLDETTI, *Osservazioni sopra i Cimiteri de Santi Martiri*, p. 102), and may be observed, together with the same emblem of victory, in the sepulchral epitaphs of the martyrs SS. Alexander and Marius (*Ibid.*, pp. 232-233), the first of whom suffered under the Emperor Antoninus, the latter under Hadrian. The assertion of the Protestant Basnage, that no monument bearing this monogram of a date anterior to the reign of Constantine the Great could be produced from the catacombs, is now completely exploded. It was for some time a favourite but totally unfounded hypothesis with several Protestant writers, that this cruciform monogram of Christ was the invention of the first Christian emperor, who, by ordering it to be inscribed upon the standard called the Labarum, and affixed, instead of the eagle and thunderbolts of Jove, upon the shields and helmets of the Roman legions, first gave rise to its adoption by the faithful as a symbol of belief in Jesus. The substitution of Christian in place of Pagan ornaments, in the dress and armour of the soldiery, is noticed by Prudentius, who introduces Constantine as thus addressing the city of Rome :—

> Agnoscas, regina, libens mea signa, necesse est,
> in quibus effigies Crucis, aut gemmata refulget,
> aut longis solido ex auro praefertur in hastis.

> Christus purpureum gemmanti textus in auro
> signabat labarum, clypeorum insignia Christus
> scripserat, ardebat summis Crux addita cristis.

PRUDENTIUS, *Contra Symmachum*, lib. I.

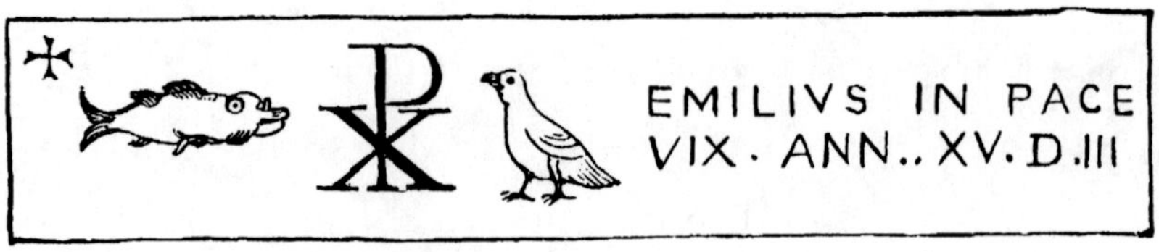

Inscription found in the Catacombs at S. Agnes's. See BOLDETTI, lib. II, p. 453.[1]

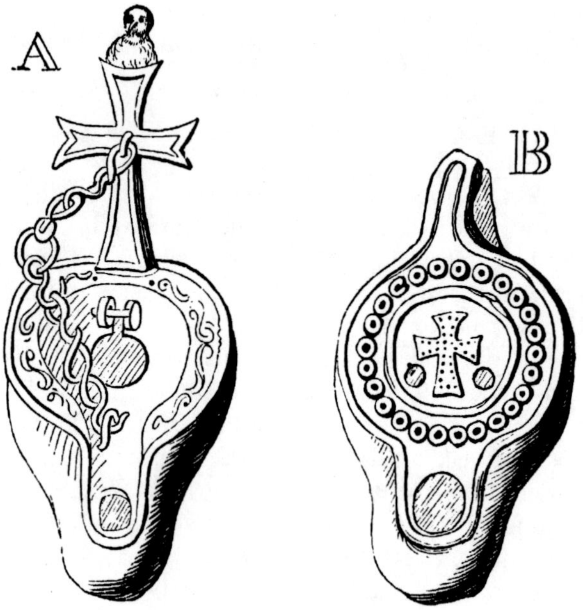

A. Bronze lamp found in the Catacombs. See ARINGHI, *Roma Subterranea*, vol. I, p. 511.

B. Terra-cotta sepulchral lamp found in the Catacombs. *Ibid.*, vol. I, p. 519.

---

[1] The figure of a fish, as a Christian hieroglyphic, is of very frequent recurrence on the monuments of primitive antiquity. The Greek term ΙΧΘΥΣ, which signifies a fish, is composed of the initial letters of the sacred name and titles of our Divine Redeemer, as written in the Greek language: 'Ιησοῦς Χριστός Θεοῦ Υἷος Σωτὴρ—Jesus Christ the Son of God, the Saviour. It was on account of that spiritual regeneration which man received by being born, as it were, again by water, and initiated into the faith of Jesus, and from the conviction that if they did not continue in that vivifying belief they would be spiritually dead and must infallibly lose their salvation, that the first Christians delighted to employ this symbol, and designate themselves by the enigmatical appellation of *Pisciculi*, or little fishes. This we learn from Tertullian, who

1. A ring discovered in the Catacombs. See ARINGHI, vol. II, p. 708, and
SEROUX D'AGINCOURT, vol. V, p. 318.
2. The Labarum of Constantine, taken from a terra-cotta lamp.—MAMACHI,
Origines et Antiq. Christianae, tom. III, p. 50.[1]

observes : 'Nos Pisciculi secundum ΙΧΘΥΣ nostrum Iesum Christum in aqua nascimur ; nec aliter quam in aqua permanendo salvi
sumus.' (*De Bap.*, c. I.) Amongst the several religious emblems
which S. Clement of Alexandria, in his work entitled *The Tutor*
(written c. 190-195), recommends the Christians of Alexandria to
have engraved upon their rings, he enumerates the fish, and remarks that such a sign will prevent them from forgetting their
origin. (*Paedag.*, lib. III, c. XI.) S. Optatus of Milevis (c. 365) likewise refers to the name and symbol of the fish in the following
passage : 'Hic est piscis, qui in baptismate per invocationem fon-
talibus undis inseritur, ut quae aqua fuerat, a pisce etiam piscina
vocitetur. Cuius piscis nomen, secundum appellationem Graecam,
in uno nomine per singulas litteras turbam sanctorum nominum
continet, Ἰχθύς, quod est Latinum, Iesus Christus, Dei Filius,
Salvator.' *De Schismate Donatistarum adversus Parmenianum*,
lib. III.

[1] The biographer of Constantine the Great has left an accurate
description of the celebrated standard called the *Labarum*. Eusebius
(*Vita Constant.*, lib. I, c. 29-31) tells us that this imperial banner
was fashioned in the following manner. Near the top of the shaft
of a lance sheathed in plates of gold was affixed a small transverse
rod forming the figure of a cross. From this cross-bar was suspended a small square of purple stuff of the finest texture, embrio-

Portion of a bas-relief in one of the sarcophagi found in the Catacombs, at the Vatican. See ARINGHI, vol. I, p. 295. In all probability a monument of the fourth century.

dered with gold thread and precious stones. Above this banner arose the sacred monogram of Christ, composed of two letters, the Greek X or *chi* intersecting P or *ro*, and encircled with a wreath or chaplet of gold profusely gemmed with precious stones. Just below the monogram of Christ it became the custom, a little later, to insert the effigy of the reigning emperor, and of his son and consort. Fifty men, the most conspicuous amongst the imperial guards for their valour and their piety, were selected and embodied into a particular band, to whom was confided the distinguished office of carrying and defending the Labarum, which was borne by them singly in turns before the emperor whenever they went to battle. Banners partially resembling the imperial model, but of somewhat smaller

That it was customary with the primitive Christians to wear about their persons crosses made of gold and silver, or of wood, is evident from the incident which led to the martyrdom of S. Orestes, a soldier in the Roman legions during the reign of Diocletian. Orestes was distinguished in his cohort for his agility in every martial exercise, and in particular for the precision with which he cast the disc. Once, as he was displaying his activity in presence of his commander Lysias, a cross which the Christian soldier wore around his neck by accident escaped from between the folds of his garment, where it lay concealed, and proclaimed the religion of Orestes, whose resolute refusal to sacrifice in honour of the gods was crowned with martyrdom.[1]

V.—INTRODUCTION OF THE CRUCIFIX.

Though from the very birth of Christianity it was a pious custom with the faithful to make the sign of the Cross upon their foreheads, and to impress the same holy emblem upon the walls of their places of religious assembly—in the cemeteries, upon their altars, and upon the tombs of

---

dimensions, and wrought of less costly materials, were distributed through the whole army to be the future ensigns of the Roman cohorts. Figures of those standards frequently occur upon the coins of the empire in the time of Constantine and his more immediate successors.

[1] SURIUS, *De probatis Sanctorum Historiis.* Coloniae, 1575, tom. VI, p. 885, Dec. 13; and ARINGHI, vol. II, p. 545.

their martyred brethren; yet it was not until long after the promulgation of the Gospel that they ventured to exhibit any representation of Christ nailed to the Cross. Nothing could be more discreetly cautious than the manner of proceeding adopted by the Church as regards this matter. She manifested the most studious anxiety that the recently converted Gentiles should not experience any scandal, nor suffer the slightest detriment to their belief, from the use of images. The Cross was regarded by the Pagans with the greatest horror, and the deepest shade of infamy was cast upon the character of him who suffered death upon it. Christ crucified was, therefore, 'to the Jews a stumbling-block, and to the Gentiles foolishness.'[1] This it was that withheld the Christians of the first centuries from painting the figure of our Blessed Redeemer on the Cross[2] and made them exercise their ingenuity to invent the most appropriate methods of insinuating what

---

[1] 1 *Corinthians*, I, 23. Minucius Felix (c. 234), in his beautiful dialogue between the Pagan Caecilius and the true believer Octavius, introduces the heathen as thus vituperating Christ and His followers: 'Nescio an falsa, certe occultis ac nocturnis sacris apposita suspicio; et qui hominem, summo supplicio pro facinore punitum, et crucis ligna feralia, eorum caeremonias fabulantur; congruentia perditis sceleratisque tribuit altaria, ut id colant quod merentur.'—M. MINUCII FELICIS *Octavius*, cap. IX.

[2] CIAMPINI, *Vetera Monimenta*, tom. I, p. 201. Representations of the Crucifixion of earlier date than the sixth century are extremely scarce, and appear only as part of a series of representations of events in the life of Christ.

kind of death our Saviour underwent, without wounding the piety of the neophyte or startling the prejudices of the unbeliever. The book of the Apocalypse furnished them with a most happy as well as most beautiful illustration of the fact. Christ had been pointed out as the 'Lamb of God' by the Baptist,[1] but it was for the well-beloved disciple John to draw the magnificent picture of the 'Lamb which was slain from the beginning of the world';[2] while he tells us that he beheld, 'In the midst of the throne, and of the four living creatures, and in the midst of the ancients, a Lamb standing, as it were slain, . . . and He came and took the book out of the right hand of Him that sat on the throne.'[3] They delighted to copy this description of S. John; and oftentimes translated it into colours on their walls, in fresco paintings and mosaic work; or imaged it in sculpture on their sarcophagi; and even represented it upon their articles of furniture, as may be instanced in those fragments of drinking cups occasionally discovered affixed to the tombs of the martyrs in the catacombs,[4] many of which are now deposited at the Vatican library, in the Museum of Christian Antiquities. In these venerable monuments of early piety the Lamb, the emblem of Jesus crucified, is figured as bearing a

---

[1] *S. John*, I, 29. [2] *Apocalypse*, XIII, 8. [3] *Ibid.*, v, 6, 7.
[4] BUONARRUOTI, *Osservazioni sopra alcuni frammenti di Vasi antichi di vetro*, p. 38.

cross upon its forehead; sometimes as slain, at other times reposing on a splendid throne; but in painting and mosaic invariably encircled with an azure field, sprinkled with stars of gold to represent the heavens,[1] and to signify that Christ by His death had conducted afflicted humanity to those happy regions. In progress of time the Lamb began to be represented as stretched upon the ground, or leaning against a cross, and not unfrequently as standing at the foot of it, and bleeding.[2] This we learn from a couplet in the epistle addressed by S. Paulinus of Nola[3] to Severus, in which the prelate says:

> 'Neath a red cross, see Christ our Saviour stand,
> veil'd in the figure of a snow-white lamb;
> the lamb-like victim, unoffending, immolated
> by unjust death for our offences.[4]

---

[1] As may be observed in the mosaic in the apse of the Church of SS. Cosmas and Damian in the Forum at Rome.

[2] The accompanying engraving of an ancient mosaic which adorned the apse or tribune of the old church of S. Peter at Rome is copied from J. B. CASALIUS, *De veteribus sacris Christianorum Ritibus*, p. 3. For further observations, see List of the Plates.

[3] S. Paulinus was born in 353 or 354. See p. 321, note 1.

[4] Sub cruce sanginea niveo stat Christus in agno
Agnus ut innocua iniusto datus hostia leto.
Epist. XXXII, ad Severum.

Continuing the description of the church which he had just erected and ornamented, S. Paulinus informs his friend Severus that in the vestibule of this Basilica there were several crosses painted in red colour, and over them the following inscription: 'Item dextra laevaque crucibus minio superpictis haec epigrammata sunt:

Ardua floriferae crux cingitur orbe coronae
et Domini fuso tincta cruore rubet.

*From an ancient Mosaic which adorned the Apse or tribune
of the old Church of S. Peter at Rome.*

displayed in public, without hesitation or reserve, especially from that period when Constantine prohibited throughout the empire the cross from ever being employed as an instrument of punishment; and to eradicate as speedily and with as much effect as possible, the withering germs of heathenism, that emperor erected crosses along the public ways at those different points denominated *Ubivilia* by the Romans, and Ἑρμῆς τρικέφαλος by the Greeks, and thus made the symbol of Christianity supplant the Mercurii and terminal gods of Polytheism.   To an incident which manifests the religious zeal of Constantine we must refer a custom, at present very generally observed in almost every Catholic country on the Continent, of placing a large Crucifix[1] by the roadside at the entrance of the towns and villages.[2] That such was anciently the custom in England when the nation was Catholic is a well-attested fact.   In a treatise on the ten commandments, entitled '*Dives et Pauper*,' and printed

---

[1] The Crucifix properly so called, *i.e.*, the Cross with the figure of our Lord nailed to it, was certainly not in use before the end of the sixth century, and for a long time after only as an object of private devotion. The earlier crosses with figures represent our Lord reigning on the Cross, clad in a tunic and crowned, and with a footstool beneath His feet, symbolising the redemption of mankind, and the triumph of Christ over sin and death ; the Crucifix properly so called, with the historical representation of our Lord nailed to the Cross and crowned with thorns, was certainly not introduced until much later.

[2] PELLICCIA, *De Christianae Ecclesiae Politia.*   Coloniae, 1829, tom. II, p. 340.

at Westminster by Wynken de Worde in 1496, the real and pious object for erecting the Cross by the roadside is thus expressively assigned: 'For this reason ben Crosses by ye waye, that whan folke passynge see the Crosse, they sholde thynke on Hym that deyed on the Crosse, and worshypp Hym above all thynge.'[1]

A writer notorious for his hostility to the ancient faith observes: 'From the earliest ages of Christianity the Cross has very naturally been made the *emblem* of our holy Faith. It was the *private mark* or signal by which the Christians used to distinguish each other among their Pagan adversaries during the times of persecution, as it was afterwards their *public emblem* when their danger became less imminent; and it is yet the 'sign' with which all Christian Churches, however widely differing in other respects, mark those who are admitted to the benefits of Baptism. Wherever the Gospel was first spread, a pious care caused crosses to be erected as standards, around which the faithful might assemble the more conveniently to hear the Divine truths inculcated, and by degrees those symbols were

---

[1] It is passing strange that in a land where it is boastingly de-clared that Christianity is part and parcel of the law, and in the calendar of whose 'Book of Common Prayer' the *Invention* and *Exaltation of the Cross* are registered and ordained to be kept as festivals, there should have been permitted such an indiscriminate destruction of this particular emblem of its religion.

fixed in every place of public resort. Every town
had its cross, at which engagements, whether of
a religious or worldly interest, were entered into.
Every churchyard had one whereon to rest the
bodies of the deceased, from which the preacher
gave his lessons upon the mutability of life. At
the turning of every public road was placed a
cross, for the twofold purpose of rest for the
bearers of the pious defunct, and for reminding
travellers of the Saviour who died for their salvation. The boundaries of every parish were
distinguished by crosses, at which during the
ancient perambulations the people alternately
prayed and regaled themselves. Every grant
from sovereigns or nobles, every engagement
between individuals, was alike marked with the
Cross; and in all cases where the parties could
not write, that emblem alone was deemed an
efficient substitute for the subscription of a name.
Crosses, in short, were multiplied by every means
which the ingenuity of man could invent; and
the people were thus kept in constant remembrance, both at home and on their journeys, as
well as in every transaction of their lives, of the
foundation of the Christian faith.'[1]

---

[1] J. BRADY, *Clavis Calendaria; or, A Compendious Analysis of the
Calendar.* London, 1812, vol. I, p. 331.

VI.—ANTIQUITY OF THE CUSTOM OF USING CRUCIFIXES IN CHURCHES.

The most ancient memorial we have of any representation of our Divine Redeemer hanging on the Cross is furnished by the author of the poem 'De Passione Domini,' which certainly bears upon its style the impress of the fifth century. The poet says:[1]

'Whoe'er thou art that seek'st this temple's bound,
arrest thy step; and, ere thou gazest round,
oh, look on Me: without one fault of Mine,
I suffer'd for thy sinfulness—thy crime.
Mark how these hands with savage nails are bor'd,
these limbs distent; this back with lashes gor'd.
See where the lance has prob'd My heaving side;
see how the wound pours forth a crimson tide;
see how these feet of Mine are dug, and how
blood stains each limb, and trickles from My brow.'

From these lines we may collect that at the period when their author composed them his-

---

[1] Quisquis ades, mediique subis in limina Templi
siste parum, insontemque tuo pro crimine passum
respice Me;

Cerne manus clavis fixas, tractosque lacertos
atque ingens lateris vulnus: cerne inde fluorem
sanguineum, fossosque pedes, artusque cruentos.
De Passione Domini.

The pseudo-council in Trullo, so denominated from its having been held in a cupola-covered hall in the emperor's palace at Constantinople, in 692, decreed in its eighty-second canon that, as in many instances Jesus Christ had been represented under the figure of the Lamb, as He was pointed out by the finger of S. John, for the future He should be imaged under His human form, such a way being more becoming.

torical or narrative representations of the Crucifixion were placed in churches; the earliest known examples, however, date from the latter half of the sixth century, and in the same composition with these the Resurrection is frequently introduced.[1]

VII.—WHY THE CRUCIFIX IS PLACED UPON THE ALTAR.

As the altar is the emblem of Mount Calvary, the Cross supporting the figure of Christ is erected in the centre of it, to call to remembrance that it was Jesus crucified who paid the ransom of our sins with His most precious blood, and that 'There is no other name under heaven given to men, whereby we must be saved.'[2]

VIII.—WHY THE SACERDOTAL GARMENTS AND THE SACRED VESSELS ARE MARKED WITH A CROSS.

A figure of the Cross is inserted on each individual article of the vestments appointed for the priest, and is affixed upon the several vessels dedicated to the sacred service, in order to announce the use to which they have been appropriated.[3]

---

[1] See MARTIGNY, *Dictionnaire des Antiquités Chrétiennes* p. 190, § v.

[2] *Acts*, IV, 12.

[3] The *Liber Pontificalis* often applies the epithet *stauracinus* to vestments and church-ornaments marked with the figure of the Cross.

IX.—WHY MADE SO OFTEN BY THE PRIEST AT MASS.

In the administration of Baptism and the other sacraments, as well as during the Sacrifice of the Altar, the Church prescribes that the sign of the Cross be frequently employed, to publish her belief that all grace is derived only from the blood which Jesus shed upon the Cross.

X.—BY CATHOLICS IN GENERAL.

The devout Catholic, studious to emulate the fervour of S. Paul, who gloried in the Cross of Christ,[1] is accustomed, at the commencement and conclusion of every pious action, to sign himself with the sign of the Cross, at the same time reverently pronouncing these words: 'In the name of the Father, and of the Son, and of the Holy Ghost, Amen,'—and thus not only makes profession of acknowledging the existence of one God in three persons, but attests his belief in the mysteries of the Incarnation and Atonement. And furthermore, Catholics so frequently employ the sign of the Cross, not only to proclaim to the world that they are not ashamed of the Cross of Jesus, and to make their public profession of belief in a crucified Redeemer, but for their private devotion and spiritual advantage. It helps them to bear perpetually in mind the death and passion

---

[1] *Galatians*, VI, 14.

of Christ. It assists them to nourish in their souls the three Divine virtues of faith, hope, and charity. In the first place, faith is exercised, because the sign of the Cross recalls to our remembrance one of the fundamental articles of Christian doctrine, namely, that the Son of God, the second person of the most Holy Trinity, took upon Himself our human nature, and died on the Cross for our salvation. In the second place, it nourishes and fortifies our hope, because this holy sign continually reminds us of the Passion and the Blood of Christ, on which the Christian reposes all his hope for grace at present, and for mercy and happiness hereafter. In the third place, charity, or the love of God, is enkindled in us by this sacred emblem, which represents to us that ardent affection of the Almighty for us poor sinners, since He sent down from heaven His well-beloved Son to die upon the Cross and thus rescue us from an eternity of punishment.

XI.—THE MANNER OF MAKING THE SIGN OF THE CROSS.

In blessing ourselves, we form the sign of the Cross by lifting our right hand to the forehead, and afterwards drawing as it were a line to the heart, and then another line crossing the former from the left shoulder to the right, at the same time pronouncing, in order to attach a meaning to the action, these words : 'In the name of the Father, and of the Son, and of the Holy Ghost.'

Thus we publish a solemn declaration of our faith in the Blessed and undivided Trinity. The pastor who imparts his benediction to his flock, or who is dedicating anything to the service of the altar or to sacred purposes, forms a cross in the air with his right hand extended towards the object he is going to bless. Another mode of making this sign is practised, especially by priest and people at the celebration of Mass, just before the reading of the Gospel. It is then customary to sign, with a distinct cross, the forehead in the name of the Father, who is the Head of all, then the lips in the name of the Son, who is the Word of the Father, then the heart in the name of the Holy Ghost, who is the bond of love.

Amongst the Greeks and Oriental Christians the sign of the Cross occurs as often in their respective liturgies, and is in as familiar use as in the Latin Church. A slight difference, however, exists between the modes employed by the members of the Western and Eastern Churches in signing themselves with this emblem of Christ's atonement. The Greeks, pressing the thumb against the ring finger of the right hand, make the sign of the Cross with the other three united fingers, thus joined to signify one God and three distinct persons. The Latins extend the thumb, second and middle finger, and bend the other two down on the palm. Both anciently raised the hand, first, to the forehead, then drew it down to the breast; and afterwards, not to the left shoulder as we at present do, but, on the contrary, to the right, and ultimately to the left, repeating the same form of words as we employ now.[1] Pope Leo IV. (847–855) ordered the sign of the Cross to be made, not 'with various fingers as many do, but with two fingers extended and the thumb bent up underneath, by which the Trinity is signified.'[2] Pope Innocent III. (1198–1216) notices the manner which was generally followed throughout the Latin Church in his time, and says: 'The sign of the Cross is to be made with three fingers, so that it may descend from top to bottom, and then pass over from right to left;'[3] but the pontiff adds: 'Some persons, however, draw the sign of the Cross from left to right.'[4]

To these may be superadded many pictorial documents which attest this fact with regard to England and the other portions of the Western Church. In paintings executed anterior to

---

[1] Χρεωστῆ ὁ καθεὶς εὐσεβὴς χριστιανὸς πρῶτα μὲν να συμάζωξει τὰ τρία του δάκτυλα διὰ τὴν ἁγίαν Τριάδα, τὸν μεγάλον δάκτυλον καὶ τὰ ἀλλὰ δύο ὁποῦ εἶναι κοντάτου, ἔπειτα πρῶτον μὲν νὰ τὰ θέσῃ εἰς τὸ βλέφαρόν του, δεύτερον εἰς τὴν κοιλίαν του, τρίτον εἰς τὸν δεξιὸν ὦμον, καὶ τέταρτον εἰς τὸν ζαρβον ὦμον.—DAMASCENUS *Hypodiaconus Thessalonicensis,* Serm. XXVI.

[2] MANSI, *Supp'ement. ad coll. Concil. Labbei,* tom. I, p. 911.

[3] Est autem signum Crucis tribus digitis exprimendum, . . . ita quod de superiori descendit ad inferius, et a dextra transeat ad sinistram; quia Christus de caelo descendit in terram, et a Iudaeis transivit ad gentes. *De Sacro Altaris Mysterio,* lib. II, c. 45.

[4] Quidam tamen signum Crucis a sinistra producunt in dextram quia de miseria transire debemus ad gloriam. *Ibid.*

the sixteenth century,[1] in the miniatures of
ancient manuscripts, in stained-glass, on sepulchral monuments,[2] and in the official seals of
religious houses, cities and corporations, may be
observed figures, sometimes that of our Blessed
Redeemer, at others of the patron saint of
the particular town, or church, or monastery,
giving the blessing in the manner ordered by
Leo IV.[3]

We impress the sign of the Cross upon the
forehead, not only in reference to that mystic
Tau, which, on the Day of Judgment, will be the
characteristic of Divine election, to distinguish
the favourites of Heaven from the objects of its
vengeance, but to manifest a desire that the
wisdom of the Cross may beam upon and illuminate the darkness of our minds, and make us
understand the words of God which are about to
be spoken to us. It is imprinted on the mouth,
in order to bring to our remembrance that saying
of the Royal Prophet: 'Set a watch, O Lord,

---

[1] Numérous instances also occur in the ancient mosaics in the
churches at Rome, as may be verified by consulting CIAMPINI
Vetera Monimenta.

[2] For many instances of this see the plates of monuments in
BRITTON, *Cathedral Antiquities.* The effigy in Exeter Cathedral of
Simon de Apulia, of which we give a cut in chap. XII, on Vest-
ments, is an example.

[3] Honorius of Autun, in his *Gemma Animae,* Pope Innocent III.
and other mystic writers, all agree in assigning the same spiritual
meaning to this way of making the sign of the Cross. It is intended
to express the mystery of the Blessed Trinity.

before my mouth: and a door round about my lips;'[1] and to instruct us to keep such a guard upon our tongue that it may never utter anything irreverent towards God, or uncharitable towards our neighbour. It is signed upon the bosom in order to banish from the heart every disorderly affection, every dangerous inclination, and every sentiment of pride or vanity that ill become the followers of Jesus, 'Who humbled Himself, becoming obedient unto death, even to the death of the Cross.'[2]

Psalm CXL, 3. [2] *Philippians,* II, 8, 9.

CHAPTER X.

ON IMAGES.

I.—THE USE OF IMAGES IN THE HOUSE OF GOD AUTHORISED BY SCRIPTURE.

THE practice of employing images as ornaments and memorials to decorate the temples of the Lord is in a most especial manner approved by the word of God Himself. Moses was commanded to place two cherubim upon the Ark,[1] and to set up a brazen figure of the fiery serpent, that those among the murmuring Israelites who had been bitten might recover from the poison of their wounds by looking on the image.[2] In the description of Solomon's temple we read of that prince not only that he made in the Oracle two cherubim of olive tree of ten cubits in height,[3] but that 'all the walls of the temple round about he carved with divers figures and carvings.'[4]

In the first book of Paralipomenon we observe that when David imposed his injunction upon

---

[1] *Exodus*, XXV and XXVI.   [2] *Numbers*, XXI, 8.
[3] *3 Kings*, VI, 23.   [4] *Ibid.*, VI, 29.

Solomon to realise his intention of building the house of the Lord, he delivered to him a description of the porch and temple, and concluded by thus assuring him : 'All these things came to me written by the hand of the Lord, that I might understand all the works of the pattern.'[1]

The isolated fact, that images were not only directed by Almighty God to be placed in the Mosaic tabernacle and in the more sumptuous temple of Jerusalem, but that He Himself exhibited the pattern of them, will be alone sufficient to authorise the practice of the Catholic Church in regard to a similar observance.

II.—RECOMMENDED BY ANTIQUITY.

A venerable antiquity instructs the Catholic to ornament with paintings and crosses those places which religion has dedicated to public worship. The primitive Christians were studious to represent a variety of subjects selected from Holy Scripture, or allusive to their religion, upon the walls of those subterranean oratories to which they were accustomed to resort in times of persecution. These paintings still remain visible at the present day; and as they possess an inestimable value in the eyes of the pious Christian, of the artist, and the theologian, they have

---

[1] *Paralipomenon* XXVIII, 11–19.

been copied and illustrated by several learned writers.[1]

It is demonstrated by Seroux d'Agincourt that some of them are the productions of the second century. He arrived at this conclusion by comparing together the fresco paintings of the sepulchre of the Nasoni family with those which decorate the catacombs that have been discovered in the neighbourhood of Rome, particularly on the Latin and Salarian Ways. This able antiquary identifies the style of painting in several of the Christian cemeteries with that of the heathen sepulchre, and observes a similar elegance, grace, and correctness of design manifested in the various subjects which severally adorn these Gentile and Christian burial places; and hence he justly concludes the paintings of both to be the productions of contemporary artists.[2] The antiquity of the pictures in the Christian cemeteries is also

---

[1] Bosio was one amongst the first to notice them. The labours of that zealous ecclesiastical antiquary were rendered still more valuable by the learning brought to a new arrangement of his book, and the addition of many important observations made to it by Aringhi in his new edition of the *Roma Subterranea.* The learned prelate Bottari afterwards treated the same subject with his usual ability, and shed a new lustre over it by his elegance and archæological erudition. Seroux d'Agincourt, in his invaluable work, *L'Histoire de l'Art par les Monumens,* derived much assistance, and extracted a variety of materials for the compilation of his book from the fresco paintings of the Roman catacombs.

[2] See SEROUX D'AGINCOURT, vol. v, plates 5 and 6. Concerning the paintings in the Roman catacombs, Flaxman, who studied at Rome several years, observes : 'Even during the reigns of those

established by the fact that in many instances
they have been cut through, in order to make
niches in the walls which they ornamented for
the bodies of the martyrs : an incident which
demonstrates that they were finished anterior to
the later persecutions endured by the Church.

It should not be forgotten that these subterranean chambers, in which were deposited the
bodies of the martyrs, served the double purpose
of dormitories for the dead and churches in which
the living assembled to pray and celebrate the
sacrifice of the Mass upon the very tombs of their
heroic brethren. These ancient paintings triumphantly refute the assertions of Bingham, who
labours hard to prove that 'no pictures or images
were allowed in the churches for the first three
hundred years;' and that they were 'first
brought in by Paulinus and his contemporaries,
privately and by degrees, in the latter end of the
fourth century.'[1]

---

emperors by whom the Christians were cruelly persecuted, when
they were obliged to perform their sacred worship in subterrains
and sepulchral chambers, they ornamented those retreats with
sacred portraits and subjects from Scripture.' J. FLAXMAN, *Lectures
on Sculpture.* London, 1829, p. 302.

[1] Book VIII, chap. VIII, sect. 6 and 7.

On many occasions Protestant writers explicitly, though uninten-
tionally, admit that the use of pictures in churches prevailed at the
earliest periods of Christianity. Dr. Russell, whose book on Egypt
was just now noticed, while speaking of the architectural remains
which still adorn the great Oasis, remarks : 'In regard to what
appeared at first as the ruins of an Arab town, we are informed that,
upon a closer examination, it proved to be a necropolis or cemetery,

What Bingham is pleased to designate the
beginning was, however, only the extension of
an ancient practice.[1] It is certain that the
Christians, from the earliest epoch, were careful
to ornament with pictures, according to their

---

consisting of a great variety of buildings, not fewer than two or three
hundred, each the receptacle of a number of mummies. . . . One
building, in particular, is divided into aisles like our churches ;
and that it has been used as such by the early Christians is clearly
evinced by the traces of saints painted on the walls.' *View of
Ancient and Modern Egypt*, p. 290.

[1] Canon XXXVI of the Provincial Council held in 305 at Eliberis,
in Spain, immediately refutes the error of Bingham. The pastors
of the Spanish Church beheld the grievous persecution that Diocletian had commenced to wage against the Christian faith, which had
for a lengthened period enjoyed comparative repose under the for-
bearing reign of Constantius Cæsar, father of Constantine the Great.
They assembled to concert precautionary measures, and, amongst
other things, they determined that in the provinces under their
immediate jurisdiction there should be no fixed and immovable
pictorial monuments, such as fresco-paintings or mosaics ; no images
of Christ whom they adored, nor of the saints whom they venerated,
on the walls of the churches which had been erected and ornamented
during the long interval of peace which the Christians had enjoyed.
'Placuit,' says the council, 'picturas in ecclesia esse non debere ;
ne quod colitur et adoratur, in parietibus depingatur.' (*Conc. Elib.
apud* LABBEUM, *Concil. Gen.*, tom. II, col. 11.) This economy was
prudent, and adapted to the exigency of the period : the figures of
Christ and of His saints were thus protected from the ribaldry and
insult of the Pagans. But this well-timed prohibition demonstrates
that the use of pictures and images had been already introduced into
the Spanish Church. That they were equally employed in other
Churches is evident. With regard to Africa, we have the authority
of Tertullian (*de Pudicitia*), who particularly instances the figure
of the Good Shepherd, which was almost invariably to be observed
upon the chalices. The catacombs of Rome sufficiently indicate
what was the practice of the Christians in the imperial metropolis,
by the numerous sepulchral chambers, used also as chapels, which
are entirely covered with fresco-paintings, ascertained to have been
executed a long time previous to the epoch assigned by Bingham.

humble means, those chambers that were dedicated to religious uses for the common benefit. During the first three centuries these halls were comparatively private chapels. But the same style of decoration continued to be followed when Christianity was recognised as the religion of the State; and the obscure and retired oratories of the faithful became the public sanctuaries of their triumphant worship, openly resorted to without dread or molestation.

At this period, when peace was given to the Church by the accession of Constantine to the throne of the Cæsars, the temples of the Christians were ornamented with tenfold splendour; and not only painting, but her sister arts, sculpture and architecture, with their respective handmaids, were invited to celebrate the victory and adorn the triumph of the Christian Faith.

III.—WHY THE CHURCH EMPLOYS THEM.

It cannot be denied that the image of Jesus Christ suspended from the Cross must awaken in our minds the most affecting remembrance of Him 'who hath loved us so, as to deliver Himself up to death for us.'[1] As long as the religious sentiments created by this image keep possession of the mind we are naturally prompted to manifest, by some exterior token, the ardour of that

---

[1] *Galatians*, II, 20.

grateful piety with which the heart is glowing; and while we humble ourselves in presence of the image, we express our love and testify our submission towards its glorious and heavenly original. Such is the idea of the Church, as we may collect from the Council of Trent,[1] where she thus admonishes her children : 'The honour which we give to images is referred to their prototypes or originals ; so that, by the images which we kiss, or before which we bow or uncover our heads, we adore Christ.' In reality, the spirit of the Church, in honouring images, may be ascertained from the motives which induce her to exhibit a respect to the Cross and the book of the Gospels. It must be evident to everyone that, by kneeling before the Cross, we adore Him 'who His ownself bore our sins in His body upon the tree.'[2] If

---

[1] Mandat, sancta synodus omnibus episcopis, et caeteris, docendi munus curamque sustinentibus, ut, iuxta Catholicae et Apostolicae Ecclesiae usum, a primaevis Christianae religionis temporibus receptum, . . . de legitimo imaginum usu fideles diligenter instruant, docentes eos, . . . imagines Christi, Deiparae Virginis, et aliorum sanctorum, in templis praesertim habendas et retinendas ; eisque debitum honorem et venerationem impertiendam ; non quod credatur inesse aliqua in iis divinitas, vel virtus, propter quam sint colendae ; vel quod ab eis sit aliquid petendum ; vel quod fiducia in imaginibus sit figenda, veluti olim fiebat a gentibus, quae in idolis (Psal. cxxxiv, 18, et cxxiii, 8) spem suam collocabant ; sed quoniam honos, qui eis exhibetur, refertur ad prototypa, quae illae repraesentant : ita ut per imagines, quas osculamur, et coram quibus caput aperimus et procumbimus, Christum adoremus ; et sanctos, quorum illae similitudinem gerunt, veneremur.—Sessio xxv, De Invocatione Sanctorum, et Sacris Imaginibus.

[2] 1 Peter, ii, 24.

we stand up, from motives of respect, when the book of the Gospels is carried past us, or when any portion of it is recited; if we kiss it in a court of justice, or during the celebration of Mass; if we carry lights before it, or perfume it with incense, such attributes of religious honour are not rendered to a piece of wood, but to Him who died upon the Cross to save us; not to the ink and paper of a book, but to the word of God, and those eternal truths which are propounded to us in the sacred volume.[1]

We Catholics adorn our altars and our churches with the pictures and images of Christ and His sainted servants, and preserve them with decent and pious respect, not only through a reverence for their illustrious prototypes, but that the sight of them may recall to our remembrance those heroic virtues which made their lives so celebrated, and

---

[1] That, long before the Council of Trent was assembled, precisely the same doctrine as that delivered in one of its decrees just noticed was inculcated with much solicitude by the pastors of the English Catholic Church, is manifest from their writings. Lyndewode, who affixed some learned annotations to the collection which he published in 1422 of the Constitutions promulgated at different epochs by the several archbishops of Canterbury, passes the following remark upon the use of images: 'Ipsarum tamen imaginum pictura non est adoranda, sed res per ipsam repraesentata. . . . Et nota, quod triplex fuit ratio institutionis imaginum: una est ad instructionem rudium, qui eis quasi quibusdam libris edoceri videntur. Secunda est, ut Incarnationis mysterium, et sanctorum exempla magis in memoria nostra essent, dum quotidie oculis nostris repraesentantur. Tertia est ad excitandum devotionis affectum, quae ex visis efficacius excitatur quam ex auditis.'—LYNDEWODE, *Provinciale*, p. 252. Oxoniae, 1679.

quicken us, if not to emulate, at least to follow their example at an humble distance, by some faint imitation of their holiness.

The loyal subject, or the patriot, who ornaments his residence with the portrait of his sovereign, or of those amongst his fellow-citizens whose achievements in the field, or whose abilities in the senate, no matter what character they may have borne through private life, have won for them the admiration of their countrymen, cannot surely advance any reasonable objection against the conduct of the Catholic for rendering in his churches a similar homage to the 'author and finisher of his faith,'[1] Christ Jesus, and to such among His disciples as have shed a glory round His religion by the lustre of their brilliant virtues, or have carried the tidings of it to the heathen, and recorded with their life-blood, in presence of the tyrant and the persecutor, their intrepid adherence to all its doctrines.

That pictures and images in churches are particularly serviceable in informing the minds of the humbler classes, and, for such a purport, possess a superiority over words themselves, is certain :

'Segnius irritant animos demissa per aurem,
    quam quae sunt oculis subiecta fidelibus, et quae
    ipse sibi tradit spectator.'[2]

---

[1] *Hebrews*, XII, 2.   [2] HORATIUS, *De Arte Poetica*, v. 180.

> What's through the ear convey'd, will never find
> its way, with so much quickness, to the mind,
> as that, when faithful eyes are messengers,
> unto himself the fix'd spectator bears.

The remark of a heathen poet is corroborated by the observations of the most celebrated amongst ancient and modern Christian writers.[1] So persuaded was S. Paulinus of Nola, fifteen hundred years ago, of the efficacy possessed by paintings for conveying useful lessons of instruction, that he adorned with a variety of sacred subjects the walls of the church which he erected and dedicated to God in honour of S. Felix :

> ' Propterea visum nobis opus utile cunctis
> Felicis domibus pictura ludere sancta,' etc.[2]

---

[1] That what is now quite harmless was, half a century ago, intrinsically evil, will require much logical acumen and some eloquence to demonstrate. Not many years since, Barry the artist volunteered to enliven the drear and gloomy walls of S. Paul's Cathedral with paintings, but his generous offer was rejected by the dean and chapter of the metropolitan cathedral.

This instance ought not to awaken our astonishment. With writers of the Established Church and other Protestant sects it has always been a favourite occupation to stigmatise their Catholic fellow-countryman, most unjustly, as the worshipper of a wooden God—a Crucifix, and to denounce his religion, the olden faith, as damnable and idolatrous—no gentle epithets. It was this profound abhorrence, hitherto manifested by the heads of the English Protestant establishment, against ornamenting the temple of the Lord with statues and pictures, that defeated the laudable proposal of this British artist. But how men and men's ideas have changed ! This very Church of England is now busily adorning her pinnacles and domes and steeples with crosses, and ornamenting her communion-tables and her chancel-windows with pictorial and sculptured images.

[2] S. PAULINUS, *De S. Felice Natalitium carmen IX.*

To us it seem'd a useful work to paint
with sacred scenes the temple of this saint.

Prudentius assures us how much his devotion
was enkindled as he gazed upon the sufferings of
the martyrs, so feelingly depicted around their
tombs and in their churches. On his way to
Rome, about the year 404, the poet paid a visit
to the shrine of S. Cassian [1] at Forum Cornelii,
the modern Imola, where the body of that Christian hero reposed, under a splendid altar, over
which were represented, in an expressive picture,
all the sufferings of his cruel martyrdom. So
moved was Prudentius, that he threw himself
prostrate upon the pavement, kissed the altar
with religious reverence, and, numbering up with
many a tear those wounds that sin had inflicted
upon his soul, concluded by exhorting everyone
to unite with him in entrusting their petitions
for the Divine clemency to the solicitude of the
holy martyr Cassian, who will, he assures us, not
only hear our request, but will afford us the
benefit of his patronage.

'Stratus humi, tumulo advolvebar, quem sacer ornat
  martyr dicato Cassianus corpore.

---

[1] He was a schoolmaster, and suffered death for the Catholic
religion under Julian the Apostate. His own scholars were selected
to be the executioners of his martyrdom. The youths were directed
to surround and stab their teacher with their styles, or metal pens,
with which, as was then the custom, they learned to write upon
little tablets of wood covered with wax. His body is still venerated at Imola, under the high-altar of the cathedral.

Dum lachrymans mecum reputo mea vulnera, et omnes
    vitae labores, ac dolorum acumina,
erexi ad caelum faciem ; stetit obvia contra
    fucis colorum picta imago martyris,
plagas mille gerens, totos lacerata per artus,
    ruptam minutis praeferens punctis cutem.' [1]

Prone to the ground, the sacred tomb I press'd,
    that holy Cassian's bones were tenanting.
With many a tear my sorrow I express'd
    for all my sins, as grief my heart did wring.
Upwards I gazed,—before me shone the scene
    wrought in fair colours by the painter's art,
that told so well the cruel martyring
    of blessed Cassian, by the schoolboys' dart.

Arrived at Rome, Prudentius observed and applauded the piety which induced its citizens to ornament the tombs of the martyrs. The Church of S. Hippolytus particularly attracted the poet's attention, and he has described with much minuteness the paintings which decorated that Christian hero's tomb.

' Exemplar sceleris paries habet illitus, in quo
    multicolor fucus digerit omne nefas.
Picta super tumulum species liquidis viget umbris
    effigians tracti membra cruenta viri.' [2]

The painted wall, with many a tint that glows,
    reveals the horror of the impious deed,
And o'er his tomb proclaims the martyr's throes,
    imaging each tortured limb to bleed. [3]

---

[1] Περὶ Στεφάνων *liber*, Hymnus IX, v. 5.

[2] Hymnus XI, v. 123.

[3] From these passages in the hymns composed by Prudentius, it may be gathered that the custom of decorating the tombs of the martyrs with paintings, and of placing what in modern language is

IV.—RELIGIOUS FEELINGS CAUSED BY IMAGES.

Not only can sculpture and painting furnish the knowledge, and exhibit the detailed account of every fact recorded in the Old and New Testaments, to the man who cannot read, but not unfrequently the eye, by their assistance, conveys to the imagination a more impressive and accurate idea than could be imprinted by a perusal of the passage itself in which it is registered, or by listening attentively to a disquisition on the subject from some learned commentator.

This is particularly applicable with regard to the Crucifix. That virgin brow of Christ enwreathed with thorns; those lips disparted, not with plaintiveness, but sighing forth with their latest breath a supplication and a pardon for His executioners; that serenity of agonising painfulness; those feet and hands bored through with rugged nails; that blood, welling from His open side; and, as we stand gazing on the 'Word made flesh,' those whispers of the still inward voice of conscience that upbraid us,—I too joined

---

denominated an altar-piece above the altar where their relics were enshrined and mass was celebrated, was introduced before the fifth century. Noticing the above verses, extracted from the hymn on S. Hippolytus, a Protestant French writer, Le Clerc, passes the following remark : 'It ought to be observed, that upon the grave there was a table, or an altar, on which they celebrated the Eucharist (v. 170), so that the image was placed precisely upon the altar, where they are wont to place images now in the Church of Rome.' —*Bibliothèque universelle et historique de l'année* 1689, pp. 316, 317.

to crucify my God!—yes, all these possess a sad, silent, but powerful eloquence, that speaks to the heart of the most giddy worldling, and finds its way to the intelligence of the learned philosopher as well as to the comprehension of the lowly uneducated rustic.[1]

There are few persons, however slightly familiar with the productions of the fine arts, who do not

---

[1] How inferior in pathetic expression, and how much less capable of awakening sympathy in the heart of the spectator, are the sublimest specimens of classic Greek sculpture when compared with innumerable productions of the Christian artist's chisel. The weeping Niobe—the almost childless mother—stands motionless with grief amid the scene of desolation, with her youngest child, a girl, clinging round her knees, the last of many sons and daughters dead around her: the Laocoon writhes as the serpent's poison is envenoming his blood in every vein, and he hears the wailings and the cries for help that are ejaculated by his sons, without the power to succour them, or scare away the monsters that entwine their deadly coil around them all. But both of these justly celebrated groups fall infinitely short of the agonising, yet undisturbed and serene expression, legible on many a figure of our crucified Redeemer. The Niobe exhibits a countenance that is beautiful, indeed, and expressive of much grief, but that is all. The expressions of the Laocoon's head and figure are indicative of personal concern; they exclude every other feeling but that for self: no father's eye, beaming parental tenderness through tears, is cast down on either of two sons, moaning for a father's help; no arm is outstretched to tear the reptile from his boys, but both his hands are employed in grappling with the serpent that is about to inflict a second wound upon his own person. Upon the sacred features of our Blessed Saviour there are stamped, indeed, the throes and tortures of suffering humanity, but they are overmastered by the Divine nature which beams out through all the countenance, and lights it up with every characteristic of heavenly love—forgiveness—patient resignation—ideal, angelic beauty, that announce a God-man expiring under the severest torments, but undisturbed and sighing out a prayer with His latest breath to obtain a pardon from His Father for His murderers.

call up before their imagination, during a perusal of the sacred volume, those paintings and sculptures they have seen illustrative of the subject; or on contemplating a sacred picture, or piece of sculpture, do not recollect the part of Scripture which suggested it. This is, indeed, only natural, for sculpture and painting are but the translations of ideas or language into forms and colour.

V.—OBJECTION AGAINST THE USE OF IMAGES ANSWERED.

To such a custom some have raised objections, and have adduced a precept in the Decalogue in support of their hostility. The commandment, however, does not prohibit the making of images; for, if it really did, God would have been the first to violate His own injunctions by directing Moses to make and set up the figures of the cherubim; but what it forbids is the making of idols, that is, of images to be adored and served as gods. Such a caution was necessary for the Hebrew people, surrounded as they were by nations that followed the most ridiculous idolatry. Thus the Canaaneans worshipped the sun, and moon, and stars; an ox was the principal amongst the Egyptian deities, some of which were mice, and even beetles; and the Philistine would arise from his worship of Dagon to pay his adoration to serpents and to fishes.

VI.—NO VIRTUE RESIDENT IN IMAGES THEMSELVES.

Not only are Catholics not exposed to such dangers, but they are expressly prohibited by the Church[1] from believing that there is any divinity or virtue resident in images for which they should be reverenced, or that anything is to be asked of them, or any confidence placed in them, but that the honour given should be referred to those whom they represent; and so particular are their religious instructors in impressing this truth upon the minds of their congregations, that if a Catholic child, who had learned its first catechism, were asked if it were permitted to pray to images, the child would answer: 'No, by no means; for they have no life, nor sense to help us;' and the pastor who discovered anyone rendering any portion of that respect, which belongs to God alone, to a Crucifix, or to a picture, would have no hesitation in breaking the one, and tearing the other into shreds, and throwing the fragments into the flames, in imitation of Ezechias, who broke the brazen serpent, on account of the superstitious reverence which the Israelites manifested towards it.

VII.—THE USE OF IMAGES DEFENDED BY SIR HUMPHRY DAVY.

That celebrated philosopher, Sir Humphry Davy, in his 'Consolations in Travel,' puts into

---

[1] *Concilium Tridentinum*, Sessio XXV, just now quoted, p. 155.

the mouth of his Catholic friend Ambrosio the following remark in his reply to the objections urged against Christianity by the sceptic Onuphrio: 'It seemed as if the grossness of our material senses required some assistance from the eye in fixing or perpetuating the character of religious instinct; and the Church to which I belong, and I may say the whole Christian Church in early times, allowed visible images, pictures, statues and relics, as the means of awakening the stronger devotional feelings.

'We have been accused of worshipping merely inanimate objects, but this is a very false notion of the nature of our faith; we regard them merely as vivid characters representing spiritual existences, and we no more worship them than the Protestant does his Bible, when he kisses it under a solemn religious adjuration.'[1]

VIII.—ANCIENT CUSTOM IN ENGLAND.

In our old churches, built in Catholic times, there was a gallery which ran across the nave, at the entrance of the choir or chancel, and received the appellation of rood-loft, from the circumstance that a great Crucifix, or, as it was anciently denominated, Rood, was always erected there, facing the people.

But the iconoclastic mania, which during the

---

[1] H. DAVY, *Consolations in Travel, or the last days of a Philosopher.* London, 1830, p. 90.

sixteenth and seventeenth centuries unhappily infected the inhabitants of our islands, quickened their zeal against images into fury, and stimulated them to vie with, nay, to surpass, the Vandals in dilapidation and barbarism. In England, Ireland, and Scotland the Rood was precipitated from its pinnacle on the screen, and its niche within the chancel; the costly and elaborate shrine was broken down and desecrated; the statue of 'the Mother of our Lord'[1] was hurled, by generations that did *not* call her blessed,[2] from its fretted canopy; the pictorial image of the apostle or the patron saint was shattered as it glowed upon the rich and storied window that shed a moral light —a light of virtue and of holiness upon the heart and understanding, as well as poured its rays upon the eye of him who entered our venerable churches and cathedrals. Thus was for ever obliterated a precious and a brilliant page in the annals of British arts and cultivation. This mania, however, did not lay hold on Luther, the Father of the miscalled Reformation; nor has it yet infatuated any of the followers of that apostate monk. The traveller in Germany will be very often at a loss to decide, at his first entrance into what is in reality a Lutheran place of worship, whether it be not a Catholic instead of a Protestant church, for he will observe the Crucifix and lights arranged

---

[1] *S. Luke*, i, 43.   [2] *Ibid.*, 48.

precisely according to the Catholic ritual, upon the communion table.[1]

The Rood or Crucifix was taken down from the churches throughout England in consequence of an order to that effect issued by the Government in the year 1548, and from that period the royal arms have been substituted for the Cross of Jesus; and in many places the lion and the fabled unicorn occupy the precise spot where, in olden time, might be observed the more appropriate device of Christianity, the image of our bleeding Saviour.[2]

IX.—INCONSISTENCY OF PROTESTANTISM.

It is curious to observe the infatuation of prejudice. Such portions of the Word of God as bore the appearance of condemning the custom of employing images were eagerly selected and written on the walls of the church by those very persons who, immediately after, set up the figures of Moses and Aaron holding the tables of the Law, which it was pretended contained the prohibition; and

---

[1] The writer, on entering the beautiful old Gothic pile of S. Sebald's at Nuremberg, now in possession of the Lutherans, could not, for some minutes, determine whether it was a Catholic church, or dedicated to the Protestant form of worship. A handsome Crucifix, and lofty bronze candlesticks, with wax tapers burning, were conspicuous on the ancient altar; folding pictures, then unclosed, representing the Blessed Virgin Mary with the sacred Infant, and subjects from Scripture and the saints' lives ornamented the walls and pillars.

[2] See J. KENDALL, *An Elucidation of the Principles of English Architecture.* Exeter, 1818, p. 47.

who removed the Crucifix, in order to substitute
in its place the insignia of royalty ; or, in other
words, who pulled down the symbol of Jesus, and
the sign of His humility, to make room for the
symbol of a man, and the emblem of worldly
grandeur.   James I. was so forcibly struck with
this impropriety that he observed to the Scottish
bishops who objected to his ornamenting his chapel
at Edinburgh with statues and paintings : 'You
can endure lions, dragons (the supporters of the
royal arms) and devils (the armorial griffins of
Queen Elizabeth) to be figured in your churches,
but will not allow the like place to the patriarchs
and apostles.'[1]   Protestants can discern in various
texts a condemnation of the Catholic custom of
adorning their churches with paintings and statues;
and yet, in total disregard of their own principles,
they embellish their Common Prayer-books with
many images of the saints.   The writer has in his
possession a book of Common Prayer[2] decorated
with a number of such engravings.   That man
must be endowed with most penetrating logical
acumen who can distinguish it to be idolatrous
and contradictory to Scripture to ornament with
images the temple we pray *in*, but perfectly harmless, nay, useful, to do so with regard to the book
we pray *from*.

---

[1] J. SPOTSWOOD, *History of the Church of Scotland*, p. 530.

[2] Printed by the assigns of T. Newcomb and H. Hills, printers to
the Queen's most excellent Majesty, 1711.

X.—ON THE DIVISION OF THE DECALOGUE.

It may be proper to observe that both Catholics and Protestants receive the ten commandments as they are delivered in Exodus and Deuteronomy, though they differ in the manner of arranging them. The commandment which, according to the Catholic enumeration, is considered as the first, is improperly divided into two precepts by Protestants; and those two really distinct precepts which, in the Protestant division of the Decalogue, are condensed into one — the tenth commandment — the Catholic Church more properly separates into two, the ninth and tenth.[1] Hence it not unfrequently happens amongst

---

[1] *The First Commandment in the Catholic division of the Decalogue.*

I. Thou shalt not have strange gods before Me. Thou shalt not make to thyself a graven thing, nor the likeness of any thing that is in heaven above, or in the earth beneath, nor of those things that are in the waters under the earth. Thou shalt not adore them, nor serve them. I am the Lord thy God, mighty, jealous, visiting the iniquity of fathers upon their children, unto the third and fourth generation of those that hate Me; and shewing mercy unto thousands of those that love Me, and keep My commandments.

[1] *The First and Second Commandments in the Protestant division of the Decalogue.*

I. Thou shalt have none other gods but Me.

II. Thou shalt not make to thyself any graven image, nor the likeness of any thing that is in heaven above, or in the earth beneath, or in the water under the earth. Thou shalt not bow down to them, nor worship them; for I the Lord thy God am a jealous God, and visit the sins of the fathers upon the children, unto the third and fourth generation of them that hate Me, and shew mercy unto thousands in them that love Me, and keep My commandments.

Protestants even of intelligence and information that we are accused of omitting the second commandment to apologise for our pretended worship of idols. The Scripture, however, while it assures us that the words of the Law were ten,[1] nowhere furnishes us with the manner in which they were divided. The division therefore of the Decalogue is left to the Church, and is in itself a matter of inferior importance. The Catholics, with S. Clement of Alexandria, S. Augustine, and S. Jerome, divide the commandments into two parts, as given by God to Moses on two tablets of stone; on the first table were written the first three, which prescribe the worship of God, and the sanctification of the Sabbath, or day of rest; on the other table were engraven the remaining seven, which expound the duty of men to each other. This division is to be preferred to that made by Origen, which assigns four to the first table, and six to the second. First, because the prohibition to make idols or to adore them is an explanation and consequence of adoring one

---

Ninth and Tenth Commandments in the Catholic division of the Decalogue.

IX. Thou shalt not covet thy neighbour's wife.

X. Thou shalt not covet thy neighbour's house, nor his servant, nor his ox, nor his ass, nor any thing that is his.

Tenth Commandment in the Protestant division of the Decalogue.

X. Thou shalt not covet thy neighbour's house, thou shalt not covet thy neighbour's wife, nor his servant, nor his maid, nor his ox, nor his ass, nor any thing that is his.

[1] *Deuteronomy,* IV, 13.

only true God, and not having strange gods before Him, and should therefore be joined with it. Secondly, because, as the sixth commandment, which forbids the outward crime of adultery, is different from the seventh, which tells us not to steal our neighbour's goods ; so, in like manner, the ninth, which prohibits the sin of desiring our neighbour's wife, is properly separated from the tenth, in which we are forbidden to covet any part of his possessions.[1]

These cursory observations, it is trusted, will disabuse the reader of any erroneous preconceptions he may heretofore have entertained concerning the doctrine and the practice of the Catholic Church in the employment of images. Such observations will have helped him to detect the calumnious accusations of those amongst her adversaries who unhesitatingly prefer against her, without having ascertained the truth of their denunciation, the serious charge of having mutilated and abridged the Decalogue,[2] in order to

---

[1] See *Deuteronomy*, v, 21 ; also the Septuagint version of Exodus.

[2] That up to the change in religion the ten commandments were taught, and divided in the same way as at present, by Catholics all over the world ; and that the division now in use amongst English Protestants was introduced, not immediately along with the new religion, but some years after, are facts that may be easily substantiated.

There is a very curious and scarce work, entitled *Dives et Pauper*, at the end of which is inserted the following explanation of its contents : 'Here endeth a compendyouse treatyse dyalogue of Dives and Pauper. That is to saye, the ryche and the poore fructuously

keep out of sight a condemnation of her idolatry; for such is the language which some zealots employ to designate a rite which is so harmless; as if such an erasure in the commandments could

---

treatynge upon the x commaundementes, fynysshed the iij daye of Decembre. The yere of our lorde god M.CCCC.LXXXXVI. Emprentyd by me Wynken de Worde at Westmonstre. Deo Gracias.'

In this work the first and second commandments are enumerated in the following words and order:

'Here begynneth the fyrste commaundemente. *Dives.* In the fyrste commaundement as I have lerned, God sayth thus. Thou shalte have none other straunge goddes byfore me. Thou shalte make to the noo graven thynge, noo mawmette, noo lykenesse that is in heven above, ne that is bynethe in erthe, ne of ony thynge that is in the water under therthe. Thou shalt not worshyppe theym with thy bodye outwarde, ne within thyn herte inwarde. Exodi xx. c.' After a long explanation of the first commandment, he proceeds to the second, thus: 'In the seconde commaundement God byddeth that we sholde not take his name in vayne, for who so doth shall be gylty and shall not passe unpunysshed.'

This same method of dividing the commandments continued several years after the expulsion of the ancient faith. This may be verified, in the first place, from a catechism drawn up by Erasmus and entitled: 'A playne and godly exposition or declaration of the commune Crede (which in the Latyn tonge is called Symbolum Apostolorum) and of the x commaundementes of Goddes law, newly made and put forth by the famouse clerke, Mayster Erasmus of Roterdame, at the requeste of the moste honorable lorde, Thomas Erle of Wyltshyre: father to the most gratious and vertuous Quene Anne wyfe to our moste gracious soveraygne lorde kyng Henry the viii.

'The fyrste commaundement.—The fyrst precepte therfore is this. Thou shalt not have any straunge goddes in my syght, thou shalt not make the any graven ymage, nor any maner similitude, or lykenes, which is in the fyrmament above, or whiche is in the earthe benethe, neyther of those thynges whiche are in the waters under the earth.

'The secound precept.—Thou shalt not take the name of God in vayne.

'Imprynted at London in Fletestrete, by me Robert Redman.

justify the crime in the eyes of any Catholic, or tranquillise his conscience. They will have satisfied him, too, that instead of being forbidden, the use of images is positively recommended by the

---

n the second place, Cranmer's 'Catechismus, That is to say, a shorte Instruction into Christian religion for the singuler commoditie and profyte of children and yong people. Set forth by the mooste reverende father in God Thomas Arch-byshop of Canterbury, Primate of all England and Metropolitane. Gualterus Lynne excudebat. 1548,' in which the arch-reformer thus gives the Commandments according to our present Catholic enumeration :

These are the holy ten commaundementes of the Lorde our God.

The firste.

'I am the Lorde thy God, thou shalt have none other Goddes but me.

The seconde.

'Thou shalt not take the name of the Lord thy God in vayne, etc.

. . . .

The nynthe.

'Thou shalt not covet thy neyghbours house.

The tenth.

'Thou shalt not covet thy neyghboures wyfe, nor hys man servaunte, nor hys mayde servaunt, nor hys oxe, nor hys asse, nor anye thynge that is thy neyghboures.

. . . .

'Ye have herd, good children, in the former sermon, that all maner of Idolatrie is forbyd by this commaundement. Thou shalt have none other Gods but me. Where also it was declared unto you, howe you may commit spirituall ydolatrie, by over much fearyng, trustynge, and lovyng of creatures. But nowe I wyll speake of the moost grosse ydolatrie, whiche standeth in wourshyppynge of ymages, eyther of creatures or of God himselfe.

'And this ydolatrye is forbyde by expresse wordes in this commaundement, where God sayeth thus :

word of God ; and he will conclude that the utility of those religious memorials is evident, as they serve to call to our remembrance some of the most sacred mysteries taught by our religion —help to keep our thoughts from wandering at the time of prayer ; and, while they point towards heaven, silently remind us of the sufferings, and the death on the altar of the Cross, of God made man—our Jesus—our crucified Redeemer.

Thou shalt make the no graven ymage, nor any lykenesse of anye thynge whiche is in heaven above, or in earth benethe, or in the water under the earthe.   Thou shalt not bow downe unto it, nor wourship it.

'These wordes (by most interpretors of late tyme, belonge to the first commaundement, althoughe after the interpretation of manye auncient autors they be the seconde commaundement), etc.'

In the Book of Common Prayer, published in 1549, we find the Decalogue divided just as it is at present in Protestant catechisms.

CHAPTER XI.

ON THE USE OF LIGHTS.

I.—LIGHTS COMMANDED TO BE USED IN THE JEWISH TABERNACLE.

THE use of lights in the service of the Jewish temple is a fact too well authenticated to require any proof. Such is the historical celebrity, both religious and profane, belonging to the seven-branched candlestick [1] which the Almighty Himself commanded to be made, 'according to the pattern that was shown to Moses in the Mount,' [2] that it immediately presents itself to our attention; nor will it escape the remembrance of anyone, however partially conversant with the con-

---

[1] The taking of Jerusalem by the Roman legions under Titus was regarded as an occurrence of so much magnitude, that the honours of a public triumph were decreed by the senate to that imperial conqueror. Amongst the trophies of his victory which were selected to adorn this military pomp, the seven-branched candlestick belonging to the Jewish temple was by far the most conspicuous. This is evidenced by the triumphal arch of Titus, which still exists at Rome, and stands between the Forum and the Colosseum; and exhibits so accurately, at the present day, the image of this celebrated candlestick sculptured on one of the beautiful bas-reliefs which ornament the inner part of that splendid monument.

[2] *Exodus,* XXV, 31-40.

tents of the sacred volume, that, in order to keep a lamp always burning in the tabernacle, a constant supply of the purest oil of olives was particularly enjoined.[1] Among the vessels which Solomon made for the house of the Lord were 'the golden candlesticks, five on the right hand, and five on the left.'[2]

II.—ADOPTED BY THE APOSTLES.

But without referring to the ceremonial of the Jewish Temple, we have an authority for the employment of lights in the functions of religion

---

[1] *Ibid.*, XXVII, 20.

[2] 3 *Kings*, VII, 49. The twofold use of lights, to manifest a civic respect and exhibit a religious veneration, was conspicuous amongst the Jews. The employment of such a method to manifest a reverence towards things that were dedicated to the service of religion is instanced by a circumstance which Josephus mentions in his 'Antiquities' (lib. XVIII, c. 6). We gather from the pages of that Jewish historian that whenever the stole, or mantle belonging to the high-priest, was deposited within the walls of a certain tower called Antonia, a lamp was kept daily burning there.

That they considered the burning of lights as an emblem of civic homage and a testimonial of public respect may be gathered from an incident in the history of their nation mentioned by the author of the second book of Machabees, XXII. While recording the magnificent reception which Antiochus met with on his visit to Jerusalem, he informs us that Jason, who had obtruded himself into the dignity of high-priest, and the whole city awaited at the gates that prince's approach, and on his arrival there 'came out with torch-lights and praises.' So conspicuous indeed was this Hebrew custom, that a heathen poet particularly mentioned it. Persius, as he notices how the Jews celebrated the birthday of King Herod, says :

At cum
Herodis venere dies, unctaque fenestra
dispositae pinguem nebulam vomuere lucernae.
Satira V, v. 180.

presented to us in the Apocalypse. In the first chapter of that mystic book, S. John particularly mentions the golden candlesticks which he beheld in his prophetic vision in the isle of Patmos. By commentators on the sacred Scripture it is generally supposed that the Evangelist, in his book of the Apocalypse, adopted the imagery with which he represents his mystic revelations from the ceremonial observed in his days by the Church for offering up the Mass or Eucharistic sacrifice of the Lamb of God, Christ Jesus.

That the use of lights was adopted by the Church, especially at the celebration of the sacred mysteries, as early as the time of the Apostles, may likewise, with much probability, be inferred from that passage in their Acts which records the preaching and the miracles of S. Paul at Troas: 'And on the first day of the week, when we were assembled to break bread, Paul discoursed with them, being to depart on the morrow: and he continued his speech until midnight. And there was a great number of lamps in the upper chamber, where we were assembled.'[1] That the many lamps, so particularly noticed in this passage, were not suspended merely for the purpose of illuminating, during the night-time, this upper chamber, in which the faithful had assembled on the first day of the week to break

---

[1] *Acts*, xx, 7, 8.

bread, but also to increase the solemnity of that function and betoken a spiritual joy, may be lawfully presumed from everything we know about the manners of the ancient Jews, from whom the Church borrowed the use of lights in celebrating her various religious rites and festivals.

III.—LIGHTS EMPLOYED FROM PRIMITIVE TIMES AT DIVINE SERVICE.

The custom of employing lights, in the earlier ages of the Church, during the celebration of the Eucharist and other religious offices is authenticated by those venerable records of primitive discipline which are usually denominated the Apostolical Canons.[1]

In several of these ordinances a distinct men-

---

[1] Of the authenticity of these canons, it may not be amiss to present the reader with the following observations :—The Apostolical Canons comprehend a collection of regulations respecting the discipline observed by the primitive Church, and amount to the number of eighty-five, of which the last thirty-five are not admitted to possess any claims to authority. While it is universally allowed that the first fifty were not drawn up by the Apostles themselves, nor promulgated by them in the form in which we now possess them, their testimony as to the discipline of the Church in the first ages is generally admitted to be incontrovertible. Daillé and a few Protestants have, it is true, bestowed, but thrown away, much labour and some learning in endeavouring to prove that these canons are supposititious, and that they were not even known, much less cited, before the fourth century. Among the successful advocates who have come forward in their vindication should be particularly noticed Dr. Beveridge, a learned Protestant divine, Bishop of S. Asaph, who in a couple of treatises of great learning entitled *Iudicium de Canonibus Apostolicis* and *Codex canonum Ecclesiae*

tion is made of these offerings of oil which were intended for nourishing the lamps employed in the assemblies of the faithful; and the third of these canons expressly prohibits that anything should be offered at the altar during the holy oblation excepting oil for the lights and incense.[1]

Some amongst the Fathers of the Church, by the incidental notice they have taken of the use of lights in the sanctuary, have rendered an important attestation in favour both of the

---

primitivae vindicatus (published in 1678, and reprinted by Cotelerius in his collection of Apostolic Fathers, tom. I, p. 432, and tom. II, Appendix) has clearly demonstrated that the regulations embodied in these canons were enacted, in conformity with the traditions handed regularly down from the Apostles, by various Synods assembled in different places and at various times during the latter part of the second or the earlier part of the third century, and that they were brought together and formed into a collection during the third century.

To pretend that these canons are supposititious is an equivocation of which some amongst those who reject the doctrines of the Catholic Church have, without reason, endeavoured to avail themselves.

Though these canons be apocryphal, inasmuch as they were neither committed to writing by the Apostles themselves, nor drawn up by S. Clement from their directions, still this does not prevent them from being a true and authentic memorial of the discipline which prevailed during the first and second centuries.

If these canons more immediately record the practices of discipline, they likewise lend their attestation to the dogmas insisted on, to the morality recommended, and to the outward worship piously exercised by the teachers of Christianity during the first two ages subsequent to its promulgation. It is, moreover, worthy of remark that in these venerable documents of religious antiquity we continually meet with the terms 'altar' and 'sacrifice,' observe the various gradations in the hierarchy, and perceive that to the pastors of the Christian Church were assigned all the attributes of a veritable order of priesthood.

[1] Μὴ ἐξὸν δὲ ἔστω προσαγεσθαί τὶ ἔτερον εἰς τὸ θυσιαστήριον ἢ ἔλαιον εἰς τὴν λυχνίαν, καὶ θυμίαμα, τῷ καιρῷ τῆς ἁγίας προσφορας.

employment of them and of the antiquity of the practice. S. Athanasius, writing in 341, complains feelingly against the Arians, whose impiety was such that they afforded access into the Church to the heathens, who plundered the oil and burned before their idols the very tapers that had been the offerings of the faithful.[1]

S. Augustine, in one of his discourses,[2] thus exhorts his auditors: 'Let those who are able present either wax-tapers or oil which may supply the lamps.'

IV.—DEFENDED BY S. JEROME AGAINST VIGILANTIUS, AND NOTICED BY S. PAULINUS AND PRUDENTIUS.

It happens not unfrequently that those very calumnies which have been propagated, and the attacks that have been directed by the enemies of our holy faith in ancient times against certain practices of discipline then followed by the Church, are the most triumphant testimonials which can be adduced at the present day, both to establish the venerable origin of such observances and to warrant a continuation of them. In the present instance this remark is strikingly observable; for the strictures which Vigilantius passed on the use of lights in churches, as well

---

[1] Τὸ ἀποκείμενον ἔλαιον ἥρπαζον· τὰς θύρας καὶ τοὺς καγκέλλους ὡς σκῦλα ἕκαστος ἐλάμβανε· . . . τοὺς κηριάλους τῆς ἐκκλησίας τοῖς εἰδώλοις ἀνῆπτον.—S. ATHANASII *Epistola encyclica.*

[2] *De Tempore Sermo* 215.

as at the shrines of the martyrs, and the energetic
refutation by S. Jerome of the charge of superstition preferred by that apostate against this pious
usage, may be adduced as an irrefragable argument in the nineteenth century to establish the
remote antiquity of this religious custom. After
mentioning as a fact of public notoriety, and in
a manner which defied contradiction, that the
Christians at the time when he was actually
writing, which was about the year 403, were
accustomed to illuminate their churches during
midday with a profusion of wax-tapers, Vigilantius proceeds to turn this practice into ridicule.
But he met with a learned and victorious op-
ponent, who, while he vindicated this practice of
the Church against the objurgations of her enemy,
took occasion to enumerate the reasons which
induced her to adopt it. That holy and learned
Father observes: 'Throughout all the Churches
of the East, whenever the Gospel is to be recited
they bring forth lights, though it be at noonday;
not, certainly, to drive away darkness, but to
manifest some sign of joy, that under the type of
corporal light may be indicated that light of which
we read in the Psalms: "Thy word is a lamp
to my feet, and a light to my paths."' [1] The information which was casually furnished by S. Jerome

---

[1] Per totas Orientis Ecclesias, quando legendum est Evangelium,
accenduntur luminaria, iam sole rutilante : non utique ad fugandas
tenebras : sed ad signum laetitiae demonstrandum . . . ut sub typo

concerning a practice invariably observed throughout the Eastern portion of the Church has, with
reference to the West, been conveyed to us in
some beautiful lines of S. Paulinus of Nola, who,
in his verses in honour of S. Felix, writes thus:

> Aurea nunc niveis ornantur limina velis,
> clara coronantur densis altaria lychnis.
> Lumina ceratis adolentur odora papyris,
> nocte dieque micant, sic nox splendore diei
> fulget: et ipsa dies caelesti illustris honore,
> plus micat innumeris lucem geminata lucernis.
> > *De S. Felice Natalitium carmen III.*

> With crowded lamps are these bright altars crown'd,
> and waxen tapers shedding perfume round
> from fragrant wicks, beam calm a scented ray
> to gladden night, and joy e'en radiant day.
> Meridian splendours thus light up the night,
> and day itself, illumined with sacred light,
> wears a new glory, borrow'd from those rays
> that stream from countless lamps in never-ending blaze.

Prudentius, another Christian poet, furnishes
in several places of his works, especially in his
hymns, the clearest testimony as to the use of
lights throughout the Churches of Gaul, Spain,
and Italy at the time he wrote, which was
towards the decline of the fourth century. So
far is he from regarding their introduction into
the liturgy as an event of recent date, that he

---

luminis corporalis illa lux ostendatur, de qua in Psalterio legimus:
Lucerna pedibus meis verbum Tuum, Domine, et lumen semitis meis.
S. HIERONYMI *contra Vigilantium liber.*

tacitly asserts the practice to have been derived from antiquity, by the notice which he takes of lights while describing the assemblies of the early Christians in the times of persecution. In his hymn on the martyrdom of the holy deacon S. Laurence, he introduces the persecuting proconsul as describing the meetings of the Christians in the catacombs, and puts these with several other verses into the mouth of that Roman magistrate :

> Argenteis scyphis ferunt
> fumare sacrum sanguinem ;
> auroque nocturnis sacris
> adstare fixos cereos.
> Περὶ Στεφάνων *liber*, *Hymnus* 11, v. 69.

> In silver chalices, 'tis said,
> fuming the sacred blood is shed ;
> and fixed on gold, the tapers' light
> illumes their midnight solemn rite.

V.—PROVED FROM THE LITURGIES AND OTHER MONUMENTS.

That lights were anciently as now employed at the celebration of the sacred mysteries and at other portions of the public service may be gathered, not only from the ritual constitutions of the Church, but from a variety of incidental circumstances. The form that was employed in the Church of Carthage for the ordination of acolytes has already been quoted in another part of this work.[1] The person to be initiated into that last of the four minor orders was admonished that one amongst his future offices would be to take care of the lights in the church. S. Isidore testifies what was the function more particularly incumbent on acolytes in the Spanish Church, when he says that they are denominated in Latin ceroferarii, or taper-bearers, from their carrying wax-lights not only when the Gospel is read, but whenever sacrifice is to be offered up.[2] Micrologus[3] asserted that, according to the Roman ordinal, Mass was never celebrated without lights, which were employed not to dispel darkness, since the service is performed during the broad day, but rather as a type of the light of Him whose sacrament we there celebrate, and without whom we grope about at midday as though it were night.[4]

The use of lights at Mass is not peculiar to the

---

[1] See vol. I, p. 73.

[2] 'Acolythi Graece, Latine ceroferarii dicuntur, a deportandis cereis quando Evangelium legendum est, aut sacrificium offerendum. Tunc enim accenduntur luminaria ab eis, et deportantur,' etc. S. ISIDORI *Orig.* lib. VII, c. 12.

[3] Such is the name assigned to an unknown author who wrote (A.D. 1080) a very valuable book on the celebration of Mass, to which he affixed the modest title of the '*Little Discourse;*' in Greek, *Micros Logos.*

[4] 'Iuxta Ordinem Romanum nunquam Missam absque lumine celebramus : non utique ad depellendas tenebras, cum fit clara dies : sed potius in typum illius luminis, cuius sacramentum ibi conficimus, sine quo et in meridie palpabimus ut in nocte.'—*Micrologus de Eccles. observat.* c. II.

Latin Church, and without reproducing the testimony of S. Jerome[1] concerning the practice at his time of all the Churches in the East, we may refer at once to the Oriental liturgies themselves, and we shall observe that in all of them there are rubrics which especially prescribe that waxtapers should burn at the altar at which the Holy Sacrifice is offered. In the Syriac liturgies it is directed that lights be arranged on the right hand and on the left previously to the approach of the priest to the altar;[2] and the commentators on the various liturgies in use amongst the other Churches in the East have particularly noticed this ritual observance in all of them.[3] A section of the Protestant denomination still preserves this ancient rite in its public service, for the Lutherans, like the Catholics, have wax-tapers burning at their celebration of the Lord's Supper.[4]

---

[1] See the passage p. 182 of this volume.

[2] 'Igitur post primas illas breves orationes accenduntur cerei, a dextra parte primum, mox a sinistra. . . . In Missali Chaldaico notatur, sacerdotem ubi cerei accensi sunt, vasa sacra collocare in altari, et mox oblatam et calicem disco imponere.'—RENAUDOT, *Liturgiarum Orientalium Collectio*, tom. II, p. 53.

[3] 'Accenduntur cerei : quorum saepe mentio fit in pompis, solennibusque processionibus Christianorum, quarum memoria est in Historia Alexandrina. Gabriel filius Tarich Patriarcha in Constitutionibus ita definit: *Liturgia non celebretur absque cereis duobus maioribus aut minoribus, qui circa altare luceant.* Idem praecipiunt autor Scientiae Ecclesiasticae, Abulbircat, omnesque Liturgiarum expositores.' RENAUDOT, *Lit. Orient. Coll.*, tom. I, p. 196.

[4] Everyone who has travelled through any part of Lutheran Germany is aware of this. A visit to the Lutheran chapel in S. James's Palace, or to any of the other Lutheran chapels distributed through London, will satisfy the untravelled reader of this fact.

To this custom of employing lights at the
Divine Service must be referred many of those
magnificent donations which the more wealthy
of the faithful carried to the sanctuary even in
the times of persecution, and which sometimes
quickened the diligence, or rather sharpened the
cupidity, of the magistrates to whom was entrusted the execution of those cruel edicts issued
by the Cæsars for the extermination of the Christian name.[1]   The presents of gold and silver
lamps and candlesticks which pontiffs and princes
offered at the tomb of the Apostles, and distributed at various times amongst the other
churches at Rome, are frequently noticed in the
Liber Pontificalis, from which we gather that the
piety of those times was not always satisfied with
burning common wax and oil about the sanctuary,
but that the most costly and odoriferous unguents
were on many occasions provided.[2]

---

[1] This is partly testified by Prudentius in those verses we have just
now given.   In the Proconsular Acts are sometimes enumerated the
lamps and candlesticks delivered up to the imperial authorities.

[2] The number and variety of the lamps and candlesticks anciently
employed in churches may be gathered from their denominations.
In old writers we continually find mentioned Candelabrum, Cereos-
tata, Pharus, Cantharus, Cicindela, Lucerna, and Lampades cum
delphinis.   The *Liber Pontificalis* is particularly minute in the
enumeration of the golden lamps and crosses which Constantine
the Great bestowed upon the basilicas at Rome; and the names
of the various estates in Africa and the East with which that pious
emperor endowed those dedicated to S. Peter and to S. Paul have
been preserved in the same work, which, in the account of that
splendid temple erected on the Ostian way by Constantine over the
tomb of the Apostle of the Gentiles, tells us : 'Omnia enim vasa

VI.—MYSTIC SIGNIFICATION OF LIGHTS AT MASS.

In the holy Sacrifice of the Mass the Christian has the most abundant cause imaginable for joy. The altar then becomes the throne of God made man, and angels and cherubim surround it in prostrate adoration. The Church, in her primitive days, to manifest her lively, glowing faith and joyfulness, produced this emblem of lights. She still continues to retain their use. While these wax-tapers, therefore, proclaim our exultation for the actual presence of our Blessed Redeemer, they typify the light and glory of the Gospel diffused throughout the earth by that Orient from on high, Christ Jesus. S. Jerome, as we have already

sacrata aurea, argentea, aut aenea ita posuit, sicut et in Basilicam Sancti Petri Apostoli, ita et Beati Pauli Apostoli ordinavit. Sed et crucem auream super locum Beati Pauli Apostoli posuit pensan libras centum et quinquaginta. Possessio Fronimusa praestans oleum nardinum libras septuaginta, aromata libr. quinquaginta. Cassia libr. centum. Sub civitate Ægypti possessio Cyrias praestans oleum nardinum libr. septuaginta, balsamum libr. triginta, aromata libr. septuaginta, storace libr. triginta, stacten lib. centum et quinquaginta. Possessio Basilea praestans, Aromata libr. quinquaginta oleum nardinum libr. sexaginta, balsamum libr. viginti, crocos libr. septuaginta.'

The brilliancy and fragrance which were often shed around a martyr's sepulchre at the celebration of his festival by multitudes of tapers and lamps fed with aromatic oils are noticed by S. Paulinus :—

> Ast alii pictis accendant lumina ceris,
> multiforesque cavis lychnos laquearibus aptent,
> ut vibrent tremulas funalia pendula flammas.
> Martyris hi tumulum studeant perfundere nardo,
> et medicata pio referant unguenta sepulchro.
> *De S. Felice Natalitium carmen VI.*

seen, observed in his answer to Vigilantius:
'Whenever the Gospel is to be recited, lights
are brought forth, though it be at noonday; not,
certainly, to drive away darkness, but to manifest
a sign of joy.'

VII.—LIGHTS AT BAPTISM.

Nor were lights confined to the Sacrifice of the
Mass; they were employed during other functions
of religion.

Amongst the ceremonies which were practised
immediately after baptism had been administered,
S. Gregory Nazianzen, who flourished about the
year 372, enumerates that of a lighted taper being
carried by the neophyte. 'The lamps,' he says,
in his fortieth oration on the baptized, 'the lamps
which immediately after baptism thou shalt light
are emblems of those lamps of faith with which
radiant souls shall hasten forth to meet the Bride-
groom.'

When personages of high distinction were
baptized with public solemnity, the custom of
bearing lights was observed with extraordinary
magnificence. An instance is recorded in the
splendid ceremonial which accompanied the administration of this sacrament to the younger
Theodosius: 'After the Emperor had been baptized, and had issued from the church, another
opportunity was afforded to behold the splendour
and magnificent apparel of those who were

invested with the public magistracy. Everyone
was robed with white, so that the whole assembly
appeared covered, as it were, with snow. The
patricians, illustrious personages, and the several
dignitaries, with lines of military, preceded, bearing wax-tapers in their hands, so that the stars
themselves might have been imagined to have
appeared upon the earth.'[1]

VIII.—SPIRITUAL MEANING OF THEM.

The employment of lights on this occasion
was most appropriate. The glowing taper was a
symbol beautifully expressive of the actual illumi-
nation of the recently baptized person by the
Holy Spirit, and called to his remembrance that
admonition of the Saviour: 'So let your light
shine before men, that they may see your
good works, and glorify your Father who is in
heaven.'[2]

IX.—LIGHTS USED AT FUNERALS.

An observance which was practised at the
initiation of the faithful into the mysteries of
religion was sedulously employed when their
mortal remains were consigned to the sepulchre.

Eusebius, the historian, has noticed in a parti-

---

[1] See BARONIUS, Anno 401, vol. v.

[2] Deinde cereus ardens in manum traditur, qui ostendit Fidem
charitate inflammatam, quam in baptismo accepit, bonorum operum
studio alendam atque augendam esse. *Concilium Tridentinum, Catechismus de Baptismi Sacramento,* num. 75.

cular manner, the unusual number of lights placed upon golden candlesticks which produced such a powerful effect upon the crowd of spectators who came to view the funeral obsequies of Constantine the Great.[1] S. Gregory Nazianzen,[2] in the description which he gives of the funeral honours rendered to his brother Caesarius, mentions that their mother accompanied the corpse to the place of sepulture and bore a lighted taper in her hand. Another S. Gregory, the highly gifted Bishop of Nyssa (372–395), and younger brother to the great S. Basil, referring to the obsequies of his sister Macrina, mentions that a great concourse of people encircled the bier, and that a numerous body from amongst the clergy, drawn up in long array and holding lights in their hands, preceded it. S. Jerome informs us[3] that the body of S. Paula was carried by bishops to its place of interment. Some of the prelates supported the bier upon their shoulders, and the others went before with lighted tapers in their hands. Theodoret,[4] recording the translation of S. Chrysostom's body from Comana to Constantinople, remarks that such a multitude of people proceeded in ships and every kind of vessel to meet the precious

---

[1] EUSEBIUS, *Vita Constantini.*

[2] *Oratio VII in laudem Caesarii fratris.*

[3] In his 108th Epistle, which is directed to Eustochium.

[4] He was Bishop of Cyrrhus, and author of a history of the Church from the rise of Arianism under Constantius to the death of Theodore of Mopsuestia in 429.

relics in their passage across the Bosphorus, that the very sea was radiant and twinkling with the lamps.[1]

The meaning of this custom is explained to us by S. Chrysostom himself, who informs us that it was usual to carry lights before the dead, to signify that they were champions or conquerors, and, as such, were borne in triumph to their graves.[2] This ancient custom is still kept up in Catholic countries. Everyone who has travelled in any Catholic country must have oftentimes observed that not even the poorest individual is ever conveyed to the grave without some few attendants, who walk by the bier, with lighted torches in their hands, reciting a prayer for the soul of the departed. Lamps and torches were lighted in the day to signify Christian joy, and to exhibit respect and honour to the departed, as to a victorious combatant who had vanquished this world here below, and was now proceeding to take possession of a brighter and a better world above.[3]

---

[1] By the 59th of the Justinian Novels, a prohibition was issued to the acolytes of Constantinople, by which they were forbidden to exact a fee for their torches, since, from the public fund which had been established in the imperial city for the interment of the dead, a certain stipend had been assigned to these ecclesiastics for their attendance at funerals.

[2] Εἰπὲ γάρ μοι, τί βούλονται αἱ λαμπάδες αἱ φαιδραί; οὐχ ὡς ἀθλητὰς αὐτοὺς προπέμπομεν. S. Chrysostomi in Epist. ad Hebraeos Homil. IV.

[3] Θυμιάμασι καὶ κηρίοις αὐτοὺς συνοδεύομεν, δεικνύντες ὅτι τοῦ σκοτεινοῦ βίου λυθέντες, πρὸς τὸ φῶς τὸ ἀληθινόν ἐπορεύθησαν. S. Chrysostomi Hom. CXVI.

X.—ON THE PASCHAL CANDLE.

Who was the inventor of the Paschal candle, or from what epoch may be dated its earliest adoption by the Church, are incidents both of which are equally involved in historical obscurity.[1] That its origin is very ancient may be unhesitatingly asserted, when we remember that S. Jerome and S. Augustine severally make mention of this usage—the first in his epistles, the latter in his book, *De Civitate Dei.*

That at Rome, in the fifth century, a candle was solemnly blessed upon the eve of Easter, and kept burning at Divine Service during Paschal time, or the period which elapses between the feasts of the Resurrection and Ascension, is ascertained by a permission which, the *Liber Pontificalis* informs us, was conceded by Pope Zosimus (417–418) in favour of the several parish churches throughout Rome, by which they were authorised to bless the Paschal candle, in imitation of a practice then observed in the basilicas of that metropolis of Christianity.[2] If it be permitted

---

[1] In the ancient Roman Sacramentaries, particularly in that of S. Gelasius (492–496), the solemn blessing for the Paschal candle is inserted. S. Ennodius, the learned bishop of Pavia (511–521), has left us two forms of benediction, composed in no inelegant language ; and the Fourth Council of Toledo, celebrated in 633, makes mention of the Paschal candle and its benediction, at the same time assigning the mystic sense which the Spanish Church affixed to that ceremony. LABBEI *Concil. Gen.*, tom. x, col. 620.

[2] Hic (Zosimus) fecit constitutionem per parochias, concessa licentia cereos benedici. *Liber Pontificalis.*

to hazard a conjecture, the Paschal candle may be supposed to have derived its origin from a custom which for a long time afterwards prevailed at Constantinople, and was introduced under the founder of that imperial capital, of illuminating the streets with a profusion of lights and tapers upon the eve of Easter, to anticipate the joy and shadow forth the glory of the resurrection.[1]

Representation of the Blessing of the Paschal Candle, from an illuminated Manuscript of the eleventh century.

XI.—THE EXSULTET.

That beautiful canticle, the *Exsultet*, which is chanted by the deacon on Holy Saturday while blessing the Paschal candle, has been unanimously assigned by ecclesiastical tradition to the great

---

[1] I. L. SELVAGIO, *Antiquitatum Christianarum institutiones*, vol. II, p. 33.

S. Augustine,[1] though, indeed, through the emendations and abridgements it has undergone from S. Hugh and other holy prelates, that expressive composition, as we now possess it, somewhat varies from the original.

The Paschal candle is of unusual dimensions, being generally many feet in height and several inches in diameter. Towards the middle part of it are inserted five grains of incense,[2] in the figure of a cross. On the Continent, particularly at Rome in the basilicas and the patriarchal and the richer churches, the pedestal which upholds it is usually a column of some precious marble, and sometimes elaborately wrought with sculpture or curiously tessellated in rich and elegant mosaic.[3]

---

[1] S. Augustine himself thus refers to the hymn which he composed for the blessing of the Paschal candle: 'In laude quadam cerei breviter versibus dixi.' In an old manuscript Pontifical used in the church of Poitiers, which, as appears by the style of the character, must have been transcribed about the year 800, is the following observation on the *Exsultet:* 'Usum benedicendi cereum a beato Augustino repertum tradit Ecclesia, qui benedictionem illius perficiens, a Sancto Hieronymo reprehensus est, cur Vergiliana verba inseruerit, sed sicut a beato Hieronymo emendata tunc fuit; ita nunc per ecclesias canitur.' MARTENE, *De antiquis Ecclesiae Ritibus.* Antverpiae, 1737, tom. III, col. 409.

[2] These five grains of incense are of a cubical form, and have a pin fixed in them, by which they are fastened to the candle.

[3] In many of the churches at Rome the column which supports the Paschal candle is composed of a shaft of *verde antico*, and of a Corinthian base and capital, elegantly wrought either in gilt bronze or white marble, and stands permanent and conspicuous in the sanctuary. The curiously storied column of S. Paul's, exhibiting the passion and resurrection in a series of bas-reliefs, may be seen in

The deacon, not the celebrating priest, recites the benediction over it.[1]

XII.—ITS MYSTIC SIGNIFICATION.

The twofold mystic signification which the Church attaches to this ancient rite is no less appropriate than beautiful and edifying. The Paschal candle is regarded as an emblem of Christ. While it remains unlighted, it is figurative of His death and repose in the tomb; when lighted, it represents the splendour and the glory of His resurrection. Before it is blessed the officiating deacon inserts the five grains of incense, to signify that the sacred body of our Divine Redeemer was bound in linen cloths with spices, and thus consigned to the grave, by Joseph of Arimathea and Nicodemus.[2] The five incisions made to receive the grains of incense, which are so arranged as to form the figure of the cross, represent the five wounds that were inflicted on the body of Christ at His crucifixion.

Though it be usually reserved to priests only to pronounce benediction over anything, an ex-

---

Ciampini (*Vetera Monimenta,* tom. I, p. 24, tab. xiv), who has also given those of S. Clement's and of S. Laurence's. *Ibid.,* pp. 22, 23, tab. xii, xiii.

[1] From Venerable Bede, *Liber de Temporum Ratione,* cap. xlvii, we gather that in his time it was the practice of the Church for the deacon, before commencing the benediction of the Paschal candle, to inscribe with a stylus or writing-needle the date of indiction and the occurring year upon it.

[2] *S. John,* xix, 38–40.

ception is made in the present instance, as it is
the deacon, not the celebrant, who blesses the
candle. This, however, is not destitute of a
mystic meaning; for it signifies that the body of
Christ was deposited in a sepulchre that had
been prepared with a mixture of myrrh and aloes,
'as was the manner of the Jews to bury,'[1]—not
by His apostles, but by the disciples.[2]

The Paschal candle has also another meaning.
Before being lighted, it is a figure of the column
of a cloud which moved before the Israelites by
day; and lighted, it represents the column of fire
that burned by night and led them through the
Red Sea.[3]   This figurative meaning, though at
present forcible and appropriate, was still more
obvious in the early ages of the Church, when it
was usual not only for the baptismal font to be
blessed, but for public baptism to be administered

---

[1] *S. John*, XIX, 39, 40.

[2] See BENEDICT XIV., *De Festis Domini nostri: de Sabbato sancto*,
lib. I, c. VIII, § 55.

[3] Such is the symbolic meaning attributed to the Paschal candle
in the Pontifical of Poitiers already referred to (p. 194 of this vol.),
which contains the following annotation on the *Exsultet:* 'Cereus
quoque statuitur in loco ubi benedicendus est, in typo columnae
egredienti populo ex Aegypto ducatum praebentis.'   MARTENE, *De
antiquis Eccl. Ritibus*, tom. III, col. 434.   In the hymn itself, after a
reference is made to the pillar which preceded the Israelites in their
exit from Egypt to the land of promise, the candle is denominated
a column: 'Sed iam columnae huius praeconia novimus, quam in
honorem Dei rutilans ignis accendit.'   In some churches on the
Continent the Paschal candle is made to weigh thirty-three pounds,
in reference to the number of years our Blessed Redeemer lived
upon earth.

on Easter eve to a crowd of catechumens, when the Paschal candle, which had been recently blessed, was carried before them in the solemn procession which they made towards the waters of regeneration. It was then the catechumens were happily assimilated to the Israelites. Like them, these new believers had escaped an Egyptian bondage, and were about to pass through the Red Sea, in the waters of baptism, in order to arrive at the real promised land, a state of grace, which was indicated by that heavenly column shining on them day and night, the Gospel-light of Christ. The column which is generally employed in the churches of Italy, but especially in those of Rome, to support the Paschal candle has a reference to the second meaning of this ceremony.

In the service peculiar to Holy Saturday, or Easter eve, the attention will be arrested by the lighting of the triple candle, the branches of which all arise from one stem, which is affixed to the top of what is denominated the reed. This three-branched candle is intended to indicate a Trinity of persons in one God, or the light and glory of the Triune God beaming forth upon mankind through the person of our Redeemer Jesus.[1]

---

[1] In the Greek ritual, each time a bishop celebrates Mass he blesses the people in a peculiar manner, holding in each hand a curious wax-taper. One of them is a three-forked candle, denominated the τρικήριον, and is intended, like that employed in the Latin

The Purification, a festival common to the Latin and Greek Churches,[1] is rendered peculiar by the blessing of wax-tapers, which are carried burning by those who form the procession which takes place afterwards. The symbolical meaning attributed to this ceremony is, that the faithful should, with the holy Simeon, recognise in the infant Jesus the salvation which the Lord had prepared before the face of all people—'a light to lighten the Gentiles, and the glory of the people of Israel'[2]—and be admonished by the burning tapers which they are carrying in their hands, that their faith must be fed and augmented by the exercise of good works, through which they are to become a light to shine before men.[3]

The reader may feel an interest in learning that a custom which, at the feast of the Purification and on some particular and solemn festivals,

---

Church on Holy Saturday, to symbolise the Triune God. The second, which is composed of two branches arising from one stem, and called δικήριον, is a symbol of Christ, who in His one person unites the two distinct natures of God and man. GOAR, Εὐχολόγιον, *sive Rituale Graecorum*, p. 125. We have given the figure of a Greek prelate blessing the people, with these lights, in a plate at Chap. XII, no. 36.

[1] This festival is very ancient, and is called in the Greek calendar Ὑπάντη, or 'the meeting,' because, as Micrologus observes, 'those venerable personages, Simeon and Anna, came forth to meet our Divine Redeemer Jesus, when He was brought, by the blessed Virgin Mary, to be presented in the temple.' One of S. John Chrysostom's homilies is composed on this festival. S. Gelasius also notices its celebration in the Latin Church.

[2] *S. Luke*, II, 31, 32.   [3] *S. Matt.* V, 14–16.

is still observed in some churches of painting the candles,[1] derives its origin from venerable antiquity, since we find S. Paulinus referring to it in a hymn composed by that prelate in honour of S. Felix. The poet says :

'Let other some the painted tapers light.'[2]

Another curious practice, of which no remnant that we know of is now discoverable, was observed amongst the ancient Christians. Not only were they accustomed to provide, when able, the richest oils and the most odoriferous balsams[3] to feed the lamps which were suspended over the sepulchres of the martyrs or illuminated the celebration of the Holy Sacrifice, but they had a method of mingling a perfume in the wax with which they made their tapers, and thus caused them to diffuse around a continual fragrance during the time they were kept burning. This is evident from passages both in Prudentius and S. Paulinus of Nola.[4] From what has hitherto been said we gather that from the earliest

---

[1] Perino del Vaga, one of Raphael's most efficient and successful scholars, commenced his profession in the workshop of an humble artist who earned his livelihood by painting candles for church-festivals.

[2] See the note on p. 187.

[3] In a note at p. 186 was cited a passage from the *Liber Pontificalis*, enumerating the various oils and aromatics produced by the estates in Africa and Asia belonging to the church of S. Paul at Rome.

[4] See p. 182.

periods of the Church the use of lights prevailed; that they were employed to shed splendour and impart a dignity to the ceremonies of religion, as well as to create a solemnity of thought and inspire reverence in the minds of the assistants.

Though on some, but not on all, occasions the employment of lights was indispensable, from either convenience or necessity, still, however, they had invariably attached to them a spiritual, a mystic signification. Lamps and glowing tapers, from their number and their brilliancy, were regarded as lively emblems of joy and exultation. Hence, to express these emotions, it was a custom of the Church to use lights at the celebration of the holy Eucharist and at the public services, at the administration of baptism and at the funeral obsequies of her spiritual children. But she particularly delighted to suspend them around the tombs of the martyrs and confessors, upon their festivals, or, to speak more accurately, upon the annual celebration of their nativity to the bliss of heaven, in order to exhibit a becoming honour to those amongst her sainted but departed children, and to stimulate her living sons and daughters to earn the glory and the happiness, by emulating the virtues and the heroism of their holy brethren.

CHAPTER XII.

ON THE VESTMENTS.

I.—ORIGIN OF THE VESTMENTS IN GENERAL.

FROM the concurrent testimony of writers who have bestowed much laborious research upon the investigation of this subject,[1] it appears that, during the infancy of the Church, the garments worn by her priesthood when employed in offering up the holy Eucharistic sacrifice were identically the same in form and composed of similar materials with those corresponding articles of dress in the ordinary apparel adopted by persons of condition at that period. One distinction, however, was observed. The garments once employed in the celebration of the sacred mysteries were for ever afterwards exclusively appropriated to the same holy purpose; and it was regarded as highly indecorous, if not a profanation, to alienate them from the service of the altar, and to wear them when otherwise engaged.

In ancient as in modern days fashion had her

---

[1] I. BONA, *Rerum Liturgicarum*, lib. I, cap. XXIV. THOMASSIN, *Ancienne et Nouvelle Discipline de l'Eglise.*

waywardness, though her changes were not so sudden nor so capricious as at present. But her innovations were not permitted to invade the precincts of the sanctuary, and the ecclesiastical vestments retained their original form, while the costume of civil society underwent a perfect but gradual transformation. In process of time those garments which once were universally worn, without regard to age, station, or employment, by the more respectable members of society became peculiar to the servants of the altar. This began to be discernible about the close of the sixth century.

From the moment that Constantine declared himself a Christian the ceremonies of religion were performed with splendour, and regal magnificence shone throughout the sacred ritual. Before this period the vestments of the priesthood at the altar, though not always, were more frequently composed of the less expensive materials, and decorated merely with a scarlet stripe, which was then denominated *latus-clavus*. This was now exchanged for a vesture the same, indeed, in form, but manufactured of the richest stuffs.[1]

---

[1] The sacred habit presented by Constantine to Macarius, bishop of Jerusalem, to be employed by that prelate in administering the sacrament of Baptism, was made of cloth of gold, as we gather from the testimony of Theodoret (*Hist.*, lib. II, c. 22). In progress of time, such was the splendour of some of the sacerdotal ornaments that they were not only almost stiff with gold, but literally ponderous with the pearls and precious stones that studded them. L. CICOGNARA, *Storia della Scultura*, Prato, 1824, tom. I, pp. 223, 224.

It would, however, be wrong to conclude that anterior to the reign of Constantine the functions of religion had been wholly divested of magnificence :[1] so far, indeed, is this from being the case, that on some occasions the precious ornaments of the Church aroused the cupidity of her persecutors.[2]

Religion suggests and propriety insists on the appropriation of a distinctive habit to the priest and his attendants at the altar while occupied in the public functions of their ministry. That amid the other members of the commonwealth its public functionaries should be distinguished by some appropriate costume is, and, from time

---

[1] The Evangelist S. John was accustomed to wear a plate of gold upon his forehead and put on a linen tunic, as we gather from the testimony of the historian Eusebius (lib. v, c. 24) in his notice on a fragment of the letter of Polycrates, bishop of Ephesus, to Pope Victor. A similar golden ornament was worn by S. James the Apostle and first bishop of Jerusalem, as Epiphanius, on the authority of Clement of Alexandria, informs us (EPIPHANIUS, *Haer.* XXIX, 2).

[2] The persecutor of S. Laurence was not more eager to contaminate the faith of that holy deacon than to possess himself of the gold and silver ornaments belonging to the altar confided to his custody, as appears from those verses of Prudentius in which the poet (see p. 183 of this vol.) represents the persecutor enumerating the golden vessels and candlesticks employed at Mass. S. Optatus of Milevis, who flourished c. 365, not many years after Diocletian's persecution, particularly notices the various gold and silver ornaments of the Church, which the bishop Mensurius could neither conceal nor take away with him, to prevent them falling into the hands of the persecutors. 'Erant ecclesiae ex auro et argento quam plurima ornamenta, quae nec defodere terrae, nec secum portare poterat (episcopus Mensurius).' *De Schismate Donatistarum, adversus Parmenianum,* lib. I.

immemorial, has been everywhere acknowledged. For in every government, whether it be a republic or a monarchy, a distinctive uniform is assigned to a soldier, whilst the civilian is recognisable by his peculiar habit. The chief of an army differs in his outward appearance from the common soldier; the judge when seated on the tribunal of justice and the advocate while pleading at the bar before him may be severally distinguished by their forensic robes of office. The nobleman on State occasions in the senate, or when he approaches the presence of his sovereign in a formal manner, is marked by some peculiar badge, which notifies his rank of Earl or Baron, Duke or Marquis. Similar motives of propriety have influenced the Church in ordering her ministers to array themselves in certain vestments while employed in the public celebration of her liturgy and the administration of her sacraments. Even those sects which stand widest apart in doctrine and discipline from the Catholic Church recognise, in fact, the propriety of her principles on this point, since their ministers not only assume a distinctive dress in society, but in general put on a surplice or a gown, or may be distinguished by the colour at least of their garments, when employed in the midst of their respective congregations in the offices of the public ministry.

II.—THEIR USE WARRANTED BY THE OLD LAW.

In the Old Law we find that the Almighty instructed Moses with minute precision relative to the sacred vestments: 'And thou shalt make a holy vesture for Aaron thy brother, for glory, and for beauty. And thou shalt speak to all the wise of heart, whom I have filled with the spirit of wisdom, that they may make Aaron's vestments, in which he, being consecrated, may minister to Me; and these shall be the vestments that they shall make: a Rational and an Ephod, a Tunic and a straight linen garment, a Mitre and a Girdle. They shall make the holy vestments for thy brother Aaron, and his sons, that they may do the office of priesthood unto Me. And they shall take gold, and violet, and purple, and scarlet twice dyed, and fine linen. And they shall make the Ephod of gold, and violet, and purple, and scarlet twice dyed, and fine twisted linen embroidered with divers colours. . . . And beneath at the feet of the same tunic round about, thou shalt make, as it were, pomegranates of violet and purple, and scarlet twice dyed, with little bells set between.' [1]

Describing the vision in which it was given him to see the rebuilding of the temple, the prophet Ezechiel says: 'And when the priests shall have entered in, they shall not go out of the holy places

---

[1] *Exodus*, XXVIII, 2–6 and 33.

into the outward court; but there they shall lay their vestments wherein they minister, for they are holy, and they shall put on other garments, and so they shall go forth to the people.'[1]

III.—VINDICATED FROM THE STRICTURES PASSED UPON THEM BY MODERN PURITANISM.

The stern and melancholy religionist may morosely criticise the practice of arraying the minister who officiates in the Christian sanctuary with splendid garments of an ancient fashion. The self-opinionated sophist may congratulate himself that his spirit of devotion does not feel the want of such material auxiliaries to keep it animated; but the reasoning man, the pious and humble Christian, will acknowledge that the bulk of mankind is constituted not of philosophers, but of individuals who stand in need of something removed from the usages of ordinary life, before they will exhibit a becoming reverence for the functions of religion, and who require external aids to elevate and purify their thoughts and to rivet their attention at the hour of prayer.[2] Insensible, indeed, must be the soul of that man to all the holiest emotions of devotion who can assist at the more solemn celebration of the Eucharistic sacrifice, and not experience how it lends a glow to fervour and excites religious

---

[1] *Ezechiel*, XLII, 14.   [2] See note, p. 118 of this volume.

sentiments, nor feel how beautifully appropriate
to the Christian priesthood and the public service
of the Christian temple is the passage of the
sacred writer in which he describes the venerable
son of Onias, the high priest, Simon, who shone
' as an olive-tree budding forth, and a cypress-tree
rearing itself on high, when he put on the robe
of glory, and was clothed with the perfection of
power. When he went up to the holy altar, he
honoured the vesture of holiness; and when he
took the portions out of the hands of the priests,
he himself stood by the altar. And about him was
the ring of his brethren; and as the cedar planted
on mount Libanus, and as branches of palm-trees,
they stood round about him, and all the sons of
Aaron in their glory. . . . He stretched forth his
hand to make a libation, and offered of the blood
of the grape. He poured out at the foot of the
altar a divine odour to the Most High Prince. . . .
Then all the people together made haste, and fell
down to the earth upon their faces, to adore the
Lord their God. . . . And the singers lifted up their
voices, and in the great house the sound of sweet
melody was increased. . . . Then . . . he lifted up
his hands over all the congregation of the children
of Israel, to give glory to God with his lips, and
to glory in His name.' [1]

---

[1] *Ecclesiasticus*, L, 11–22. The Protestant Bible enumerates this
book amongst the Apocrypha. That it is, however, the genuine
and Divinely inspired word of God is demonstrated by the same

IV.—PROPRIETY SUGGESTED THEIR ADOPTION BY THE GENTILES.

What was inspired to the Israelites by the Spirit of God decorum suggested to both idolater and Gentile. The Pagan priesthood was scrupulously solicitous to assume a particular kind of garment when occupied in performing the rites of their superstitious worship or in sacrificing to their imaginary deities. This is equally attested by the poets and historians of antiquity, as well as by the statues, paintings, and medals of that period, which faithfully illustrate the customs of Greeks, Romans, and barbarians.

V.—MOTIVES OF THE CHURCH FOR USING THEM.

The instruction which the Church delivers to her pastors is as beautiful as it is eloquent. In exchanging his ordinary garments for the habit of the sanctuary, she admonishes the priest to express his desire before God of being invested with all those graces requisite for the due performance of his awful ministry. For she assures him that the sacerdotal vestments, as Pope Innocent III. has remarked,[1] signify those virtues

---

authority upon which Protestants believe in the inspiration of those books which they place in their Canon of Scripture, namely, the tradition and authority of the Catholic Church. For a vindication of the Catholic Canon of Scripture see Appendix III.

[1] *De sacro Altaris Mysterio*, cap. x.

with which the priest of God should be decorated, according to the pious prayer of the psalmist : ' Let Thy priest put on justice, and let Thy saints exult.' Nor, in these instructions, does she forget the people. She tells them to behold in the varied ornaments in which their pastors, while officiating at the altar, are arrayed a lively emblem of those several virtues which should adorn each Christian.[1]

---

[1] From the writings of the Fathers, and in those monuments of primitive Christianity which remain, we observe that from the very earliest periods of the Church the faithful were accustomed to affix a symbolical and spiritual meaning to almost everything employed in the service of religion. Orpheus was painted in the chapels in the catacombs as an emblem of Christ, who, by the melodious sounds of the Gospel, was to tame the human passions and draw around Him men from every nation. The figure of a fish or of a dove upon the tombs of the primitive Christians is a favourite symbol. Both mystically indicate Christ. The fish, for one amongst other reasons, because its name in Greek—'Ιχθύς—is composed of the initials of 'Ιησοῦς Χριστὸς Θεοῦ 'Υιός Σωτήρ—'Jesus Christ, the Son of God, the Saviour ;' the dove, because Christ was innocence itself, as we have already noticed more at length in Chapters VII and IX (see pp. 82 and 130). Not only the form in which churches were erected, but their several ornaments, and even the colour of the materials, and of the columns about the altar, were determined and selected on account of some emblematic meaning assigned to them. The works which go under the name of S. Dionysius the Areopagite, but which were certainly written in the fifth century, especially the book on the Celestial Hierarchy and the treatises on Mystic Theology, afford an interpretation to these symbols. The sacraments themselves were signs or symbols. We cannot, therefore, be surprised that, although the vestments were, in their original form, nothing more than the common dress of Greece and Rome at the birth of Christianity, the Church very soon assigned to them appropriate mystic significations. That she does so now, and has done for many centuries, is attested by the very prayers which she directs her ministers to recite when they array themselves in these sacerdotal garments.

VI.—THEY CHARACTERISE THE ANTIQUITY OF THE CHURCH.

The peculiarities of style in building will help to fix the era in which an edifice was erected; the form of character, together with the material on which it is written, will materially assist the antiquary in detecting the date of an inscription; the costume of a statue or the accessories of a picture will serve to ascertain the period when the individual represented flourished, as well as to announce his rank or particular condition. So it is with the Catholic Church; view her under the semblance of a vast and spiritual edifice, the scriptural order of her hierarchy declares that her architect was Christ, whilst His apostles were the builders; the same ancient languages which are, and ever have been, used within her almost boundless limits, by men of every age, of diverse speech, from every nation of the earth, in administering the sacraments and while offering up the Eucharistic sacrifice, proclaim what tongues were common to the world at the period of her birth, and have ever been familiar to her from her infancy upwards; while the antiquated fashion of those garments which her ministers put on when officiating at the altar not only speaks to us of centuries and centuries gone by, and can alone furnish us with any remnants of the dress of republican or imperial Rome,

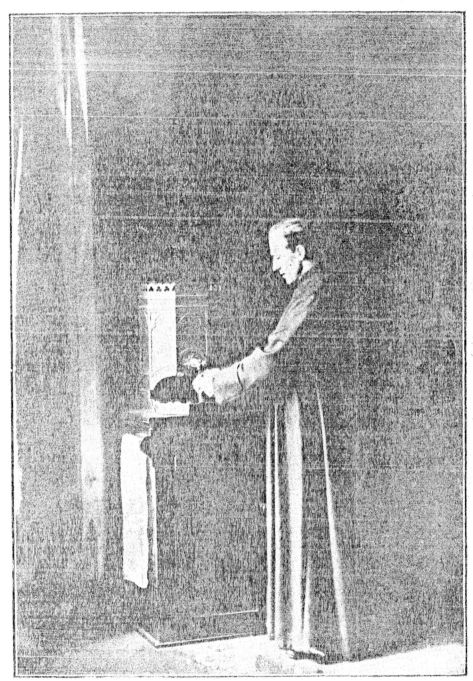

The Priest in his cassock, washing his hands before vesting.

but announces to us her jealousy, not only of guarding the deposit of faith, but of retaining the use of things in themselves indifferent. From passing these preliminary remarks upon the justness of appropriating a distinctive habit to the Christian priesthood, in which its members may offer up the sacrifice of the new law—that clean oblation spoken of by Malachias—we will now proceed to notice separately each article of this sacerdotal dress.

VII.—WASHING OF HANDS. VIII.—FIGURATIVE MEANING.

Before he robes himself in the eucharistic vestments, the priest, clad in his cassock, washes the tips of his fingers. It has been invariably the custom, at all times and in every nation, for the ministers of the altar to wash their hands previously to offering up sacrifice. The old law expressly commanded this observance.[1]

VIII.—Though respect alone for the decorum of religion would inspire such a practice, still, however, the Church attaches a spiritual signification to it, and studies to convey to her ministers, by the symbol of exterior ablution, instructions to cleanse the heart by an interior purity, which she teaches them to solicit in a prayer particularly adapted to the purpose. 'Grant,' exclaims the

---

[1] *Exodus*, XXX, 18-20.

priest while washing his fingers, 'grant to my hands, O Lord, a virtue that shall cleanse away every stain, so that I may be able to serve Thee without impurity of body and of soul.'

IX.—THE CASSOCK.

The Cassock is common to every order of the clergy, only varying in colour according to the dignity of the wearer. Priests wear black; prelates and bishops, purple; cardinals, scarlet; and the Pope, white. Over the cassock is placed the amice.

X.—THE AMICE. XI.—ITS FORM. XII.—FIGURATIVE MEANING. XIII.—WHY SO CALLED.

The Amice is an oblong piece of fine white linen. The priest rests it for a moment, like a veil, upon the crown of his head, and then adjusts it round his neck so that it hangs down over his shoulders, reciting meanwhile the following prayer: 'Place upon my head, O Lord, the helmet of salvation, that I may be enabled to repel all the fiery darts of the wicked one,'—remembering the exhortation of the Apostle: 'Put you on the armour of God, that you may be able to stand against the deceits of the devil, . . . and take unto you the helmet of salvation.'[1] It is not without a mystic signification. The act of resting

---

[1] *Ephesians*, VI, 11, 17.

The Priest putting on the Amice.

it for a moment on the head, as well as the prayer which the priest is directed to pronounce on assuming it, render it strikingly allusive to that helmet of salvation with which each Christian warrior should arm himself to extinguish and repel the fiery darts of the wicked one.

XI.—Formerly the amice was worn upon the head in the manner of a hood while vesting, and until the priest arrived before the altar, when it was lowered and thrown back upon the shoulders, a custom which is still retained in some churches on the Continent, as well as by the Dominican and Capuchin friars.

XII.—By some ecclesiastical writers the amice has been likened, and not without reason, to the ephod[1] of the Jewish priesthood; others have assimilated it to the sackcloth of penance which the prophets of the Old Testament so often recommended to the people. The corresponding garment in the Coptic liturgy of S. Basil is called Epomis, which is mentioned by Gabriel, patriarch of Alexandria, and by other ecclesiastical writers of the Eastern Churches,[2] amongst the sacerdotal vestments. Amices were formerly richly em-

---

[1] Hinc humerale, quod intellige Ephod, apud nos Amictus dicitur, sibi imponit, et illo caput, et collum et humeros, unde et humerale dicitur, cooperit. HONORIUS, *Gemma Animae*, lib. 1, cap. 201.

[2] Epomis sive amiculum, instar Aaronis sacerdotis, quem Deus in tabernaculo legali, superhumerali amictum esse iussit. ABUSEBAH, *Tractatus de Scientia Ecclesiastica*, cap. 61, quoted by RENAUDOT, *Lit. Orient. Coll.*, tom. 1, p. 178.

broidered with gold and silk, or adorned with an oblong piece of silk stuff called an apparel. Apparelled amices were in use until the end of the sixteenth century, since which they have gradually dropped out of use.

XIII.—The term 'amice' is derived from the Latin verb, *amicire*, to cover; being introduced in the eighth century to cover the neck, which until that period was usually bare.

XIV.—THE ALB: ITS FORM AND COLOUR.

To the amice succeeds the Alb, which is an ample linen tunic reaching to the feet, and so called from the Latin word *alba*, white. Long garments were usually worn not merely in the States of ancient Greece and by the separate nations of the East, but throughout the empire of Rome, and were not peculiar to any certain class of Roman citizens. Some, however, were plain and made of common stuff, as they were employed for ordinary use; others were more costly, and appropriated to days of religious ceremony and to State occasions. The priests and Levites, under the Mosaic dispensation, were undistinguished in ordinary life from the rest of society by any particular garments. They assumed, however, a different and official vesture to distinguish them while discharging the functions of their sacred ministry. This, no doubt, the Church of Christ, along with several other things, borrowed from the synagogue.[1] The Church has now consecrated the alb or linen tunic to the use of her priests, her deacons, and her sub-deacons who are ministering at the altar.

The lower edge of the alb and the wrists were anciently ornamented with one or several stripes of scarlet attached to it. The number of these stripes affixed peculiar appellations to the alb. Albs which had but one were denominated 'Albae Monolores;' if they had two, 'Dilores;' if three, 'Trilores,' etc.[2] From the Life of Benedict III. it would appear that albs were sometimes fringed with gold and made of silk, as we are informed that the king of the Saxons presented to the Church of S. Peter at Rome, amongst other magnificent donations, certain albs of this description.[3] A remnant of the scarlet border is still preserved by some of the religious orders, who trim the bottom and the sleeve-cuffs of the alb with lace, under which they attach scarlet silk.[4] In the Middle Ages the alb was adorned with apparels embroidered in silk and gold, sometimes enriched with pearls and precious stones, or with four pieces of rich silken stuff, two at the wrists and two at the foot, one in front and one behind.

---

[1] L. Thomassin, *Ancienne et Nouvelle Discipline de l'Eglise*, tom. I, p. 367.

[2] Vopiscus, *Historiae Augustae Scriptores, Aurelianus.*

[3] *Liber pontificalis.*

[4] A. A. Pelliccia, *De Christianae Ecclesiae Politia*, tom. I, p. 226.

Still later the custom of contracting the alb, by plaiting it in long folds, was introduced, and is still observed.[1]

This long linen garment, which is called alb in the Latin or Western Church, is also used amongst the Oriental Christians by priests, deacons, and sub-deacons in the celebration of Mass. By the Greeks it is denominated χιτώνιον ;[2] by the Syrians, 'Koutivo ;'[3] and by the Arabs, 'Tunia,'[4] and is always white. Amongst the seven sacerdotal vestments used in the Coptic liturgy of S. Basil, it is particularly enumerated by Abusebah, who observes that the alb appropriated to the use of the bishop should be edged with a rich border.[5] The perfect resemblance of the Greek to the Latin alb may be observed by a view of those plates which we have given in this chapter in illustration of the Greek vestments.[6]

---

[1] Albs are now often far from being in accordance with ecclesiastical tradition, the lower portion sometimes even up to the waist being composed of paltry crochet-work or machine-made lace. The appearance of a priest thus habited is anything but dignified.

[2] RENAUDOT, *Liturg. Orient. Coll.*, tom. I, p. 178.

[3] *Ibid.*

[4] *Ibid.*, tom. II, p. 54.

[5] Camisia, sive Alba, quae, si fuerit episcopus, limbo ad summum pretioso praetexetur ; secus, eo carebit. ABUSEBAH, *Tract. de Scient. Eccles.*, cap. 61, quoted by RENAUDOT, *Liturg. Orient. Coll.*, tom. I, p. 178.

[6] The Fourth Council of Carthage (398) decreed that the deacon should use the alb only during the oblation or the lecture. 'Ut diaconus tempore oblationis tantum vel lectionis Alba utatur.' LABBEI *Concil. Gen.*, tom. I, col. 120. This long white linen tunic

The Priest vested in his Alb putting on the Girdle.

XV.—FIGURATIVE MEANING.

This long and snow-white garment which envelops the whole person of the wearer is beautifully emblematic of that stainless candour and purity of soul which should shine, in a conspicuous manner, in all those who officiate around the altar where the Lamb without spot is immolated. The priest, therefore, very appropriately says the following prayer in putting on the alb: 'Cleanse me, O Lord, and purify my heart, that, sprinkled with the blood of the Lamb, I may enjoy eternal felicity;' where the blessed are for ever clothed in robes of white, standing before the throne of God, and serving Him day and night in His temple.[1]

The priest now confines the alb with the girdle.

XVI.—THE GIRDLE.   XVII.—ITS ANCIENT FORM.

XVII.—It is in more modern times only that the girdle has been generally made like a cord with tassels at the end; anciently it was flat; and, whilst it wore the appearance, was indiscriminately denominated by the terms of belt and zone, as well as girdle. It was formerly made of various coloured silks, not unfrequently interwoven with

---

may be observed as one of the vestments with which bishops, priests, and other ministers of the altar are arrayed in the mosaics of the old churches at Rome and in the illuminations of MSS. and other monuments of ecclesiastical antiquity.

[1] *Apocalypse*, VII, 9–15.

gold and decorated with embroidery, and sometimes studded with precious stones, as may be
gathered from various authorities.[1]

XVIII.—MENTIONED IN SCRIPTURE.

In several passages of Holy Scripture mention
is made of the girdle. The prophet Isaias, speaking of the Messiah, pronounces of Him: 'Justice
shall be the girdle of His loins; and faith the
girdle of His reins.'[2] Christ, while preaching to
His disciples, thus exhorted them: 'Let your
loins be girt, and lamps burning in your hands.'[3]
S. Paul, in admonishing the Ephesians to take
unto themselves the armour of God, instructs
them to 'stand, having your loins girt about with
truth.'[4]

XIX.—FIGURATIVE MEANING.

The girdle, therefore, is very appropriately made
a portion of the ceremonial attire belonging to
the sanctuary, and is eloquently emblematical of

---

[1] Riculfus, bishop of Perpignan (887-915), bequeathed to his see
five zones, four of which were ornamented with gold and embossed
with jewels; the remaining one was simply of gold (DOM.
GEORGIUS, *De Liturgia Romani Pontificis*, tom. I, p. 132). Among
other legacies which Talco Vigilensis made to the Church of S.
Margaret was a zone of crimson silk (UGHELLI, *Italia sacra*, VII,
p. 1275). The antiquity of this article among the sacerdotal vestments is evident by the devotion with which the people emulously
strove to kiss the girdle of the Roman pontiff S. Gregory the Great,
according to John the Deacon, who wrote his life.

[2] *Isaiah*, XI, 5.   [3] *S. Luke*, XII, 35.

[4] *Ephesians*, VI, 14.

that chastity and unsullied purity with which both priest and people should anxiously endeavour to array themselves before they dare to pass the threshold of a temple sacred to the Lord of spotless holiness.[1] 'Gird,' says the minister as he binds it on, 'gird my reins, O Lord, with the girdle of purity; extinguish in my heart the fire of concupiscence; and may the flames of Thy holy love consume every earthly affection, everything therein that is unworthy of Thee.'

The zone or girdle with which the priest girds himself round the waist, over the alb, is noticed in all the Greek and Oriental liturgies.[2]

Having finished the above prayer, the priest affixes, just above the wrist of his left arm, an ornament which is called the Maniple.

---

[1] From the girdle used by the Pope at the celebration of Mass hangs, on the left side, an ornament called the Succinctorium, which somewhat resembles a small maniple (GEORGIUS, *De Liturgia Rom. Pontificis*, tom. I, p. 146). This vestment, peculiar amongst us to the sovereign pontiff, corresponds to a similar appendage appropriated to bishops and dignified ecclesiastics of the Greek rite, and denominated ἐπιγονατιον. Balsamon (A.D. 1180) observes that the epigonation is considered by the Greek Church to typify the napkin with which our Blessed Redeemer girded Himself at the Last Supper when He washed the feet of His disciples. At present it is ornamented with the cross, or more usually bears the head of our Saviour either painted or wrought in embroidery upon it (GOAR, Εὐχολόγιον, *sive Rituale Graecorum*, p. 111), as may be observed by inspecting our plates of the Greek prelates.

[2] GOAR, Εὐχολόγιον, p. 111. RENAUDOT, *Litury. Orient. Coll.*, tom. I, p. 178, and tom. II, p. 55.

XX.—THE MANIPLE.　XXI.—ITS ANCIENT FORM AND
USE.　XXII.—HOW GRADUALLY CHANGED.

XXI.—Originally the maniple was a narrow strip of linen suspended from the left arm, which supplied the place of and was used as a handkerchief.

XXII.—Gradually, however, it received embellishments. First of all it was bordered by a fringe, then decorated with embroidery, till at length it became too precious to be employed for its original purpose. But although it ceased to be used as a handkerchief, it was retained as an ornament to which could be appropriately attached a spiritual meaning. A little later, from being made of linen, it began to resemble in colour and to be composed of the same splendid materials of which the chasuble was formed;[1] and we find that about

---

[1] It even came to be esteemed a badge of honour and distinction about the sixth century, when John, archbishop of Ravenna, referred the urgent solicitations of his minor clergy to Pope S. Gregory the Great, in order to obtain his permission to wear, in imitation of the clergy at Rome, the maniple while waiting on their archbishop. The Roman pontiff yielded to this prayer, but restricted his favour to the first deacons only of the church at Ravenna (S. GREGORII MAGNI *Epist. LIV, ad Ioannem episc. Ravennatum*). During the ninth century it was an ornament common both to priests and deacons without distinction (PELLICCIA, *De Christianae Ecclesiae Politia*, tom. I, p. 229), and after the eleventh century its use was extended to sub-deacons (*Ibid.*), to whom it was now delivered at the time of their ordination, as the insignia of their order and their ministerial office (*Caeremoniale Episcoporum*). It would appear, from the illuminations of ancient MSS. and Missals, that formerly it was of the same breadth, and was not widened, as now, at its extremities.

the eighth century it was enumerated among the sacerdotal vestments.[1]

XXIII.—ITS FIGURE AND SIGNIFICATION.

Its ancient service is not by any means forgotten amid the ornaments which decorate it, but in the accompanying prayer is happily alluded to in order to afford a useful, no less than a pious and consoling admonition to the priest that he should bear the evils of this life, and endure the toils and anxious labours of his ministry, with the anticipation of a certain and eternal recompense. It is on this account that the Church directs her ministers to recite the following prayer as they assume this ornament: 'O Lord, may I be found worthy to bear the maniple of sorrow and affliction, that I may reap with joy the reward of my labours.' In the Greek Church the maniple is not used, but the $\dot{\epsilon}\gamma\chi\epsilon\dot{\iota}\rho\iota o\nu$ worn by deacons attached to the girdle is, in fact, a parallel. The $\dot{\epsilon}\pi\iota\mu\alpha\nu\dot{\iota}\kappa\iota o\nu$, worn by the Greeks as well as Maronites, one on each arm, though apparently similar to the maniple, is really quite different, and was long worn only by bishops; but in later times its use was extended to priests, and in the present century to deacons. Among the Greeks it is, like the Epigonation, almost always ornamented with the head of our Saviour, which

---

[1] BONA, *Rerum Liturgicarum*, lib. I, cap. XXIV, § 5.

the prelate holds out to such as approach him to be kissed by them. The introduction of this custom was owing to the zeal of the Greek Church to propagate amongst the people a due respect for holy images.[1]

XXIV.—THE STOLE. XXV.—ORIGINAL SIGNIFICATION OF THE NAME. XXVI.—FORM OF THE CLASSIC STOLE. XXVII.—HOW ORNAMENTED.

The word stole comes from the Greek στολή, and was employed anciently to signify clothing in general, and especially the outer or best robe.[2]

XXVI. This outer robe was usually a short-sleeved white tunic which fell in folds and reached nearly to the feet.

XXVII. It was adorned with two vertical stripes or bands, and was worn originally by both men and women, but among the Romans it was thought effeminate for men to wear it, and it became the characteristic dress of the matron. It was, however, worn by the early Christians of both sexes.

XXVIII.—THE STOLE REALLY AN ABRIDGMENT OF THE ORARIUM.

Over the Stole and round the neck was worn an oblong piece of linen called the Orarium,[3]

---

[1] GOAR, Εὐχολόγιον, sive *Rituale Graecorum*, p. 111.

[2] 'Stola Graece vocatur, quod supermittatur.' S. ISIDORUS, *Etymolog.*, lib. XIX, c. 25.

[3] By some the word 'orarium' is derived from the use to which it was applied of wiping the face, 'ora ;' by others from the Latin

which served the purpose of a handkerchief, and was by females spread, in time of prayer, over the head and shoulders, falling around the body like a veil.

A female at prayer, clad in a stole and veiled with an orarium. This figure is painted on the wall of the fourth chamber in the cemetery of Callistus, on the Appian way. See BOTTARI, *Sculture e Pitture*, tom. ii, plate lxxii.

orare, to pray, as it was a robe which the primitive Christians invariably wore during the time of public prayer, and with which the female portion could veil their heads, according to the admonition of S. Paul (1 *Corinthians*, XI, 5). The paintings of the catacombs and the ancient mosaics of the churches of Rome favour the supposition.

The orarium worn by ecclesiastics was bordered with stripes of purple, and when, in course of time, its dimensions were contracted, those ornaments were retained as marks of honour, while the plain linen portions were cut away in such a manner that it was reduced to a band which surrounded the neck and fell down below the knees on both sides of the body. It afterwards exchanged the denomination of orarium for that of stole, by which name it is now known.

A figure clad in a tunic ornamented with stripes of purple cloth, called 'Clavi.' From a fresco-painting in the Catacombs, Cemetery of SS. Marcellinus and Peter. See ARINGHI, *Roma Subterranea*, tom. II, p. 105.

XXIX.—THE STOLE ANCIENTLY THE INSIGNIA OF THE ORDER OF DEACONS.

Before the use of the tunic called 'Colobium' and the later privilege of wearing the Dalmatic were accorded to the deacons in general, the Stole

was the insignia of their order.[1] Thus in the
ancient mosaic which adorns the apse of the
Church of S. Laurence in Rome, that martyred
deacon and S. Stephen are represented with

---

[1] Formerly the deacon wore his stole, or, as it was anciently called,
'Orarium,' floating down and suspended from his left shoulder.

A Bishop in the act of blessing, attended by a Deacon who wears the Stole hanging
from the left shoulder. From a Miniature in a Pontifical of the ninth century, in
the Library of the Minerva at Rome. See SEROUX D'AGINCOURT, *Hist. de l'Art*,
tom. V, plate XXXVII.

This ancient rite is noticed, and the reason for it is assigned
by the fourth Council of Toledo (A.D. 633) : Unum igitur Orarium
oportet Levitam gestare in sinistro humero, propter quod orat,
id est, praedicat. LABBEI *Concil Gen.*, tom. v, col. 629. The use
of the orarium or stole was by the Council of Laodicea (A.D. 364)
prohibited to lectors and sub-deacons, and exclusively reserved for
deacons and for priests. *Ibid.*, tom. I, col. 568. Though the use of
the Dalmatic was granted to the deacons who ministered around the
person of the Roman pontiff, and to such as were attached to a few
privileged churches, it was not until several centuries had elapsed
that this vestment was generally employed. This we may collect
from various ecclesiastical pictorial monuments which exemplify the
manner in which the deacon anciently wore the orarium upon the
left shoulder, at the same time that they exhibit proofs of the more
recent introduction of the dalmatic into general use. In the Pontifical of Landolf, bishop of Capua, 856–879, now in the Minerva
Library at Rome, there are several illuminations illustrative of the
ceremonies of the ordinations. The figure of the deacon in these

stripes of linen attached to and flowing from their left shoulders, a custom to which the author of a Homily formerly attributed to S. John Chrysostom, and certainly not much later than his time, alludes, when he mentions that the deacons, while ministering in their holy office during the tremendous sacrifice of the Mass, appear to move and glide about like angels with their wings expanded.[1]   When the stole became peculiar to the ministers of the altar, it ceased to be made of linen, and was composed of the same materials as the chasuble or upper garment.

---

paintings is always represented in an ample and ornamented alb, with the orarium or stole descending from the left shoulder, as in the accompanying cut.   Towards the commencement, however, of the tenth century the dalmatic seems to have been everywhere adopted as the officiating vestment of the deacon.   (See p. 242.)

[1] 'Επίστασθε τὴν πνευματικὴν εὐφροσύνην, οἱ ταύτης γευσάμενοι καὶ μεμνημένοι τῶν φρικτῶν μυστηρίων, τῶν λειτουργῶν τῆς θείας ἱερουργίας, τῶν μιμουμένων τὰς τῶν ἀγγέλων πτέρυγας, ταῖς λεπταῖς ὀθόναις ταῖς ἐπὶ τῶν ἀριστερῶν ὤμων κειμέναις, καὶ ἐν τῇ ἐκκλησίᾳ περιτρεχόντων.   *Hom. in Parabolam de Filio Prodigo.*   When vesting for Mass the bishop lets his stole hang straight down from around his neck on the right and left; the priest crosses it on his breast; and the deacon, ever since the twelfth century, wears it resting on the left shoulder transversely, uniting itself like a belt under the right arm.   The stole may be seen on all the monumental effigies of bishops pontifically vested in our old cathedrals; and it should be remarked that it is not crossed upon the breast, but always falls parallel, just as it is worn at the present day by prelates.   It is usually fringed, but does not expand so much at its extremities as the modern stole.

The Priest with the Maniple on his left arm arranging the Stole in the form of a cross on his breast.

XXX.—THE STOLE IN THE GREEK CHURCH.

As in the Latin, so in the Greek and Oriental Churches, the Stole is a very conspicuous ornament amongst the vestments peculiar to the higher ministers of the altar. It is mentioned

A Greek Deacon vested as was anciently the manner in the Latin Church with regard to the Stole, and is still the case among the Orientals.

in all their liturgies. In the Greek rite the stole assigned to the priest is carefully distinguished from that allotted to the deacon, not only by a difference of appellation, but by the manner in which it is worn. The sacerdotal stole is termed Ἐπιτραχήλιον, and put round the neck ;[1] the deacon's stole continues, as anciently, to be termed Ὠράριον. It has inscribed upon it, in three several places, the word ἅγιος, or holy, and is cast over the left shoulder, from which it hangs unconfined both before and behind,[2] except at Communion, when it is folded in the form of a cross upon the breast, and its extremities are bound round the waist.[3] The Syrian liturgy denominates the stole by the term *Ouroro*; the Coptic gives it the same appellation as the Greeks.[4]

XXXI.—ITS SPIRITUAL MEANING.

The mystic signification which the Church attaches to this vestment is beautifully expressed in the words of the prayer which the priest is directed by her to recite when he puts it on: 'Restore to me, O Lord, the robe of immortality, which was forfeited by the prevarication of our first parents ; and though unworthy to celebrate so august a mystery, grant that I may attain to everlasting glory.'

XXXII.—THE CHASUBLE.   XXXIII.—ITS FORM.

The sixth and last garment which the priest who is about to offer up the holy sacrifice of the

---

[1] It may be distinctly seen in our plates of the Greek vestments in this chapter.

[2] GOAR, Εὐχολόγιον, p. 59.   [3] *Ibid.*, p. 147.

[4] RENAUDOT, tom. II, p. 54.

The Priest vested and taking up the Chalice about to proceed to the altar.

Mass puts on is called the Chasuble, from the Latin *casula*, diminutive of *casa*.

XXXIII.—This upper vestment descends both before and behind, some way down the person of the wearer. In England, France, Belgium, Holland, and Germany a cross is marked upon the back; whilst in Italy, and in other parts of the Catholic world, it is more generally affixed upon the front part.

XXXIV.—THE VESTMENTS OF THE JEWISH PRIESTHOOD.

Amongst the vestments which were assigned by the Almighty to the Jewish priesthood when employed in sacrificing we discover a garment corresponding to our chasuble in the 'Tunic of the Ephod all of violet, in the midst whereof above shall be a hole for the head, and a border round about it woven, as is wont to be made in the outmost parts of garments.' [1]

XXXV.—ORIGIN OF THE CHASUBLE.

The chasuble derives its origin from a species of cloak which, amongst the ancient Romans, was called Paenula, and is supposed by many commentators on the Scriptures to be the same kind

---

[1] *Exodus*, XXVIII, 31, 32.

of mantle as that left by S. Paul at Troas with Carpus, and which he requested Timothy to bring with him to Rome.[1] The toga was a majestic but cumbersome species of habiliment which began to fall into disuse as early as the time of Augustus. That emperor frequently expressed his regret upon

A male figure in the act of prayer; taken from a fresco in one of the chambers in the Catacombs, Cemetery of SS. Marcellinus and Peter. See ARINGHI, *Roma Subterranea*, tom. II, p. 105.

The garment is the ancient Paenula, now called the Chasuble, and exhibits its ancient form. It is adorned with Clavi.

the subject, and by the promulgation of a law ordaining that every senator who appeared in public should be arrayed in the toga, endeavoured, but in vain, to rescue the garment peculiar to the

----

[1] 2 *Timothy*, IV, 13.

A Greek Priest muffled in the Phelonion or Chasuble.

Roman people from that neglect into which it was rapidly declining. For the toga was substituted the Paenula, which in shape was perfectly circular, with an aperture in the middle to admit the head, while it enveloped the arms and entire person of the wearer; and precisely such was the chasuble worn by the priest at Mass during more than twelve hundred years. The toga resembled the segment of a circle, and usually left the right arm uncovered and at liberty.[2] There were two kinds of paenulae: the more ancient, short and narrow, was usually reserved for travelling; the other, which descended to the feet and was very ample, became the ordinary, and at first the distinctive, habit of the senatorian order, but in process of time was assumed by every person of respectability throughout the Roman Empire. From this, and not from the toga nor the shorter paenula, is derived our chasuble.

XXXVI.—PRESENT FORM AMONG THE GREEKS.

In the Greek Church this vestment still retains its ancient form of a large round mantle covering the whole figure, and is not unfrequently starred all over with a multitude of small crosses.[3]

---

[1] Gens togata. VERGILII *Aeneis*, I, 282.

[2] See A. LENS, *Le Costume des Peuples de l'Antiquité prouvé par les Monumens*, liv. V, c. II, p. 247.

[3] As may be observed in the plate (representing a Greek prelate blessing the people).

XXXVII.—ONCE COMMONLY WORN BY LAICS AND ECCLESIASTICS, THEN BY THE LATTER ONLY.

Up to the sixth century the paenula was a civic habit, and worn, without discrimination, by laymen and ecclesiastics. But after the fashion of the age had invented some other vesture which superseded, in its turn, the paenula or chasuble, it continued unaltered in its form amongst the clergy, who, during many years after its use had been laid aside by the secular portion of the community, retained it as their ordinary garment.

XXXVIII.—ITS USE RESTRICTED TO THE SANCTUARY.

Its reservation to use within the sanctuary seems to have obtained towards the close of the sixth century; for the third Council of Toledo, celebrated in the year 589, ordained, that in restoring degraded ecclesiastics to their former dignity: 'If a bishop, he was to receive the stole, the ring, and crosier; if a priest, the stole and chasuble; and if a deacon, the stole and alb.' For more than a thousand years the chasuble has been assigned to the priest, at the time of ordination, as the habit peculiar to his order when about to offer up the Eucharistic sacrifice.[1]

---

[1] See the *Sacramentary of Senlis*, written in 880; now preserved in the Library of S. Geneviève, at Paris. P. LE BRUN, *Explication des Prières et des Cérémonies de la Messe*, tom. I, p. 53.

XL.—THE CROSS SUPPLANTED THE LATUS-CLAVUS.

The ancient Romans, as was observed when speaking of the stole, were accustomed to ornament their garments with scarlet stripes, which were either composed of pieces of linen tinged with that colour and sewed on, or were interwoven with the material itself. With such stripes they were particularly careful to adorn the paenula, or outward garment, as thus the importance or dignity of the wearer was more especially discernible. Amongst those ancient monuments still existing which so eminently serve to illustrate the manners, civil as well as religious, of the early Christians, there are various examples of this custom. In the frescoes which adorn the catacombs at Rome may be seen several figures with their hands uplifted in the act of prayer, clad in the paenula, adorned with two broad parallel and vertical stripes of scarlet.[1]

XLI.—WHY CURTAILED.

The graceful and symbolical amplitude of the chasuble at first produced no inconvenience to the movements of the sacrificing priest, both because of the lightness of its material and the

---

[1] See the figure at p. 230.

presence of assistants ready at hand to arrange and sustain it according to circumstances.[1] But when cloth of gold and heavy brocaded stuffs were introduced and the celebration of Low Masses became frequent, the priest experienced the inconvenience of the ample chasuble, which formed, when extended out, a perfect circle unbroken by any opening, and fell round the body in such a manner as completely to envelope it.[2] Before, therefore, the hands and arms could be at liberty, it was requisite either that someone should hold it elevated, or that it should be gathered up and folded on both sides above the shoulder. To adjust in this way a vestment of rich damask, or of cloth with embroidery and ornament, was almost impossible. As a remedy to the inconvenience, it was gradually abridged of its flowing and majestic circular dimensions, and cut so as to assume the form it naturally took when sup-

---

[1] Traces of this are still discernible. At High Mass the deacon and sub-deacon continue to take hold of the border of, and sometimes slightly elevate, the chasuble of the celebrant whenever he performs such ceremonies as require the movement of the arms to be uncumbered, and which, at the period when the chasuble was circular, would have rendered necessary the attendance of some minister to gather up and sustain the ample folds of his vestment. Bishops to this day do not put on the maniple till after the 'Confiteor,' because it was then that the assistants anciently gathered up and arranged the borders of the encircling chasuble upon the shoulders, preparatory to the bishop's ascending the steps of the altar.

[2] This may be seen in the plates of the Greek pontiffs, who still retain the ancient form of the chasuble.

ported by an attendant minister, or collected and gathered on the shoulders of the celebrant.[1]

Monumental effigy of Simon of Apulia, Bishop of Exeter, 1214-1223, Exeter Cathedral. See J. BRITTON, *Exeter Cathedral*, plate XX, B.

---

[1] The chasuble during more than a thousand years retained its amplitude, for up to the thirteenth century it still continued unabridged and without any incision, and at the present moment retains its ancient form in the Greek and Eastern Churches. In some particular places in France, Belgium, and Germany the chasuble in its ancient form still remains in use.

XLII.—TRACES OF ITS ANCIENT FORM.

Examples of this sacerdotal habit, fashioned according to its uncurtailed and ancient form, may be seen on the monumental effigies of priests and bishops, as well as on the figures in the paintings, miniatures, and stained-glass windows which so eloquently attest the magnificence of former days, and supply such splendid and authentic vouchers for the success with which the arts were cultivated by Englishmen before the change of religion miscalled the Reformation.[1]　Two interesting works,

---

[1] The Church is undoubtedly the nursing mother of the fine arts, and had she not been banished from this island the English school of art might at this day have been pre-eminent. This is no idle boast, dictated by the spirit of an overweening patriotism. It is suggested by a review of our national literature, which exhibits such splendid coruscations of all those higher mental powers—fervid and poetic imagination, felicitous invention, pathos, loftiness of soul, a feeling exquisitely alive to all those various charms of inanimate or animated nature, endowments which are requisite to constitute a people that shall be capable either of appreciating what is grand and beautiful in architecture, sculpture, and painting, or of producing it and giving to sublime ideas, to 'airy nothingness, a local habitation and a name,' in colours or in marble. The land which produced such artists with the pen as Shakespeare and Milton surely may furnish others equally excellent with the chisel and the pencil. It is suggested by those magnificent cathedrals which adorn the country, and while they extort the admiration of foreigners by their impressive style of architecture, by the profusion of their sculpture and the richness of their painted glass, attest the capabilities of English genius and the effects of ancient piety. It is a memorable circumstance, not generally known, as Flaxman, in his *Lectures on Sculpture*, remarks, that England was almost the first, on the revival of the arts, to cultivate sculpture, and that we possess some of the earliest and finest specimens of the art. 'Sculpture,' he observes (p. 13), 'continued to be practised with such zeal and

The Regal and Ecclesiastical Antiquities, by Strutt,
and the *Cathedral Antiquities of England*, by

success that in the reign of Henry III. efforts were made deserving
our respect and attention at this day. . . . It is very remarkable that
Wells Cathedral was finished in 1242, two years after the birth of
Cimabue, the restorer of painting in Italy, and the work was going
on at the same time that Nicolo Pisano, the Italian restorer of
sculpture, exercised the art in his own country. It was also finished
forty-six years before the cathedral of Amiens, and thirty-six years
before the cathedral of Orvieto, was begun ; and it seems to be the
first specimen of such magnificent and varied sculpture, united in a
series of sacred history, that is to be found in Western Europe. . . .
The long and prosperous reign of Edward III. was as favourable to
literature and liberal arts as to the political and commercial interests
of the country. So generally were painting, sculpture, and architecture encouraged and employed, that, besides the buildings raised
in this reign, few sacred edifices existed which did not receive addi-
tions and decorations. The richness, novelty, and beauty of architecture may be seen in York and Gloucester Cathedrals and many
of our other churches ; besides the extraordinary fancy displayed in
various intricate and diversified figures which form the mullions of
windows, they were occasionally enriched with a profusion of foliage
and historical sculpture, equally surprising for beauty and novelty '
(p. 18). Speaking of the monument of Richard Beauchamp, Earl of
Warwick, in S. Mary's Church at Warwick, which is composed of
one large and several small gilt bronze statues standing on niches,
supporting canopies over them (see R. GOUGH, *Sepulchral Monuments in Great Britain*, vol. II), the same eminent sculptor says
(p. 22) : 'The figures are so natural and graceful, the architecture
so rich and delicate, that they are excelled by nothing done in Italy
of the same kind at this time, although Donatello and Ghiberti were
living when this tomb was executed, in the year 1439.' Referring
to the iconoclastic fury which maddened the lustful and tyrannical
Henry VIII., the regal baby, Edward VI., and ambitious Somerset,
the pillars of England's modern Church, Flaxman observes (p. 28) :
'The commands for destroying sacred painting and sculpture effec-
tually prevented the artist from suffering his mind to rise in the
contemplation or execution of any sublime effort, as he dreaded
a prison or the stake, and reduced him in future to the miserable
mimicry of monstrous fashions, or drudgery in the lowest mechanism
of his profession ;' so that, 'after the spirit of liberal art had been

Britton, as well as those illuminations which
adorn many ancient manuscripts, will supply a

---

extinguished among the natives, it was found necessary to engage
celebrated artists from other countries.'

With these facts before him, who can help compassionating the
prejudices and puerility of certain weak but book-learned men who
draw a circle round the globe, beyond which they dogmatically assert
that the fine arts cannot flourish, and, as they pretend that this
zone of the beautiful which girdles the paradise of genius passes
through the fiftieth degree of latitude, point to England as necessarily existing in the desert. Alas for systems! It is a fact well
authenticated that to Great Britain is Europe principally indebted
for a new era in the arts, and their emancipation from that ignorance, deformity, and affectation to which they had been subjected
by Bernini and his followers in Italy, and his imitators in Northern
Europe, the French school. This is attested not by native, but by
the most eminent foreign writers on the fine arts, Cicognara, in his
Storia della Scultura, and Missirini, in his *Vita di Canova*, men
who are as competent as they are impartial in delivering their
opinion. It was by following the directions of Gavin Hamilton, in
studying perfect and elegant nature and the ideal beauty stamped
on works of Greek art, that Canova, notwithstanding the sneers and
the opposition of every other artist in Rome at the time, whether
native or foreigner, succeeded in producing a new and chastened
style in Italy and Europe (MISSIRINI, *Vita di Canova*, pp. 39-42,
53, 54), while our Flaxman, by his inimitable designs in illustration
of Homer, Hesiod, the Greek tragedians, and of Dante, very much
contributed to achieve this glorious revolution in the arts. These
designs procured for our countryman the admiration of all Europe,
and extorted from artists in every country the admission that he
approached one of the nearest to the ancient Greeks, and earned for
him the title of 'the classic Flaxman.' These facts demonstrate that
Great Britain does possess native talent, which, if heartened forwards
by a patronising Church, such as the Catholic is and always has
been, would place her as a nation amongst the very first in Europe
for her cultivation and perfection in the arts.

Some time after penning this note the author was gratified on
discovering how precisely his opinion on this subject coincided with
that of the eloquent and sensible Denina, who remarks: 'Fu molto
bene osservato che l'Inghilterra, produttrice insigne di tante egregie
manifatture, e d'ingegni in ogni sorte di scienze sublimissimi, non
produsse però pittori nè in numero molti, nè di qualità eccellenti:

A Greek Pontiff vested in the Phelonion or Chasuble which is gathered up over the shoulders.

large variety of examples.[1] The vestments and
ceremonies of the Mass, as celebrated at the present
day according to the Greek rite, will exhibit the
chasuble in its primitive form, and exemplify the
manner in which its ample and graceful folds were
adjusted upon the shoulders of the celebrant.[2]

XLIII.—MEANING OF ITS SEVERAL NAMES.

Our English term 'chasuble' for this vestment is
derived, as we just now remarked, from the Latin
casula, which signifies a small dwelling. This
name was given to it on account of its fulness,
and because it encircles the whole of the person,
and thus constitutes, as it were, a shed or covering
for the entire figure. It is as frequently denominated *planeta,* an appellation borrowed from the

---

perciocchè quando le arti s'andarono propagando dall' Italia nelle province settentrionali, già s'era in quell' isola abolito il pubblico culto
delle immagini ; onde si tolse ai geni nati al disegno e l'opportunità
d'imparare, e lo stimolo del guadagno e della gloria per applicarvisi.
Al contrario in Italia il numero cosi de' pittori, come degli altri artisti,
fu grandissimo : perocchè nel primo risorgimento della pittura non
solamente vi era comunissima e grande la divozione alle sacre immagini ; ma fors' anche perchè i frati trovando la pietà de' popoli,
spezialmente nelle città libere, più disposta che altrove a secondare le
loro idee, ebbero agio grandissimo d'impiegar l'opera de' primi ristau-
ratori del disegno ad innalzar fabbriche, a storiare e dipigner, or le
tavole per gli altari, or le mura, e le volte delle chiese, de' chiostri,
de' capitoli e de' refettorii : e la riuscita de' primi die di animo ed
impulso agli altri di coltivare le stesse arti.' C. DENINA, *Delle
Rivoluzioni d'Italia,* vol. III, l. XII, c. 6, p. 252. Torino, 1769.

[1] See J. BRITTON, *Cathedral Antiquities: Canterbury,* pl. XXIV ;
Exeter, pl. XX ; *York,* pl. XXXVI ; and *Salisbury: Monuments,* pl. I
and II.

[2] See the accompanying plates of the Greek vestments.

Greek Πλανητή, and which likewise bears a reference to its circling amplitude, and so forcibly ex-
presses the wideness of its dimensions; for the
word originally signifies anything that is cir-
cuitous.

XLIV.—ITS FIGURATIVE SIGNIFICATION.

More than one spiritual meaning has been attached by ecclesiastical writers to the chasuble.
Our countryman, Alcuin, who flourished about the
year 800, regards it as emblematical of charity;
for, as this virtue covers a multitude of sins, it is
happily figured by the chasuble, which encircles
the entire person of the priest. It is likewise said
by S. Germanus to represent the purple garment
which the soldiers threw around our Blessed Redeemer when He was going to immolate Himself
a sacrifice for man upon the Cross, and is, therefore, very properly assumed by the priest when
about to reiterate that sacrifice, and make an unbloody commemoration of the bloody Passion of
our Lord and show forth His death.

Marked as it is with the sign of the Cross, the
chasuble is likewise said to express the yoke of
obedience, which is rendered so agreeable to the
truly pious Christian by his fervent love of God,
and to signify the burden of the law, which becomes so light when carried with the proper spirit,
and for the sake of Him who thus entreats us:

'Take up My yoke upon you; . . . for My yoke is sweet, and My burden light.'[1]

XLV. PRAYER AT PUTTING IT ON.

The latter signification is more immediately referred to in the prayer which the priest is directed by the Church to recite while he puts on the chasuble : 'O Lord, Thou hast declared that Thy yoke is sweet and Thy burden light ; grant that I may carry that which Thou dost now impose upon my shoulders in such a manner as to merit Thy grace.'

XLVI.—THE DALMATIC.   XLVII.—ITS FORM.
XLVIII.—ORIGIN OF ITS NAME.

XLVI.—The Dalmatic is a vestment worn by the deacon whilst ministering at High Mass.

XLVII.—It is a long robe, open on each side, and differs from the chasuble by having wide sleeves, and instead of being marked on the back with the Cross, which superseded the senatorial Latus-clavus, it is ornamented with two stripes that were originally the Angusti-clavi, worn upon their garments by the less dignified amongst the ancient Roman people.

XLVIII.—It derives its name from Dalmatia,[2] the

---

[1] *S. Matthew*, XI, 30.

[2] Dalmatica vestis primum in Dalmatia provincia Graeciae texta est, tunica sacerdotalis candida cum clavis ex purpura.—S. ISIDORUS, *Etymologiarum liber*, XIX, 9.

people of which invented it, and was originally a

The Abbot Elfnoth presenting a book to the Monastery of S. Augustine at Canterbury,
with a Deacon, vested in the Dalmatic, holding his crosier.   From a miniature
of the tenth century in the British Museum, Harleian MS. 2908.[1]

vestment peculiar to the regal power, and, as such,

---

[1] The figure of the abbot will illustrate what we have said concerning bishops wearing the dalmatic under the chasuble, p. 243.
It would appear that Elfnoth was a mitred abbot, and consequently
was vested like a prelate of the Church.

*A Greek Pontiff vested in the Saccos or Colobium, which
resembles the Dalmatic of the Latin Church,*

was adopted, and used in public, by several among the Roman emperors.[1]

In the earliest ages of the Church the deacons wore a garment called Colobium, a kind of tight narrow tunic with very short sleeves, and which in the times of the Roman republic was worn by the more substantial citizens, but afterwards became a senatorial robe.[2]

XLIX.—WHEN ASSIGNED TO DEACONS.

In the reign of Constantine, the pontiff S. Sylvester conceded to the deacons of the Roman Church the use of the dalmatic on particular solemnities, a privilege which was gradually extended to other Churches by succeeding Popes, as we learn from S. Gregory the Great.[3] The custom of wearing the dalmatic under the chasuble was anciently peculiar to the Roman pontiff, but was afterwards allowed as an especial favour to certain prelates of the Church. For many centuries, however, every bishop has been entitled to

---

[1] LAMPRIDIUS, p. 139.

[2] *Codex Theodosianus*, lib. XIV, tit. 10. The form of the Latin colobium is still preserved in the *saccos* worn by Greek metropolitan bishops. In reality it differs very little from the dalmatic ; it was of the same shape, but its sleeves were shorter, and it was not so wide and ample.

[3] *Epistola CVII*, and BARONIUS, *ad Ann.* 508. We have already noticed the period when the use of the dalmatic probably became general throughout the Church, p. 225.

assume this, together with his other vestments, whenever he celebrates High Mass.[1]

L.—ITS ORIGINAL COLOUR AS A VESTMENT.

Anciently the dalmatic was white, and its stripes were narrow and scarlet, according to S. Isidore,[2] and, as may be observed in the fresco-paintings of the Roman catacombs, and in the mosaics which decorate so many of the venerable churches of that metropolis of Christianity.[3]

The vestment which is assigned by the Greek rite to the deacon who officiates at the Eucharistic sacrifice is denominated στοιχάριον,[4] and very closely resembles the corresponding dalmatic of the Latin Church. It extends farther down the person, and its sleeves are closer and longer than ours.[5] This garment is generally, though not always, white amongst the Orientals. With the Greeks, as in the Western Church, it is customary to employ purple-coloured vestments during the season of fasting.[6] In general, however, white still continues, as anciently, to be employed

---

[1] This may be authenticated by examining the sepulchral monuments of the prelates of the English Church.

[2] See p. 241 of this vol.

[3] See ARINGHI, *Roma Subterranea;* BOTTARI, *Sculture e Pitture;* and CIAMPINI, *Vetera Monimenta.*

[4] GOAR, Εὐχολόγιον, *sive Rituale Graecorum,* p. 110.

[5] GOAR, *ibid.,* p. 146. See figure at p. 227 of this vol.

[6] A Greek writer, Demetrius Chomatenus, observes that in the Greek Church purple vestments betoken mourning. GOAR, Εὐχολόγιον, p. 110.

amongst the Greeks, who have always regarded this colour for their vestments with particular complacency, and attach to it a symbolical meaning. Their writers notice that, as the spiritual messengers of heaven have frequently appeared to men arrayed in white and dazzling garments, we may appropriately consider the snow-white colour of those vestments in which the ministers of the sanctuary are clad to typify that angelic splendour which should emanate from the persons of those who are God's consecrated servants upon earth. Thus it was that S. Gregory Nazianzen was inspired to sing of the deacons and other attendants at the altar :

Οἱ δ'ἄρ' ὑποδρηστῆρες ἐν εἵμασι παμφανόωσιν
ἔστασαν, ἀγγελικῆς εἰκόνες ἀγλαΐης.
Somnium de Anastasiae ecclesia, v. 11.

God's ministers, in splendid vests array'd,
types of the angels by their light betray'd,
were present there.

Similar remarks have been passed by writers of the Latin Church. The ancient form, the colour, and the ornaments of the dalmatic, as used in the Latin Church, may be traced in a succession of interesting monuments, which regularly extend through many hundred years, beginning with the sixth and concluding with the nineteenth century. In the mosaic which ornaments the apse of S. Vitalis at Ravenna, erected 547 ;[1] in the apse of

---

[1] CIAMPINI *Vetera Monimenta*, vol. II, p. 63.

S. Laurence outside the walls at Rome, a work of the year 548;[1] in that of S. Mark, in the same city, executed in 774;[2] and in that of the Church of S. Praxedes, ornamented with mosaics in 818,[3] we observe various figures of deacons vested in their dalmatics. In all these valuable monuments the colour of this ecclesiastical garment is white; it has wide sleeves, and is adorned, as at present, with two clavi or stripes, which, instead of being, as now, of gold or other lace, are generally purple, and its shape almost exactly resembles that still in use at Rome, but it reaches somewhat lower down the person.

Towards the commencement of the tenth century, however, we meet with written documents which certify the use of dalmatics not only of white, but of those other various colours which are now employed.

LI.—THE TUNIC. LII.—ITS PROPER FORM.

LI.—The tunic is the vestment assigned to the sub-deacon in his ministry about the altar.

LII.—Were the regulations of the Church followed in all their precision, this garment would be longer than, but not so ample as the dalmatic of the deacon; according, however, to a custom which prevails almost everywhere, both these vestments are exactly alike.

---

[1] CIAMPINI, *Vetera Monimenta*, vol. II, p. 101.
[2] *Ibid.*, p. 123.   [3] *Ibid.*, p. 143.

LIII.—WHEN INTRODUCED.

It would appear that the use of the tunic was not until somewhat late formally appropriated to sub-deacons, since no mention of this vestment can be discovered in the writings of the early Fathers; nor is there anything resembling it discernible in the pictorial monuments of ecclesiastical antiquity; and we know, from a passage in the Letters of S. Gregory the Great, that in his time (A.D. 597)[1] the sub-deacons of the Roman Church were arrayed in a white alb when they officiated at the altar.[2]

LIV.—THE VEIL. LV.—ITS FORM.

At solemn High Mass the sub-deacon, during a part of the ceremony, has his arms and shoulders muffled with a species of scarf of an oblong shape, which is usually composed of the same material as the vestments, and is called the veil.

---

[1] *Epistolae*, lib. IX, ep. XIII, *ad Ioannem Syracusanum episcopum.*

[2] Honorius (A.D. 1130), in his enumeration of the vestments assigned at his time to the different ministers of the altar, informs us that the sub-deacon's peculiar garment, which we now call tunic, and is sometimes denominated *tunicella* by liturgical writers, was known by the term *subtile*. After noticing that the sub-deacon was permitted the use of the amice, the alb, and girdle, he says: 'Duae aliae (vestes), id est subtile et sudarium adduntur. Subtile quod et stricta tunica dicitur, portat, ut se iustitia quasi lorica induat, et in sanctitate et iustitia Deo serviat. Sudarium, quo sordes a vasis deterguntur, portat, ut transacta mala sordium a se per poenitentiam tergat.' HONORIUS, *Gemma Animae*, lib. I, cap. CCXXIX.

LVI.—ITS USE.

In the primitive ages the number of those who partook of the Blessed Sacrament every Sunday together with the priest was very great, and, in consequence, the paten or sacred disc, from which the sacramental species used to be distributed, was so large in its dimensions [1] that convenience required it to be removed from the altar as soon as the oblation had been made, and not brought back until the period arrived for giving the Communion to the people.

LVII.—WHY THE PATEN IS HELD ELEVATED.
LVIII.—AND WHY COVERED WITH A VEIL.

LVII.—Instead of depositing the paten upon the credence table which stands near the altar, or carrying it to the sacristy, the Roman ritual considered it more decorous and appropriate to consign it to the sub-deacon, who, by holding it in an elevated position, might thus announce to the assembly that the period for receiving the Blessed Sacrament would very soon approach, and silently admonish them to pray with greater fervour. [2]

---

[1] Amongst the various donations which were presented to the sovereign pontiffs and the churches at Rome by royal and illustrious visitors to the see of S. Peter, the *Liber pontificalis* enumerates several of these patens or discs of gold and silver, which weighed as much as twenty-five or thirty pounds each.

[2] At High Mass for the dead, and on Good Friday, the paten is not borne in this manner, because the more solemn ceremonies are omitted on those occasions ; and Communion is never given to the faithful on Good Friday, nor at High Mass for the dead.

LVIII. — The custom of enveloping the sub-deacon with a veil during the time he holds the paten was suggested to the Church by the ancient law, which prohibited the Levites from touching the consecrated vessels or bearing them about uncovered. 'Take,' said the Lord to Moses, 'take the sons of Caath from the midst of the Levites. . . . And when Aaron and his sons have wrapped up

Figure muffled in a veil; taken from an ancient mosaic in the Church of S. Praxedes, at Rome.—CIAMPINI, *Vetera Monimenta*, tom. II.

the sanctuary and the vessels thereof at the removing of the camp, then shall the sons of Caath enter in to carry the things wrapped up: and they shall not touch the vessels of the sanctuary, lest they die.'[1] To exhibit an equal reverence towards those instruments dedicated to

----

[1] *Numbers*, IV, 2 and 15.

the service of her altars, and used in the sacrifice of the new and better covenant, the Church directs the sub-deacon officiating at solemn High Mass to hold the paten enfolded in a veil, and forbids inferior clerics as well as laymen to touch any of her vessels. Moreover, she directs that the officiating priest who gives benediction[1] to the people with the Blessed Sacrament should also have his hands, out of reverence towards it, enveloped with the veil which he wears on the occasion, in such a manner that they do not touch the Pyx or monstrance[2] in which it is enclosed.

LIX.—THE COPE. LX.—ITS FORM.

The Cope resembles in its shape a flowing and ample cloak. It is open in the front, and is fastened over the breast by a morse, or a band of stuff with clasps. To the part which corresponds to the shoulders of the wearer is attached a piece of the same material, in form like the segment of a circle, and resembles a hood, which is usually adorned with lace and fringe.

LXI.—ITS ORIGIN.

The prototype of our cope is easily discoverable amongst the garments of the ancient Romans, since we shall soon perceive that, like the

---

[1] This ceremony has already been noticed (see vol. I, p. 153).
[2] This vessel has been described, vol. I, p. 155.

The Priest vested in a Cope, incensing the altar at the Magnificat.

chasuble, it was a mantle deriving its origin from the pacnula, which it perfectly resembled, with this variation, that, while it encircled the entire person, the cope was open in the front, and adapted to defend its wearer from the severities of the season, the variations of the weather, and from rain, by the addition of a cowl or hood. Necessity, not splendour, introduced this robe amongst the sacred vestments; and the Latin *pluviale*, or rain-cloak, the term by which it still continues to be designated, will immediately suggest its primitive use to every learned reader. Its appropriation as a sacerdotal garment may be referred to that epoch when the popes were accustomed to assemble the people, during the penitential seasons of the year, at some particular church, which had been previously indicated for that purpose, and thence proceed with them, in solemn procession and on foot, to some one or other of the more celebrated basilicas of Rome, to hold what was called a station. To protect the person of the pontiff from the rain that might overtake the procession on its way, the pluviale, or cope, was on such occasions assumed by him at the commencement of the ceremony.[1] It has

---

[1] 'Talis amictus ex necessitate primo, non ad magnificentiam receptus ab Ecclesia fuit, quando primum institutae Processiones; . . . opportuna enim tunc huiusmodi vestis ad arcendam pluviam, unde etiam habebat retro adnexum capuccium, capiti nimirum obtegendo. Hoc vero capuccium in veteribus, et a Carolo Magno Aquisgranensi

been employed at the altar ever since, and is worn by bishops and by priests on different occasions, but particularly at vespers.[1]

LXII.—COLOURS OF THE VESTMENTS.

In her vestments the Church employs five different colours. On the feasts of our Lord, of the Blessed Virgin Mary, of the angels, and of those amongst the saints who were not martyrs she makes use of white, not only to signify the stainless purity of the Lamb and of His Virgin Mother, but to figure that 'great multitude, which no man could number, of all nations, and tribes, and peoples, and tongues, standing before the throne, and in sight of the Lamb, clothed with white robes.'[2] On the feasts of Pentecost, of the Invention and Exaltation of the Cross, of the apostles and martyrs, she employs red, to typify those fiery tongues that rested on the heads of the Apostles when the Holy Ghost descended visibly among them, and in reference to the effusion of blood by Christ and His faithful

---

Ecclesiae donatis cappis pro modulo capitis compactum erat, ut videre est in bardocucullis nautarum, etc., licet nunc habeat tesserarias parmas bene amplas, inferiusque rotundas, manente adhuc, qui capucii acumen terminabat, in multis flocco.' BONANNI, *Numismata Pontificum*, tom. I, p. 2.

[1] The kings of England, at their coronation, are invested with the following ecclesiastical garments : the dalmatic or colobium, the tunic, the stole, and the cope or pall.

[2] *Apocalypse*, VII, 9.

followers. On the greatest part of the Sundays the vestments are green. Purple is the colour assigned for the penitential times of Advent and of Lent, for the Ember-days, and for the several vigils throughout the year; whilst black is reserved for the office of Good Friday, and for Masses for the dead. Rose-colour is used on Gaudete and Laetare Sundays; and on the fourth Sunday in Advent, when it falls on 24th December. Cloth of gold is allowed instead of white, red, or green, and cloth of silver instead of white. Blue is also used in many churches on the feasts of our Lady.

LXIII.—THE SURPLICE. LXIV.—ITS ANTIQUITY.

LXIII.—This is that white linen garment which is worn not only by all clerics, but also by those who, in the absence of clerics, are allowed to assist in the choir or sanctuary during the celebration of Divine Service.

LXIV.—The use of white garments by the members of the sanctuary is continually referred to by the holy fathers. This custom is most particularly noticed by S. Jerome,[1] and afterwards by the Council of Narbonne, held in 589, which, in one of its decrees, ordains that neither deacon, sub-deacon, nor lector shall lay aside the alb, or white tunic, until the Mass be entirely concluded.

---

[1] S. Hieronymus, contra Pelag., lib. i.

LXV.—ITS ANCIENT FORM.

Honorius of Autun (c. 1130) describes the surplice as a white loose vestment, that reached down to the feet;[1] and from several passages in

The form of the Surplice used in England before the change in religion.   From a miniature of the fourteenth century in the British Museum, MS. 2 B. VII.[2]

the works of ecclesiastical writers, and in the canons of various provincial synods,[3] it would

---

[1] *Gemma Animae*, lib. I, cap. CCXXXII.

[2] STRUTT, *Regal and Ecclesiastical Antiquities of England; preface to the Supplement.*   The reader will immediately see that the figure of the priest administering the Blessed Sacrament is placed on the wrong side of the Communion-cloth.   Such, however, is his position in the miniature; and the author, from his anxiety to exhibit as faithful copies as possible of those original designs from which he borrowed his illustrations, would not allow a proposed correction of this error.

[3] See L. THOMASSIN, *Vetus et nova Ecclesiae Disciplina*, pars I, lib. II, cap. LII, § 4.

appear that the surplice was a variation of the alb, from which it differed, during a long period of years, merely by being somewhat shorter and having wider sleeves. That the surplice used in Catholic England answered this description, and was long, with flowing sleeves, and, though more ample, perfectly resembled the form of the surplice in use on the Continent, in Italy, and especially in Rome, is evident from the illuminations of old English manuscripts and legends of the saints—a fact which may be authenticated by referring to Strutt's *Regal and Ecclesiastical Antiquities of England*,[1] and the engraving on page 254.[2]

---

[1] This is corroborated not only by the examination of several ancient illuminated Missals and manuals, but in the clearest manner by referring to Archbishop Robert Winchelsey's ordinance, *De Supellectili in Ecclesiis parochialibus.* (See LYNDEWODE, *Provinciale.* Oxon., 1679, p. 252.) The primate requires that each parish church be provided with 'tria superpellicia' (one for the priest, one for the deacon, and one for the sub-deacon), 'et unum rochetum.' The learned commentator remarks : 'Rochetum differt a superpellicio quia superpellicium habet manicas pendulas, sed rochetum est sine manicis, et ordinatur pro clerico ministraturo sacerdoti vel forsan ad opus ipsius sacerdotis in baptizando pueros, ne per manicas ipsius brachia impediantur.' Winchelsey was primate from 1294 to 1313.

[2] It is to be lamented that the old English surplice is not more generally used within our sanctuaries. Independently of its title to our reverence on account of being a venerable relic of our once Catholic national Church—an incident alone sufficient to demand the restoration of its ancient form—this vestment comes recommended to our good taste by its intrinsic gracefulness. Its ample and majestic sleeves and flowing drapery render it more dignified and becoming than either the French winged surplice or the Roman cotta, which are not only foreign to us, but are in themselves in-

LXVI.—ORIGIN OF ITS NAME.

Duranti, who composed his work on the *Divine Offices* about the year 1286, traces up the etymology of the Latin *Superpellicium,* whence, it is obvious, our English appellation, Surplice, is derived, to a custom which anciently prevailed in the Church of wearing tunics made from the skins of such animals as the country furnished, over which was cast a white linen alb or vestment, denominated, from that circumstance of its being worn over fur, *Superpellicium.*

LXVII.—ITS FIGURATIVE SIGNIFICATION.

Whilst indicating the derivation of its name, Duranti has also pointed out the spiritual meaning of the surplice, which, as he remarks, has been regarded as symbolical of that robe of innocence, purity, and righteousness that our Divine Redeemer purchased for the human race by the price of His glorious atonement, and with which He arrays the soul of the regenerated or repentant sinner, and effaces man's iniquities, figured by the skins of animals, since it was in garments

---

elegant. Let us hope, however, that ere long, as the study of ecclesiastical antiquities, and of those of our ancient English Church in particular, becomes more extended, the surplice will be again fashioned according to that graceful model which still prevails through Italy, and once prevailed in England, prior to the much to be lamented change of religion.

formed from such materials that fallen Adam, after being chased from Paradise, was covered.[1]

The surplice is very appropriately assigned to the Acolytes, who attend on the priest at Mass; for 'Samuel ministered before the face of the Lord; being a child girded with a linen ephod.'[2]

---

[1] Dictum est Superpellicium, eo quod antiquitus super tunicas pellicias de pellibus mortuorum animalium factas induebantur, quod adhuc in quibusdam Ecclesiis observatur, repraesentantes quod Adam post peccatum talibus vestitus est pelliciis. DURANTI, *Rationale*, lib. III, cap. I.

[2] I *Kings*, II, 18.

CHAPTER XIII.

OF BLESSED OR HOLY WATER.

THE ordinance of Almighty God, promulgated by the lips of Moses, concerning the *water* of *aspersion*, and the mode of sprinkling it, are minutely noticed in the Book of Numbers.[1] In the Book of Exodus we read that the Lord issued the following directions to Moses: 'Thou shalt make a brazen laver with its foot, to wash in: and thou shalt set it between the tabernacle of the testimony and the altar. And water being put into it, Aaron and his sons shall wash their hands and feet in it when they are going into the tabernacle of the testimony, and when they are to come to the altar, to offer on it incense to the Lord.'[2]

It is a well-attested fact that it was a practice with the Jews, not merely peculiar to the members of the priesthood, but observed amongst the people, for each individual to wash his hands before he presumed to pray.[3] The Church adopted this, as well as several other Jewish ceremonies which she engrafted on her ritual;[4] and S. Paul

---

[1] *Numbers*, XIX, 9–22.   [2] *Exodus*, XXX, 18–20.
[3] See BARONIUS, *Anno* 57, c. VIII.   [4] BARONIUS, *ibid.*

apparently borrows from such ablutions the metaphor he employs while thus admonishing his disciple Timothy: 'I will that men pray in every place, lifting up pure hands.'[1]   That in the early ages the faithful used to wash their hands at the threshold of the church before they entered, is expressly mentioned by a number of writers.[2]

I.—HOLY WATER OF APOSTOLIC ORIGIN.

The introduction of blessed or holy water must be referred to the times of the Apostles.   That it was the custom in the very first ages of the Church,

---

[1] 1 *Timothy*, II, 8.

[2] TERTULLIANUS, *De Oratione*, cap. XIII.   S. John Chrysostom (*in Ioan. Hom. VII*).   Eusebius (A.D. 320), in the description of the magnificent church erected at Tyre by the bishop of that city, Paulinus, specifies that fountains were made to spring up just before the portals, where the faithful might wash their hands previously to entering the temple (*Hist. Eccl.*, lib. X, cap. 4).   S. Paulinus of Nola mentions the fountains which, in his time, stood in the porch of S. Peter's Church at Rome, and had been constructed for a similar purpose.   Writing to his friend Severus, the same holy prelate furnishes him with a minute account of the church, the building and embellishment of which had just been finished.   He recites the verses which he had composed and affixed in various parts of this basilica; from those which were inscribed over an arch in the vestibule we gather that he had, near this spot, placed a vase containing water :—

Sancta nitens famulis interluit atria lymphis
cantharus, intrantumque manus lavat amne ministro.
Epist. XXXII, ad Severum.

In corners of the little churches in the Roman catacombs is often observed a low column supporting a shallow marble or terra-cotta vase intended to hold the blessed or holy water.   BOLDETTI, *Osservazioni sopra i Cimiteri*, pp. 16, 35.

not only to deposit vessels of water at the entrance of those places where the Christians assembled for the celebration of Divine worship, but also to have vases containing water mingled with salt, both of which had been separated from common use and blessed by the prayers and invocations of the priest, is certain. A particular mention of it is made in the Constitutions of the Apostles,[1] and the Pontiff Alexander I., the sixth pope in succession from S. Peter, whose chair he mounted in the year 109, issued a decree by which the use of holy water was permitted to the faithful in their houses.[2]

A painting in the catacombs at Rome attests the practice among the primitive Christians of sprinkling holy water at their religious assemblies.

On the ceiling of one of those sepulchral chambers which have their entrance at the church of S. Agnes outside the walls are depicted five figures each holding in one hand a vase denominated *situlus*,[3] similar to those in which holy water is at present carried about in our ceremonies. Four of these figures support in the right hand branches, as it would appear, of the palm-tree;

---

[1] Lib. VIII, c. 29, *apud* LABBEUM, *Concil. Gen.*, tom. I, col. 575.

[2] Hic (Alexander) constituit aquam aspersionis cum sale benedici in habitaculis hominum (*Liber Pontificalis*, II, p. 78). Hence it will appear that this pope did not introduce holy or blessed water, but only extended the use of a custom which he found established in the Church at his accession to the pontifical dignity.

[3] D. GEORGIUS, *De Liturgia Romani Pontificis*, t. I, p. 129.

but the fifth bears elevated a tufted aspergillum,

In the Catacombs of S. Agnes outside the walls.   See BOTTARI, *Sculture e Pitture*,
tom. III, p. 70, plate CXLVIII.

which exactly corresponds to that still employed
at the ceremony of sprinkling holy water.

II.—FORM OF BLESSING HOLY WATER.

Having signed himself with the sign of the
Cross, the priest commences the benediction of
the salt and water before him, in the following
manner : 'I exorcise thee, O creature of salt,
by the living ✠[2] God, by the true ✠ God, by the
holy ✠ God; by that God who by the prophet
Eliseus commanded thee to be cast into the water
to cure its barrenness; that thou mayst by this
exorcism be made beneficial to the faithful, and

---

[2] At those words where a ✠ is thus inserted the priest makes the
sign of the Cross, with his hand outstretched over the thing he is
blessing.

become to all those who make use of thee healthful both to soul and body; and that in what place soever thou shalt be sprinkled, all illusions and wickedness and crafty wiles of Satan may be chased away and depart from that place, and every unclean spirit commanded in His name, who is to come to judge the living and the dead and the world by fire.   Amen.

'Let us pray.

'O Almighty and everlasting God, we most humbly implore Thy infinite mercy that Thou wouldst vouchsafe by Thy power to bless ✠ and to sanctify ✠ this Thy creature of salt, which Thou hast given for the use of mankind, that it may be to all who take it for the health of mind and body, and that whatever shall be sprinkled with it may be freed from all uncleanness, and from all assaults of wicked spirits, through our Lord Jesus Christ,' etc.

After this the priest proceeds to the blessing of the water as follows :—

The Exorcism of the Water.

'I exorcise thee, O creature of water, in the name of God ✠ the Father Almighty, and in the name of Jesus Christ ✠ His Son our Lord, and in the virtue of the Holy ✠ Ghost; that thou mayst, by this exorcism, have power to chase away all the power of the enemy; that thou mayst be

enabled to cast him out, and put him to flight
with all his apostate angels, by the virtue of the
same Jesus Christ our Lord, who is come to judge
the living and the dead, and the world by fire.
Amen.[1]

'Let us pray.

'O God, who for the benefit of mankind hast
made use of the element of water in the greatest
sacraments, mercifully hear our prayers, and impart the virtue of Thy blessing ✠ to this element,
prepared by many kinds of purifications; that this
Thy creature, made use of in Thy mysteries, may
receive the effect of Thy divine grace, for the
chasing away devils and curing diseases; and
that whatsoever shall be sprinkled with this water
in the houses or places of the faithful may be
free from all uncleanness and delivered from evil:
let no pestilential spirit reside there, no infectious
air: let all the snares of the hidden enemy fly
away: and may whatever envies the safety or
repose of the inhabitants of that place be put
to flight by the sprinkling of this water, that
the welfare which we seek by the invocation
of Thy holy name may be defended from all
sorts of assaults, through our Lord Jesus Christ,'
etc.

---

[1] Similar to this is the form of blessing the water ordained in the
Constitutions of the Apostles, lib. VIII, c. 29.

Then the priest mingles the salt with the water, saying :

' May this salt and water be mixed together, in the name of the Father ✠, and of the Son ✠, and of the Holy ✠ Ghost.   Amen.

' *V.* The Lord be with you.
' *A.* And with thy spirit.

' *Let us pray.*

' O God, author of invincible power, King of an empire that cannot be overcome, and for ever magnificently triumphant ; who restrainest the forces of the adversary, who defeatest the fury of the roaring enemy, who mightily conquerest his malicious wiles : we pray and beseech Thee, O Lord, with dread and humility, to regard with a favourable countenance this creature of salt and water, to enlighten it with Thy bounty, and to sanctify it with the dew of Thy fatherly goodness, that wheresoever it shall be sprinkled, all infestation of the unclean spirit may depart, and all fear of the venomous serpent may be chased away, through the invocation of Thy holy name ; and that the presence of the Holy Ghost may be everywhere with us ; who seek Thy mercy through our Lord Jesus Christ,' etc.

III.—OBJECT OF THE CHURCH IN USING IT.

It is the never-ceasing solicitude of the Church to render her children holy and undefiled, and to preserve them from everything which can contaminate or injure them. In labouring to achieve this object she connects her prayers and aspirations with all those exterior signs and ceremonies which are most likely to express her benevolent desires. The property of water is to cleanse: it is therefore a type of purity; while salt, used as a preservative against corruption, is an emblem of wisdom.[1] Water and salt commingled, blessed, and sprinkled on the people, form a very appropriate symbol to exhibit the desire felt by the Church for our purification and preservation from everything contagious.

IV.—WHY SALT IS MINGLED WITH THE WATER.

When the men of Jericho complained to Eliseus that the waters were bad and the ground barren, the prophet said to them: 'Bring me a new vessel, and put salt into it. And when they had brought it, he went out to the spring of the waters, and cast the salt into it, and said: Thus saith the Lord: I have healed these waters, and there shall be no more in them death or barrenness'[2]

The Church, in imitation of the prophet, invokes the Divine power on the salt, that it may have an efficacy from God to preserve her members from everything that can be hurtful to them.

---

[1] *Colossians*, IV, 6.   [2] *4 Kings*, II, 20, 21.

V.—WHY EXORCISMS ARE PRONOUNCED OVER THE SALT AND WATER.

The priest exorcises the water and the salt. Exorcise is a Greek term which signifies 'to conjure, to speak imperatively.' The Church is well aware that man, by his corruption, had perverted to the service of the devil those things which were intended for the glory of God, and she hears S. Paul proclaim that 'the creature was made subject to vanity, not willingly.'[1] But she knows that everything 'is sanctified by the word of God and prayer.'[2]

Hence it is that she exorcises and blesses many creatures. She exorcises salt and water by commanding them, on the part of God and through the merits of the Cross of Jesus Christ, not only to be innocuous to man, but to become serviceable to him while labouring in the work of salvation.

This, in reality, is the object of all her exorcisms pronounced over inanimate creatures ; and it should not be forgotten that it is a pious custom with her to bless everything which is assigned for holy purposes.[3]

---

[1] *Romans*, VIII, 20.   [2] I *Timothy*, IV, 5.

[3] Protestants have retained some remnants of the ancient religion in this regard, for churches and burial-places still continue to be blessed by the bishops of the Establishment, and the oil with which the sovereign is anointed at the Coronation is particularly specified in the Protestant ritual as consecrated.

VI.—SPRINKLING OF THE ALTAR AND THE CONGREGATION.

It is usual to sprinkle the altar and the people on Sundays, immediately before commencing the celebration of High Mass. As holy or blessed water was instituted for the express design of insinuating to Christians that they were to keep a cautious guard against the attacks of Satan, and to preserve themselves, as much as possible, immaculate from the contagion of sinfulness, the purpose of this aspersion is to warn the faithful to purify themselves before they presume to assist at the holy Sacrifice—that *clean* oblation predicted by the prophet Malachias.[1] The words recited by the priest and chanted by the choir during the ceremony are quite appropriate: 'Thou shalt sprinkle me, O Lord, with hyssop, and I shall be cleansed: Thou shalt wash me, and I shall be made whiter than snow.'[2]

The blood of the Lamb was sprinkled on the door-posts of the Israelites in Egypt[3] with hyssop, as well as the waters of expiation in which were mingled the ashes of the red cow, for the purification of the unclean and leprous.[4]

The second object which the Church has in view

---

[1] *Malachias*, I, 11. [2] *Psalm*, L, 9.
[3] *Exodus*, XII, 22. [4] *Numbers*, XIX, 12, 18.

while performing this ceremony is to call to our remembrance the baptism by which we become regenerated unto Christ.

VII.—USED IN THE GREEK CHURCH.

The Greek, like the Latin, Church practises this rite, with this sole difference, that it confines the observance of it to the first, instead of every, Sunday of each month,[1] as may be observed by consulting their Missal or Euchology.[2] At the conclusion of blessing the holy water the priest is directed by the rubrics of the Euchology to sprinkle it around the church and upon the congregation, just as we do.[3]

Once in the year, on the feast of the Epiphany, the Greeks, Armenians, and other Oriental Christians perform a more solemn blessing of holy water in commemoration of the baptism of Christ in the river Jordan. The Greeks, not only at present, but from the earliest ages of the Church, have been taught to manifest a particular devotion towards this festival, and now, as anciently, provide themselves at vespers, on the vigil of its celebration, with some of the newly blessed water, which they carry home from church to their houses, where they sprinkle a part, and preserve the remainder with much care until the annual festival

---

[1] GOAR, Εὐχολόγιον, sive Rituale Graecorum, p. 451.
[2] *Ibid.*, p. 441.   [3] *Ibid.*, p. 448.

comes round again.[1] The antiquity of this custom amongst the Greek and Eastern Christians is attested by a number of their old and recent writers. From amongst the former it will be quite sufficient to adduce S. Chrysostom.[2] In a sermon delivered by him on this great festival he observes: 'This is the day on which Christ was baptized, and on which He sanctified the nature of the waters. Hence it is that everyone towards the midnight of this festival provides himself with some of the water, which he conveys home, and carefully preserves during the whole year, as the waters which were this day sanctified.'[3] The solemnity and splendour with which this blessing of water on the Epiphany is performed by the Armenians, particularly in Persia, and by the Russians at S. Petersburg, have been noticed by every traveller in those countries.[4]

---

[1] GOAR, Εὐχολόγιον, *sive Rituale Graecorum*, p. 467.

[2] A.D. 398.

[3] Αὕτη γὰρ ἐστιν ἡ ἡμέρα, καθ᾽ ἣν ἐβαπτίσατο, καὶ τὴν τῶν ὑδάτων ἡγίασε φύσιν. Διά τοι τοῦτο καὶ ἐν μεσονυκτίῳ κατὰ τὴν ἑορτὴν ταύτην ἅπαντες ὑδρευσάμενοι οἴκαδε τὰ νάματα ἀποτίθενται καὶ εἰς ἐνιαυτὸν ὁλόκληρον φυλάττουσιν ἅτε δὴ σήμερον ἁγιασθέντων τῶν ὑδάτων. S. CHRYSOSTOMI *Hom. de Baptismo Christi et de Epiphania.*

[4] This solemn blessing of water on the Epiphany was formerly observed in many dioceses of Western Christendom, but in some few, *e.g.* Augsburg and Bamberg, it took place on the Sunday within the octave of Corpus Christi.

VIII.—WHY HOLY WATER IS PLACED AT THE ENTRANCE OF OUR CHURCHES.

From the same pious motives, vases containing blessed, or, as it is denominated, holy water, are placed on the right hand at the entrance of all churches and chapels.[1]

Into these the faithful dip the tips of their right-hand fingers, and afterwards make the sign of the Cross, as they repeat the following invocation to the holy and undivided Trinity: 'In the name of the Father, and of the Son, and of the Holy Ghost.' In this manner it is that the Church endeavours to address her children at the very threshold of the tabernacle, and to exhort them to understand, by the water which she holds out to them, that they must bring a purity and cleanness of heart to the sanctuary, and thus comply with the exhortations of S. Paul, and 'lift up pure hands' to the throne of Him whose cross

---

[1] A larger vessel was also formerly placed at the west end of the nave, from which the faithful could draw supplies to take home. The Greeks and Orientals place a vase containing water at the entrance of their churches. Amongst the Greeks it has a particular place assigned to it in the vestibule, and is designed by the term of φιάλη, or fountain of springing water. (GOAR, Εὐχολόγιον, sive Rituale Graecorum, p. 13.) The Christians of S. Thomas, as the Nestorians of Malabar were at first denominated, have a vessel of blessed or holy water standing at the doors of their churches, which they take in signing themselves with the cross as they enter. (P. LE BRUN, Explication des Prières et des Cérémonies de la Messe, tom. VI, p. 567).

they have just figured on their foreheads, and
through the merits of whose death and suffering
they can alone expect to receive the pardon of
their sins and to obtain eternal happiness.[1]

---

[1] The reader will find the various rites for blessing holy water
used in the Oriental churches printed at full length in MARSILIUS,
De Fonte lustrali, seu de Aquae Benedictae praestantia.   Romae, 1603.

CHAPTER XIV.

ON THE CREED.

THE Creed is an abridgment of the Christian doctrine, and is usually denominated the Symbol of Faith.

I.—MEANING OF THE TERM SYMBOL.

The word Symbol means a sign to distinguish things from one another. To the primitive Christians the Symbol or Creed was what the watchword is to an army in the field—a signal by which a friend may be immediately discriminated from an enemy. As the Creed was the medium through which the true believer was recognised amid heretics and gentiles, it became customary to say, *Da signum, Da symbolum*—'Give the sign,' 'Repeat the Symbol or Creed.'

II.—FIVE FORMS OF CREED. III.—THE APOSTLES'.

There are five Creeds: the Apostles' Creed, the Nicene Creed, the Constantinopolitan Creed, the *Quicumque vult*, which passes, though erroneously, under the name of S. Athanasius, and the Creed of Pius IV.

III.—That the Creed which is attributed to the Apostles and bears their name was in reality drawn up by them has been ably demonstrated.[1] This was the only Creed in use amongst the primitive Christians, and for the first three centuries was not committed to writing lest it should fall into the hands of unbelievers, but was delivered down by oral tradition. With the exception of Tertullian, no author, before the reign of Constantine the Great, presumed to note down this Creed. After that period, when the danger of its being ridiculed by Jew or Gentile had passed away, it began to be penned, and first of all appeared in the works of S. Athanasius and of S. Basil.[2]

IV.—THE NICENE.

In the fourth century, Arius, a priest of the Church of Alexandria, denied the Divinity of the Word made flesh. To condemn the error of this heresiarch, the Church in the year 325 convoked a general council at Nicaea, a city of Bithynia. The assembled fathers found it expedient to develop the meaning of the second article of the Apostles' Creed by a more copious explanation of its sense and doctrine. The exposition of the council was engrafted on the Apostolic Symbol,

---

[1] See Noël Alexandre, *Historia Ecclesiastica*, Saec. i, Diss. xii.
[2] Benedictus XIV., *De Sacrificio Missae*, lib. ii, cap. viii, § 4.

which, along with this verbal addition, acquired a new denomination, and came to be entitled the Symbol of Nicaea, or Nicene Creed.

V.—THE CONSTANTINOPOLITAN.

A short time afterwards, Macedonius, bishop of Constantinople, impugned the Divinity of the Holy Ghost. The Church was again obliged to call a general council, which met at Constantinople in the year 381, and delivered to the faithful the genuine belief upon this litigated article of faith. The explanation furnished by the council was appended to the Nicene Creed, and this second enlargement of the Symbol of the Apostles was called the Creed of Constantinople.

VI.—THE ATHANASIAN.

About this time a multitude of innovators attempted to pollute the pure stream of apostolic doctrine by commingling with it their errors concerning the essence and properties of Christ's humanity. There were in the Church many zealous pastors who arose to guard the fountain-stream of faith from such contaminations, and amongst them the unknown author of that Creed which was immediately recognised as so orthodox and beautiful that it was commonly attributed to the most celebrated champion of the Faith, S. Athanasius, and still passes under his name, though ascertained not to be his production.

VII.—WHAT CREED SAID AT MASS.

The Creed which is now repeated in the Liturgy is in reality the Creed, not of Nicaea, but of Constantinople. It was not until the decline of the eighth or the commencement of the ninth century, when the discipline of the secret had long been abandoned, that the Creed began to be recited at Mass.

VIII.—WHEN SAID AT MASS.

The Creed is said every Sunday during the year, and on all those feasts which are in a manner indicated in it, such as the different festivals instituted in honour of Christ, of His Mother the Blessed Virgin Mary, and of the Apostles and Doctors of the Church, by whose arduous labours and writings the doctrine contained in this Symbol of Christianity has been disseminated through the world.

IX.—CREED OF PIUS IV.

Like the last three Creeds, that of Pius IV., so denominated from the Pope under whose pontificate it was framed, was suggested by the exigencies of the period, and was drawn up to exhibit a summary of the genuine doctrines of Christ at an epoch when the innovators of the sixteenth century were employing every expedient to decoy the faithful into error.

X.—ALL ANNOUNCE THE SAME FAITH.

It should be carefully remembered that in these several successive Creeds no new doctrines are promulgated, nor is any addition made to the code of faith delivered to the Church by the Apostles. They are all the same in substance as the Apostles' Creed, but unfold its doctrines and present an explanation of its several parts in a more precise and intelligible manner.

CHAPTER XV.

ON THE DIPTYCHS.

As the subject of the ancient Diptychs is intimately woven with some varied and useful, no less than interesting information, it is presumed that any investigation, however limited, concerning these curious monuments, which are repeatedly referred to by the fathers of the Church and writers on ecclesiastical history, will not be altogether unacceptable to the reader.

I.—THEIR NAME. II.—FORM. III.—AND USE.

As their name implies, the Diptychs[1] were composed of two folding tablets, in general made of ivory, though sometimes of wood or silver, and so connected together by hinges that they could be shut or opened like a book. It was a custom among the Romans for the newly elected Consuls, on entering upon their office, to send a diptych as a present to the governors of provinces and to

---

[1] The Greek Δίπτυχον is composed of Δύο, 'two,' and πτύξ, πτυχός, which is derived from πτύσσω, 'to fold.' Anything doubly folded is a diptych ; this term was, however, by the ancients chiefly applied to the tablets used for writing on.

their friends. The exterior surface of these consular diptychs was carved in low relief, and usually exhibited the portrait of the Consul,[1] sitting in the cushioned curule chair and wearing his full official costume; often a representation of the games which he proposed to celebrate for the public amusement during his occupation of the curule chair occupied the space below.

The interior face of each leaf, slightly sunk, was covered with wax, on which was written a list of all preceding Consuls, concluding with that of the donor, the newly elected magistrate.[2]

IV.—WHY PRESENTED TO THE CHURCH.
V.—HOW USED.

Amongst the crowds of gentiles who daily embraced the faith of Christ, there were several illustrious individuals who, along with other offerings that they bestowed upon the Church, presented these consular diptychs, which were always regarded as valuable and distinguished objects. A becoming respect for the volume containing the sacred record, as well as for all those books that were employed in the celebration of

---

[1] CLAUDIANUS, lib. III, *in Stilicon*, v. 345 *et seqq.*

[2] So much importance came to be attached to these ivory diptychs, that, by a law promulgated in 380 by Theodosius and Arcadius, all persons, excepting the ordinary Consuls, were prohibited from distributing them as official presents.—*Codex Theodosianus*, lib. xv, tit. 9, l. 1.

the holy Sacrifice and other hallowed rites of
our religion, suggested to the ancient Christians
the idea of enveloping them with every species
of covering that was precious, on account either
of the richness of its material or of the elaborate
workmanship with which it happened to be ornamented. Such magnificent covers presented themselves in the ancient diptychs; neither any demur
was made or scruple started about employing in
such a service articles that were figured with
secular practices and gentile superstitions; on the
contrary, they were esteemed as the *spolia opima*
which the temples of Christianity could exultingly
display as not the least distinguished amongst
those signal proofs of its triumphs over paganism.
From the piety of the first believers, therefore,
arose the custom of employing these consular
diptychs[1] as coverings for the sacred Scriptures,
the books of the liturgy, and other sacred
writings.

---

[1] The effect of such a practice has been that a number of consular
diptychs and several other objects connected with the fine arts,
which would have otherwise been irreparably lost, have descended
almost uninjured to us from the ancients. The magnificent sardonyx
cameo representing the Apotheosis of Augustus, the most precious
monument of its kind known to be in existence, and now in the
National Library at Paris, was once attached, as a covering, to one
of the sides of the grand Missal belonging to the Chapel Royal at
Paris. GORI, *Thesaurus veterum Diptychorum*, tom. III, p. 60. In
some cases the subject of the diptych was altered; there is an example
of this at Monza, where the Consul's head has been shaved and the
legend SCS GREGOR(ius) cut in the space beneath the arch under
which he stands.

REGISTERS OF THE DEAD WHO WERE TO BE PRAYED FOR.

Very frequently, however, these curious sculptures were employed to enclose or to serve the purpose of what, in ecclesiastical language, were denominated the sacred diptychs; for by this appellation it was usual to call those tablets[1] upon which it was the custom, commenced in the apostolic times, to inscribe, amongst other names, particularly those of such deceased members of the Church as had been benefactors to it, and for whom the priest and people never omitted to pray each time the holy Sacrifice was offered. From the ancient liturgies we gather that it was the office of the deacon to rehearse aloud this catalogue registered in the public diptychs[2] to the people, and at a certain part of the service to suggest to the priest the names of those amongst

---

[1] By the ancients all those tablets which folded up into two leaves or pages were called diptychs, or *tabellae duplices*, whether they were employed in epistolary correspondence, for holding memoranda, or any other similar purpose. Ovid, in his lamentations over the letter which had been returned to him unopened, denominates the rejected epistle *tabellae duplices;* and S. Augustine, three centuries later, referring to the two marble tables of the Law given to Moses, denominates them by the term *diptychium:* 'In illo diptychio lapideo, iam tu non corde lapideo intelligis, quid duro illi populo congruebat.' *Contra Faustum Manichaeum*, lib. xv, cap. 4.

[2] Sometimes these lists of the dead for whom public prayer was made during the celebration of the liturgy were denominated 'the sacred tables,' as we learn from various passages in those ancient works which pass under the name of S. Dionysius the Areopagite. In describing what took place at Mass immediately after the '*pax,*'

the dead for whom he was required to make more especial mention in his prayers.[1] In evidence of this, the reader is here presented with extracts from the liturgies which will serve not only to illustrate the subject under discussion, but to fortify the arguments adduced in a preceding chapter (p. 74 of this volume) in support of the ancient and apostolic doctrine of prayer for the dead.

FROM THE LITURGY OF S. MARK.

The deacon reads the Diptychs (or catalogue) of the dead. The priest then bowing down, prays:

'To the souls of all these, O Sovereign Lord our God, grant repose in Thy holy tabernacles, in Thy kingdom, bestowing on them the good things promised and prepared by Thee, which eye hath

---

or kiss of peace, that author observes: 'When all present have reciprocally saluted one another, then is made the mystic recitation of the sacred tablets: Καὶ ἀσπασαμένων ἀλλήλους ἀπάντων, ἡ μυστικὴ τῶν ἱερῶν πτυχῶν ἀνάῤῥησις ἐπιτελεῖται. *De Ecclesiastica Hierarchia,* cap. III, § 2.

[1] This custom has ceased to be observed in the Roman liturgy for some centuries, though we find it indicated there by the *Oratio supra Diptycha.* At present, when the celebrating priest arrives at that part of the canon called the 'Memento,' he secretly commemorates those for whose souls he more particularly wishes to pray. The ancient custom of reading the names of the dead from the diptychs, according to the rubric in the Sacramentary of S. Gregory the Great, was still kept up in the eleventh century, as is attested by the author of the treatise *De Divinis Officiis,* formerly attributed to Alcuin, who says: 'Post illa verba, quibus dicitur, *in somno pacis,* usus fuit anti-

not seen and ear hath not heard, and which have not entered into the heart of man. Give rest to their souls, and render them worthy of the kingdom of heaven. Grant to us such an end of life as will be worthy of Christians, pleasing to Thee, and free from sin : and give us a share and lot with all Thy saints.[1]

FROM THE LITURGY OF S: CHRYSOSTOM.

The deacon incenses the altar and the diptychs or tablets, and mentions those of the dead and the living whom he may particularly choose.

Here the priest makes particular mention of those for whom he intends to pray, both living and dead. For the living he says :

'For the safety, protection, and the remission of the sins of the servant of God, N.'

For the dead he says :

'For the repose and the remission of the soul of Thy servant N. in a place of light, from which

---

quorum, sicut etiam usque hodie Romana agit Ecclesia, ut statim recitarentur a diptychis, id est, tabulis nomina defunctorum.' The recitation of the diptychs by the deacon in the celebration of Mass according to the Greek and Oriental liturgies is still kept up, as may be seen by consulting GOAR, Εὐχολόγιον, *sive Rituale Graecorum,* p. 78 ; RENAUDOT, *Liturgiarum Orientalium Collectio ;* and P. LE BRUN, *Explication des Prières et des Cérémonies de la Messe.*

[1] RENAUDOT, *Liturgiarum Orientalium Collectio,* tom. I, p. 150.

grief and lamentation are far removed; and make him to rest where he may see around him the light of Thy countenance.'[1]

FROM THE COPTIC LITURGY, USED BY THE EUTYCHIANS, CALLED THE LITURGY OF S. BASIL.

The deacons shall read the diptychs and recite the names of the dead. The priest says, after the reading of the diptychs:

'Command those, O Lord, whose souls Thou hast received, to repose in this place, and preserve us, who are pilgrims here, in Thy faith, and graciously grant us Thy peace, to the end.'[2]

FROM THE ALEXANDRIAN LITURGY OF S. BASIL, TAKEN FROM THE GRÆCO-ARABIC.

The deacon reads the diptychs.

Priest. 'Be mindful also, O Lord, of all the sacerdotal order who are now departed, and of those who were in a secular state. Grant that the souls of them all may rest in the bosoms of our fathers, Abraham, Isaac, and Jacob. Lead them, and collect them together in a verdant pasture, on the waters of refreshment, in a paradise of pleasure.'

---

[1] GOAR, Εὐχολόγιον, p. 78.
[2] RENAUDOT, tom. I, p. 19.

After the diptychs the priest says:

'To those, O Lord, whose souls Thou hast received, grant repose in that place, and vouchsafe to transfer them to the kingdom of heaven.'[1]

VII.—CALENDARS OF THE MARTYRS AND SAINTS.

Moreover, the names of those martyrs whose relics were possessed by any particular church came to be inscribed in a particular catalogue, and those holy prelates whose habitual exercise of every Gospel virtue, whilst living, had acquired for them the reputation of heroic sanctity and induced a well-founded belief of their being admitted, by the gates of death, to the joys of heaven, received, as a public testimony of religious reverence towards their memory, the honour of being enumerated after their decease in diptychs appropriated to that exclusive purpose. Such an inscription was equivalent to the present ceremony of canonisation,[2] and, like that public act of the

---

[1] RENAUDOT, tom. I, p. 72.

[2] BENEDICTUS XIV., *De Beatificatione Sanctorum*, lib. I, cap. VI, § 7. The term canonisation is derived from that part of the Mass called the Canon, in which are mentioned the names of the saints who are always commemorated in the holy Sacrifice. On the day when the Pope, after long, most scrutinising, and satisfactory examination into the extraordinary holiness of any servant of God, formally inscribes him among the saints, and thus proposes his conduct as an example of Christian imitation, he writes down the name at the end of those already enumerated in the Canon, and invokes his intercession at the Mass which he immediately offers up to God in honour of the saint.

Church, was a warrant for the faithful to regard the subject of it as a saint, and to invoke his intercession at the throne of mercy.

VIII.—THE NAME OF THE EMPEROR INSCRIBED IN THEM.

In process of time the reigning emperor and his consort, as well as the Roman pontiff and the bishop of that individual church, the patriarchs and other dignified ecclesiastics, were enrolled upon these diptychs, that they might be severally commemorated in the public prayers. Such persons also as were in the habit of making offerings to the church for the use of the altar or the maintenance of its ministers, as well as all those who had been recently baptized, were likewise registered in the diptychs, that they might have their names announced aloud during Divine Service.

IX.—USED AS ALTAR-PIECES.

Nor were these the only purposes for which the Church employed the diptychs. It is the opinion of many ecclesiastical antiquaries[1] that during the later persecutions inflicted on the Church by the Pagan emperors a custom was introduced of painting the effigies of our Divine Redeemer and

---

[1] F. Buonarruoti, *Osservazioni sopra alcuni frammenti di Vasi antichi di Vetro*, p. 259. A. Costadano, *Dissertatio in antiquam sacram eburneam Tabulam, apud* Gori, tom. III, 63.

of the saints upon them, since upon the slightest
intimation of any one's approach they could be
folded up and instantly secreted, and thus prevent the gentile intruder from venting his fury
or pointing his derision against the representation of Christ and of His servants.[1]   When Christianity became the religion of the State and the
pastors of the Church were invested with the
means of decorating the sanctuary with splendour,
there began to be executed for its service diptychs
of ivory and of other materials, wrought with appropriate devices, subjects from the life of our
Lord and symbols of the Christian faith. The
prophets, apostles, and more illustrious martyrs
were imaged on them ; and the poetic encomium
of the pagan consul was replaced by an aspira-
tion to some Christian saint, soliciting his inter-

---

[1] The reader is not hence to conclude that there were no paintings or altar-pieces in the oratories of the ancient Christians
anterior to the epoch when these sacred diptychs commenced to
be employed for such a purpose. That those halls and sepulchral
chambers which had been dedicated to the celebration of the
Eucharistic sacrifice and the general purposes of religious worship
in the catacombs at Rome and Naples, and in the solitary tombs
of Egypt and Jerusalem (see *Appendix* iv, *on the Catacombs*), were
ornamented with pictures by the primitive faithful is evident not
only from those remnants of fresco-paintings in all these places
just enumerated that so unequivocally attest the fact, but also
from the decree of the Council of Eliberis which was noticed at
p. 153 of this volume, and from the graphic description that
Prudentius has left us of the altar-piece in the Chapel of S.
Hippolytus in the Roman catacombs which was presented to the
reader at p. 11 of this volume.

cession. But of the sainted servants of God, no one was so often introduced as the Blessed Virgin Mary.

X.—THE MODERN ALTAR-PIECE DERIVED FROM THE DIPTYCHS.

Besides all these various kinds of diptychs hitherto enumerated, it is evident, from the specimens of those which are still preserved in the museums of the curious, that there were others ornamented with the effigies of our Blessed Redeemer and of the saints, and were employed by the Church for precisely the same purpose as were afterwards the carved and painted reredoses, polyptychs, and triptychs which seem to have succeeded to these ivory diptychs, or, to speak more accurately, to have derived their origin from them. The most satisfactory proofs of this opinion may be gathered amongst those ancient altar-pieces which are still permitted to hang in some of the old churches or have been removed to museums and picture galleries. These ancient altar-pieces are composed, not of two, but of five or three folds, and hence are more accurately denominated polyptychs or triptychs. The centre is as wide as the altar for which it was destined ; the other portions are attached to its sides by hinges, and close over like folding-doors, so that when shut up the interior paintings were not only quite concealed from the eye, but protected from dust and the effects of the weather—a circumstance to which many are indebted for their present high preservation and brilliant tones of colour.[1] From the ancient, a gradual transition was made to the modern form of altar-pieces. At first these triptychs began to be always left open. Then they were formed without any hinges, so that they could not be closed, but were all of one piece. In the seventeenth century the modern style of altar-piece was introduced.[2]

As a summary of the foregoing paragraphs, we may conclude by observing that there were anciently two kinds of diptychs, profane and sacred. The sacred diptychs comprehended two grand classes: one for the dead, the other for the living, each of which, however, was distinguished into particular subdivisions. The sacred diptychs for the dead contained two catalogues: the first was a list of those for the repose of whose souls public prayer was offered up during the Liturgy of the Mass, throughout the Latin as well as the Greek and other Oriental Churches; the second contained a list of those holy prelates and other pious individuals who lived and died conspicuous

---

[1] The reader will immediately call to mind almost innumerable examples of these ancient altar-pieces. There are superb collections of painted triptychs in the National Gallery and in the Museums at Bruges, Brussels, Coeln, Berlin, Munich, and Vienna.

[2] Up to the end of the sixteenth century the centre panel of the altar-piece was generally occupied by a representation of the Epiphany, or of Calvary, or of our Blessed Lady with the Divine Infant.

for sanctity, and whose names were rehearsed in the invocation addressed to them to employ their charitable intercession at the throne of mercy in behalf of the faithful on earth. The sacred diptychs for the living included the names of the reigning pontiff, of the patriarchs, and of those bishops who were actually presiding over the more distinguished churches, as well as of emperors and princes. To insert a living prelate in this diptych was equivalent to a declaration of holding communion with him. To erase his name from it was tantamount to a sentence of excommunication or denouncement of his heterodoxy.

CHAPTER XVI.

ON ALTARS.

By the regulations of the Church it is ordained that the holy Sacrifice of the Mass be offered upon an altar of stone consecrated by a bishop, enclosing the relics of some saint or martyr, and covered with three linen cloths that have been blessed for that purpose with an appropriate form of benediction.[1] An elucidation of this ordinance will form the subject of the present dissertation, in which an inquiry will be first of all instituted concerning the antiquity of the use of altars in the Church; the formula of consecrating them will be then noticed, and the various ways of ornamenting them will be indicated to the reader.

I.—USE OF ALTARS IN THE OLD AND NEW TESTAMENTS.

The use of altars for the purpose of religion is coëval with the preservation of the human race by

---

[1] The Church now, as anciently, employs nothing in the service of religion without first dedicating it to the service of the Deity by prayer, 'For every creature of God is sanctified by the word of God and prayer' (1 Timothy, IV, 5).

Noah; and from the times of the remotest antiquity the greatest respect has been always exhibited for the place which had been more especially appropriated to the worship of the Supreme Being, as well as for the altar which was erected there.

That a particular ceremonial, accompanied by an especial form of prayer, has been invariably followed at their respective dedications seems indubitable. Everyone will remember not only the solicitude with which Noah, on issuing from the ark, immediately hastened to erect an altar for sacrifice,[1] but also the injunctions delivered by Almighty God to Jacob that he should make to Him an altar at Bethel.[2] Moses, too, was thus commanded by the Lord: 'Seven days shalt thou expiate the altar and sanctify it, and it shall be most holy;'[3] and in the Book of Numbers[4] we find enumerated the many splendid presents which were offered by the princes of Israel on the occasion of the solemn consecration of the tabernacle, in the dedication of the altar, when it was anointed.

The excellence and holiness with which the altar of the New Testament is invested are asserted by S. Paul, who admonishes the Hebrews[5] that

---

[1] *Genesis*, VIII, 20. [2] *Genesis*, XXXV, I.
[3] *Exodus*, XXIX, 37. [4] *Numbers*, VII, 12–88.
[5] *Hebrews*, XIII, 10.

'we (Christians) have an altar whereof they have
no power to eat who serve the tabernacle.' To
claim our religious respect for the temple of God,
and to assure us of the hallowed nature of the
altar there, the same Apostle first of all contrasts
the table of the Lord upon which the Eucharistic
sacrifice had been offered, with the table of devils
or the altars upon which meats had been presented in sacrifice to idols;[1] and after assuring
the Corinthians that they could not be partakers
of the table of the Lord and of the table of devils,
he thus interrogates them in a tone which announced a severe reprimand upon the slightest
irreverence towards either altar or temple : 'What,
have you not houses to eat and to drink in?
or despise ye the church of God?'[2]

II.—FROM THE TIMES OF THE APOSTLES TO THE
PRESENT DAY.

If we interrogate the various monuments of
antiquity, we shall discover that everywhere
throughout the Christian world, from the apostolic
era down to the present moment, the same idea
has prevailed that the temples of the Christian
faith were erected for the express purpose of
offering up in them the Sacrifice of the Body
and Blood of Jesus Christ, and that the table
on which this offering was made became a true,

---

[1] I *Corinthians*, X, 18–20.   [2] I *Corinthians*, XI, 22.

a hallowed altar, while the spot on which it stood was regarded as a consecrated sanctuary, the holy of holies of the New Testament, sacred from the tread of any other save the priest of God and his lawfully appointed ministers.

Commencing with the Epistles of S. Ignatius, who, venerable for his years, many of which he passed in the Apostles' society,[1] suffered martyrdom in 107, and continuing our researches down to the present time, we shall discover in the works of ecclesiastical writers, and in the customs and rituals of all the Churches, the most splendid proofs of such a doctrine. The θυσιαστήριον of the Greeks and Orientals and the *altare* of the Latin fathers are terms that most unequivocally signify a place where sacrifice is offered—in other words, an altar.[2]

To strengthen his exhortations to the Philadelphians concerning their unity of faith, their harmony of preaching, and their participation of the same Eucharist, the apostolic father S. Ignatius alleges this reason: 'The flesh of our Lord Jesus

---

[1] S. Ignatius was instructed by S. Peter and S. John; he became bishop of Antioch A.D. 67, and suffered martyrdom, being torn to pieces by wild beasts in the Colosseum, under Trajan.

[2] The term altar may be derived from the two Latin words, *altus*, 'high,' and *ara*, 'table for sacrifice;' whence *alta-ara*, or altar. Amongst the Greeks any altar was denominated θυσιαστήριον, from the verb θύειν, 'to sacrifice;' and in the Old Testament it is called מִזְבֵּחַ, from the verb זָבַה, 'to slay,' 'to kill,' or 'to sacrifice.' The table for the shewbread, on which nothing was offered in sacrifice, was not designated by this, but by another appellation.

Christ is one, and His blood is one, which was
poured out for us; one bread is broken for all,
and one chalice is distributed to all: in every
church there is but one altar, and one bishop,
with the company of elders and deacons my fel-
low-servants.'[1]

The writers of the second century, S. Justin,
Theophilus, and S. Irenæus, contribute, not indeed a direct, but only a collateral evidence on
this point. If they do not expressly use the word
altar, the terms, however, under which they
designate the holy Eucharist sufficiently imply
that, had it been their object to mention the sacred
table on which the Blessed Sacrament was celebrated, they would have called it an altar, as they
invariably denominate the Eucharist itself a sacrifice and oblation. S. Justin, in his dialogue
with the Jew Tryphon, designates the Eucharist a
sacrifice, and observes that it was of this sacrifice
of the Christians, which is offered up in every
place, that Malachias had prophesied.[2] Of the

---

[1] Μία γὰρ σὰρξ τοῦ Κυρίου Ἰησοῦ Χριστοῦ, καὶ ἐν ποτήριον εἰς ἕνωσιν
τοῦ αἵματος αὐτοῦ ἐν θυσιαστήριον ὡς εἰς ἐπίσκοπος, ἅμα τῷ πρεσβυτερίῳ,
καὶ διακόνοις, τοῖς συνδούλοις μου. S. Ignatius, *Epist. ad Philadel-
phenses.* The Protestant writer Joseph Mede acknowledges that
for the first two ages of the Church the table upon which the
Eucharist was consecrated was called by no other name than altar.
The name 'Altar' or 'Θυσιαστήριον.' London, 1637, p. 2.

[2] Διὰ τοῦ ὀνόματος τούτου θυσίας, ἃς παρέδωκεν Ἰησοῦς ὁ Χριστὸς γίνεσθαι,
τουτέστιν ἐπὶ τῇ εὐχαριστίᾳ τοῦ ἄρτου καὶ τοῦ ποτηρίου, τὰς ἐν παντὶ τόπῳ
τῆς γῆς γινομένας ὑπὸ τῶν Χριστιανῶν, προλαβὼν ὁ Θεός, μαρτυρεῖ εὐαρέστους
ὑπάρχειν αὐτῷ. S. Iustinus, *Dialogus cum Tryphone,* § 117.

Eucharistic sacrifice it is observed by S. Irenæus, that the 'oblation of the Church, which the Lord commanded to be offered up throughout the world, is considered as a pure sacrifice before God.[1] In his book on prayer Tertullian combats the scruples which began to possess a number of persons who imagined that on fasting-days it was better not to be present at the celebration of the Eucharistic sacrifice, lest by participating of the Body and Blood of Christ (for the custom of those times was that each one who assisted at Mass should also receive the Blessed Sacrament), they should thus violate the precept of fasting. He asks such persons if the participation of the Eucharist, instead of superinducing a breach of duty towards God, will not rather draw the communicant closer to Him. 'Will not,' he goes on to observe, 'will not your fasting be more solemn if you stand before the altar of God? By receiving the Body of the Lord, and reserving it, both duties will be fulfilled—the participation of the sacrifice and the discharge of your obligation.'[2]

---

[1] Igitur Ecclesiae oblatio, quam Dominus docuit offerri in universo mundo, purum sacrificium reputatum est apud Deum. *Contra haereses*, lib. IV, cap. 18, § 1.

[2] Similiter et stationum diebus non putant plerique sacrificiorum orationibus interveniendum, quod statio solvenda sit, accepto corpore Domini. Ergo devotum Deo obsequium Eucharistia resolvit? An magis Deo obligat? Nonne solemnior erit statio tua, si et ad aram Dei steteris? Accepto corpore Domini, et reservato, utrumque salvum est, et participatio sacrificii et executio officii' (*De Oratione*, cap. XIX). To understand the meaning of this passage it will be

In the same century Origen and S. Cyprian perpetually refer to the altar of the Christian Church.[1]

A crowd of writers present themselves as witnesses for the fourth century. The historian Eusebius, in describing the magnificent church erected in the city of Tyre by its bishop, Paulinus, particularly notices the altar which stood in the middle of the holy of holies, or the sanctuary.[2] S. Optatus, Bishop of Milevis, thus exclaims : 'What is so sacrilegious as to break down, to erase, to remove God's altars upon which you yourselves have once sacrificed ? . . . What is the

---

necessary to remember, first, that the ancient Christians, by the term *statio*, or station, designated their days of fasting, which, on some occasions, they rigorously observed without tasting a morsel of food until sunset ; and on others less solemn, until the first half had transpired of the time which elapses between midday and the closing-in of the evening. The term *station* was applied to indicate, amongst other things, fasting-days, because it was upon them that the faithful dedicated a greater portion of their time to prayer, which they offered up standing, and with their hands elevated and outstretched, as is exemplified in the figures which are given at pp. 223, 224, and 230 of this volume ; secondly, in the first ages of the Church the Blessed Eucharist under one kind—that of bread—used to be given to the laity, that they might convey it home with them and communicate in private. For this purpose they had little vessels called *arculae*, two of which were exhibited to the reader at p. 260 of vol. I, in which they received and carried away from the altar the Eucharistic species. To tranquillise the scrupulous, Tertullian advises that they assist at Mass and reserve the Body of the Lord, which they must receive along with the rest of the faithful, and, carrying it home, participate of it at the conclusion of the vigil, before they take their usual refection.

[1] ORIGENES, *Hom.* III.　S. CYPRIANI *Epist. passim.*

[2] 'Εφ' ἄπασί τε το τῶν ἁγίων ἅγιον θυσιαστήριον, εν μέσῳ θεὶς.—EUSEBII *Hist. Eccl.*, lib. X, cap. 4.

altar but the seat of the body and the blood of Christ?'[1] It was thus that S. Ambrose exultingly observes of the martyrs SS. Gervasius and Protasius, whose relics he had recently translated to his new church: 'Let these triumphant sufferers succeed to that place where Christ is the victim. But He who suffered for all men is upon the altar; they who have been redeemed by His passion are under it.'[2] In his reply to Vigilantius, S. Jerome asks the innovator 'if he considered that the Roman pontiffs acted wrongly when they offered up sacrifice to God over the bones of the deceased Peter and Paul, which true believers regarded as venerable but Vigilantius contemned as vile dust, or when they looked upon the tombs of the martyrs as the altars of Christ.'[3] Passages illustrative of this point from the writings of S. Paulinus of Nola and of the poet Prudentius have already been noticed;[4] and from a multitude of other authorities we will select two only, S. John Chrysostom and S. Augustine. The eloquent Bishop of Constantinople observes that 'the altar which we now use is admirable on account of the victim which

---

[1] Quid est tam sacrilegum quam altaria Dei (in quibus et vos aliquando obtulistis) frangere, radere, removere? . . . Quid est altare, nisi sedes et corporis et sanguinis Christi? *De schismate Donatistarum adversus Parmenianum*, lib. IV.

[2] See note 3 at foot of p. 26 of this volume.

[3] See note at foot of p. 33 of this volume.

[4] See above, pp. 17–24.

is deposited upon it. . . . This wonderful altar,
by its nature, is indeed of stone, but it becomes
holy after it receives the body of Christ.' 'Thou
holdest,' continues S. Chrysostom, 'the altar in
veneration because it sustains Christ's body.'[1]
'Who,' enquires S. Augustine, 'who amongst the
faithful ever heard a priest, standing at the altar,
though it was erected to the honour and worship
of God, over the holy body of a martyr, say in the
prayers, "I offer sacrifice to thee Peter, or to
thee Paul"?'[2] Though nothing could be easier,
it is unnecessary to accumulate additional authorities from the writings of the holy fathers and
other pious men to prove the use of altars in the
Church from the time of the Apostles down to
the present day, the extracts about to be made
from the various liturgies establishing this beyond
dispute.

---

[1] Τοῦτο θυσιαστήριον μὲν γὰρ θαυμαστὸν διὰ τὴν ἐπιτιθεμένην ἐν αὐτῷ
θυσίαν. . . . Θαυμαστὸν τοῦτο πάλιν, ὅτι λίθος μέν ἐστι τὴν φύσιν, ἅγιον δὲ
γίνεται, ἐπειδὴ σῶμα δέχεται Χριστοῦ. Hom. xx in 2 ad Corinthios
epistolam, cap. IX, v. 10.

[2] Quis audivit aliquando fidelium stantem sacerdotem ad Altare
etiam super sanctum corpus martyris ad Dei honorem cultumque
constructum, dicere in precibus : Offero tibi sacrificium, Petre vel
Paule. De Civitate Dei, lib. VIII, cap. 27. It should be observed,
first, that, with one or two solitary exceptions, the Greek fathers
invariably employ the word θυσιαστήριον to indicate the altar of the
Christian temple, upon which the holy and unbloody sacrifice of
the Mass is offered, while they as invariably apply the term βωμός
to signify the altars of Paganism. Amongst the Latin fathers
'altare' is more generally, though not exclusively used, since
'ara' may be very often met with. Secondly, if some of the
earliest Christian writers assured the Pagans that they had no

III.—NOTICED IN ALL THE LITURGIES.

If we turn to the several liturgies in use throughout the universal Church we shall find that they clearly demonstrate both the existence and the necessity of an altar, according to the first and general acceptation of the term, for the purposes of the true and proper sacrifice peculiar to the Christian dispensation. With regard to the liturgy in use throughout the Latin Church, the correctness of this assertion is so conspicuous, and such obvious proofs present themselves in every page of the Roman Missal,[1] that it is unnecessary to detain the reader in discussing this branch of the question. We will proceed at once to the Oriental liturgies. That which passes under the denomination of S. James's is remarkable for its antiquity.[2] In this liturgy

---

altars nor temples, we should bear in mind the motives which prompted them to produce their apologies for Christianity, and the object which they had in view while discussing the question of religious worship with idolaters. They replied to the objection in the sense in which it was propounded, and studied to adopt their language to the intelligence of Gentiles, who regarded an altar as a place where living animals were slaughtered, where bloody victims were sacrificed, and fruits and other productions of the earth were immolated. In such a sense the defenders of the Christian faith, the antagonists of Paganism and exposers of its inanities, could, as they did, assert with truth that they had no altars; but for the mystical sacrifice of the Eucharist they maintained that they had an altar.

[1] See vol. I, pp. 4, 8, 9, 44, etc.

[2] P. LE BRUN, *Explication des Prières et des Cérémonies de la Messe*, tom. II, p. 349, and III, pp. 588–590.

the priest is frequently instructed to speak of the holy, the divine altar, and the sacrifice which he is going to offer up upon it.

It would be impossible to select clearer or more splendid terms to insist upon the obligation of erecting an altar for the purpose of sacrifice than those employed in their respective liturgies by the Oriental Christians in general, whether Greeks,[1] Copts,[2] Syrians, Jacobites, Maronites,[3] Nestorians,[4] or Armenians.[5] Of this the reader may immediately satisfy himself by a perusal of the short extracts from several of the above-mentioned liturgies, which he will find noticed at the end of this volume.[6]

IV.—OF WHAT MATERIAL, AND IN WHAT FORM CONSTRUCTED.

That for the first three centuries the altar was more generally, though not always, of wood is evident from a variety of testimonies. Tradition has handed down the altar in the form of a wooden table, upon which S. Peter, as it is said, was accustomed to offer up the Eucharistic sacrifice of the Mass in the house of the patrician

---

[1] GOAR, Εὐχολόγιον, sive Rituale Graecorum, pp. 615, 618, 835, etc.

[2] RENAUDOT, Liturgiarum Orientalium Collectio, tom. II, p. 500. P. LE BRUN, tom. III, p. 591.

[3] RENAUDOT, p. 1.

[4] P. LE BRUN, tom. III, p. 597.

[5] Ibid., p. 598.

[6] See Appendix I.

Pudens at Rome, where it is still preserved
with much respect in the Church of S. Pudentiana.
S. Athanasius, in describing the sacrileges perpetrated by the Arians, enumerates, amongst other
articles of church furniture which they had burned,
the sacred table, which was of wood.[1] S. Optatus,
bishop of Milevis,[2] and S. Augustine[3] also notice
the destruction of the altars committed by the
enemies of religion. From the earliest times,
however, it is certain that it was customary to
celebrate Mass in the catacombs upon the tombs
of the Apostles[4] and martyrs,[5] not only at Rome,
but in every other portion of the Church of Christ.
The slab of marble which covered the sepulchre
was made to serve as the altar-table, and the low-
browed arched recess that spanned it merely left
sufficient space for the priest to perform the sacred
Eucharistic mysteries.[6] When the altar, as occasionally happened, was not the tomb of a martyr,
it was sometimes of an oblong cubic figure;[7] at
others it resembled a quadrangular table supported
in the centre by a single column, or upheld at its
extremities by two or at its angles by four low

---

[1] *Historia Arianorum*, ann. 356.
[2] *De Schismate Donatistarum adv. Parmenianum*, lib VI.
[3] *Epist.* CLXXXV, *ad Bonifacium*.
[4] See the passage of S. Jerome at p. 33 of this volume.
[5] See p. 17 of this volume.
[6] The form of some of these altars may be seen in the engraving given as the frontispiece to this volume.
[7] BOLDETTI, *Osservazioni sopra i Cimiteri de' Santi Martiri*, p. 35.

columns.[1] For more than fourteen centuries it
has been a universal custom to have the table of
the altar on which the Eucharist is consecrated
of stone or marble ; it should be of one piece.

V.—THE ALTAR ISOLATED IN ANCIENT CHURCHES.

When peace was given to the faithful, and
Constantine erected to the worship of the true
God those sumptuous piles in different parts of
Rome which still attest his piety, the ancient
custom was, as far as possible, preserved, and the
altar was placed immediately over the tomb of the
apostle or martyr in whose memory the basilica
itself was dedicated to the Almighty.

The tombs of the Apostles and more distinguished martyrs who were buried in the catacombs
immediately after their heroic death were employed
as altars, and became objects of particular veneration with both pastors and people, who converted
their sepulchral chambers into little churches,
and ornamented them, as far as their own re-

---

[1] Bona, *Rerum Liturg.*, lib. i, cap. xx, § i. Let us hope that in
future, whenever a church is to be erected, those who have the
superintendence of its construction will summon up the resolution
to insist that the architect not only selects his model from among
the most admired and purest specimens of the art, but that he also
carries out his design conformably to the prescriptions and traditions
of the Church.

sources and the pressure of those grievous times of persecution would allow. But as soon as the exercise of Christianity was tolerated in public these subterranean oratories were much too small, and it became necessary to construct edifices of sufficient capaciousness to contain the multitudes of those who, every day, professed themselves believers in the Gospel. The faithful were, however, unwilling to remove the bodies of the saints from the catacombs, if possible. They wished, and it was natural, to celebrate the holy mysteries on the spot hallowed by the relics of an apostle or of a glorious champion of their once persecuted but now triumphant faith, in the place rendered venerable in their eyes by having been so oftentimes frequented by crowds of saintly men and women who ultimately suffered martyrdom, and were deposited around; which, in fine, was peopled by a world of religious recollections. They consequently had recourse to this expedient of erecting churches, in and about Rome, over those places in the catacombs in which these venerable oratories stood, and contrived that the altar should be placed immediately above the tomb of the apostle or martyr in whose memory the basilica was dedicated to Almighty God. Hence it was that the altar not only stood in an isolated position, but assumed somewhat the appearance of a diminutive temple. The plain and humbly ornamented primitive altar on the tomb itself was not defrauded of any portion of its ancient honours. It was still kept up, and the oratory continued to be as much as ever frequented. To facilitate this not only a communication, by a flight of steps, was opened between the vast and sumptuous basilica and the little modest subterranean chapel, but a deep space was thrown open in front of it, sufficient to present a view of the tomb to the veneration of those above. This sunken space was denominated the *Confession*, because here reposed the remains of one who had not merely spilt his blood, but generously laid down his life itself as a martyr, a witness to the truth, a confessor of the faith of Jesus. Hence, a little later, arose the custom of denominating by the term 'confession' every similar open space in those churches that were not built over an altar in the catacombs, but whither the body of some martyr had been translated and deposited. This method of erecting a sumptuous church over an oratory in the catacombs, and converting the martyr's sepulchre into a confession, we see exemplified in many churches at Rome, but particularly at S. Laurence's outside the walls, and S. Peter's, where the hollow space at the foot of the high altar, with its hundred golden lamps that burn night and day, is celebrated through the world as the Confession of S. Peter, and around which individuals from almost every nation of the earth may be frequently observed kneeling to adore their only Saviour Jesus, and to entreat His favourite servant, the prince of the Apostles, to befriend them with his prayers.[1]

VI.—PLACED TO LOOK TOWARDS THE EAST.

From the period that the Christians were emancipated from the necessity of building their altars in caves and the gloomy windings of the catacombs, or in some retired and solitary corner above ground, to which they might resort with the least probability of attracting the notice of the Gentile and the persecutor,[2] and when they enjoyed the liberty and were in possession of the means to indulge their own ideas and wishes both in the arrangement and disposition of their churches, there are two characteristic features which may be almost invariably discovered in their religious edifices: the erection of the sacred pile so as to run due east and west, and the position of the altar arranged in such a way that it looked

---

[1] The forms of these altars and confessions in the ancient churches at Rome may be seen in a very interesting work entitled *Monumenti della Religione Christiana osia Raccolta delle antiche Chiese, o Basiliche Christiane di Roma, dal quarto, sino al decimo terzo secolo,* and in SEROUX D'AGINCOURT, tom. III, p. 32, and tom. IV, plate XIII, no. 13, etc.

[2] The writer is well aware that, from the commencement of Christianity, its professors had places of assembly dedicated to the especial and exclusive purposes of common worship. Ciampini, Mede, and Cave have ably demonstrated this fact. The position of those churches, however, and the situation of their altars were, it is presumed, in most instances, not so much the result of choice as of necessity.

directly towards the east. This we observe not only in a great many ancient churches still existing in Rome and elsewhere, but we find it noticed in the earliest as well as more recent ecclesiastical writers; Tertullian,[1] the Apostolical Constitutions,[2] Eusebius,[3] Isidorus,[4] and Walafrid Strabo[5] have severally spoken of this ancient custom.

This practice was not adopted without having a spiritual meaning attached to it. It was presumed that while the corporal eye was turned towards the east—the land where Eden's garden stood—and exiled man regretted the occasion of his banishment, the spiritual eye—the soul—would lift her gaze towards heaven, the real paradise—her own, her native home.[6] Nor was it forgotten

---

[1] Likening the church to the residence of the Dove—the Holy Ghost—this writer says : 'Amat figura Spiritus Sancti Orientem.' *Liber adversus Valentinianos*, c. III. And in another place he observes : 'Inde suspicio, quod innotuerit nos ad Orientis regionem precari.' *Apologeticus*, cap. XVI.

[2] In the Apostolical Constitutions it is prescribed that the churches be built in resemblance of a ship's hull and turned towards the east. Lib. II, cap. 57.

[3] The historian tells us that the church built by Paulinus at Tyre looked towards the rising sun.

[4] 'Antiqui, quando templum construebant, Orientem spectabant aequinoctialem ita, ut qui consuleret ac deprecaretur, rectum aspiceret Orientem.' *Etymologiarum liber*, cap. IV.

[5] Cap. IV.

[6] Τούτου χάριν πάντες μὲν ὁρῶμεν κατ' ἀνατολὰς ἐπὶ τῶν προσευχῶν· ὀλίγοι δὲ ἴσμεν, ὅτι τὴν ἀρχαίαν ἐπιζητοῦμεν πατρίδα, τὸν παράδεισον, ὃν ἐφύτευσεν ὁ Θεὸς ἐν Ἐδὲμ κατ' ἀνατολάς. S. BASILIUS, *Liber de Spiritu Sancto*, c. XXVII.

that the prophets of the Old Law delighted to designate the Messiah by the figurative appellation of the Orient, or dayspring,[1] that Sun of justice which was to arise with health in His wings,[2] and that the Evangelists and Apostles of the New Testament employ with equal complacency the same beautiful language in signification of our Divine Redeemer, as they exultingly exclaim that the Orient from on high has visited us,[3] or liken His doctrines to the dawn of morning—to the day-star which arises in the heart.[4]

It is probable that ere this a difficulty will have presented itself to the mind of the reader, who finds himself unable to reconcile with one another two such seemingly conflicting ideas as those which present themselves under the supposition that not only the entrance and whole length of the church formerly presented themselves to the east, but that the altar also looked directly towards the same quarter. It should, however, be remarked that anciently the altar did not stand, as it too often does now, against the wall of the sanctuary, but was isolated, and placed so that the priest or pontiff who offered up the unbloody sacrifice upon it should turn his face, and not, as now, his back, towards the people; hence both the altar and the portals of the church

---

[1] *Zacharias*, III, 8.   [2] *Malachias*, IV, 2.
[3] *S. Luke*, I, 78.   [4] 2 *S. Peter*, I, 19.

were directed towards the east. This we see exemplified in what are called the papal altars in the old basilicas at Rome, but particularly in S. Peter's, where the sovereign pontiff still invariably celebrates Mass on festivals at the great altar which looks towards the people, and consequently towards the portals of the church which open on the east.

VII.—THE DEDICATION OF ALTARS.

Judging from the piety of the primitive Christians, who never performed any action without hallowing it by prayer or some religious ceremony,[1] it is more than probable that, from the apostolic times, no altar was ever used for offering up the holy sacrifice of the Mass without having been previously consecrated by a solemn rite peculiar to that holy purpose; and it is no ill-founded presumption to suppose that the pastors of the Church, in the dedication of their temples and altars, copied the example of the saints of old, who were directed by Heaven itself to consecrate the altar and to dedicate the temple erected to the Deity by a particular and splendid ceremonial.[2] We have the most authentic documents to prove the use of such a rite at the commencement of the fourth century. The ceremony

---

[1] See p. 123 of this volume. [2] See p. 291.

of dedication, which must have been performed in privacy during the times of persecution, began to be celebrated with much public magnificence during the tranquil reign of Constantine. It was then a gratifying spectacle, as the ecclesiastical historian Eusebius informs us, 'to witness how the ceremony of consecration and dedication of the recently erected churches was solemnised in every city.'[1] After describing the dedication of the church of Jerusalem, the same writer informs us that it concluded by the mystical service, or offering of the unbloody sacrifice to God.[2] S. Gregory Nyssen (d. 394) observes: 'This holy altar at which we assist is constructed of stone, which, by nature, is common and nothing different from other flags of stone with which the walls of our houses are encrusted and our pavements are ornamented. But because it is consecrated and dedicated to the worship of God, and has received a benediction, it is a holy table, an immaculate altar, which is no longer to be touched by all, but by priests only, and even by them with veneration.'[3]

---

[1] De Laud. Constantini, cap. XVII.

[2] Vita Constantini, lib. IV, cap. 45.

[3] Ἐπεὶ καὶ τὸ θυσιαστήριον τοῦτο τὸ ἅγιον, ᾧ παρεστήκαμεν, λίθος ἐστὶ κατὰ τὴν φύσιν κοινὸς, οὐδὲν διαφέρων τῶν ἄλλων πλακῶν, αἱ τοὺς τοίχους ἡμῶν οἰκοδομοῦσι, καὶ καλλωπίζουσι τὰ ἐδάφη. Ἐπειδὴ δὲ καθιερώθη τῇ τοῦ Θεοῦ θεραπείᾳ, καὶ τὴν εὐλογίαν ἐδέξατο, ἔστι τράπεζα ἁγία, θυσιαστήριον ἄχραντον, οὐκέτι παρὰ πάντων ψηλαφώμενον, ἀλλὰ μόνον τῶν ἱερέων, καὶ τούτων εὐλαβουμένων. In Baptismum Christi.

S. Ambrose (d. 397) has left us a prayer which
he employed in the dedication of the churches
and altars which he erected. 'O Lord!' devoutly
prayed the holy Bishop of Milan, 'O Lord! I now
beseech Thee to look down as daily high-priest
upon this Thy house; upon these altars which are
this day dedicated; upon these spiritual stones,
in each one of which a sensible temple is consecrated unto Thee; and in Thy Divine mercy
receive Thy servants' prayers, that are poured out
to Thee in this place. Let every sacrifice which
is offered up in this temple, with an entire and
pious sedulousness, be unto Thee as an odour
of sanctification.'[1]

VIII.—THE ALTAR ANOINTED.

Not only did the Church bear in mind the
Divine command issued to Moses of celebrating
the dedication of the altar, but she also remembered that the holy table was more particularly consecrated to the purposes of religious
worship by being anointed with rich and precious
unguents. In the Book of Genesis we read that
the patriarch Jacob, awaking out of his sleep,

---

[1] Te nunc Domine precor, ut supra hanc domum Tuam, supra
haec altaria, quae hodie dedicantur, supra hos lapides spirituales,
quibus sensibile Tibi in singulis templum consecratur, quotidianus
praesul intendas, orationesque servorum Tuorum, quae in hoc loco
funduntur, divina Tua suscipias misericordia. Fiat Tibi in odorem
sanctificationis omne sacrificium, quod in hoc templo fide integra,
pia sedulitate defertur.

exclaimed concerning the spot on which he had been taking his repose : 'How terrible is this place! This is no other but the house of God, and the gate of heaven. And Jacob, arising in the morning, took the stone, which he had laid under his head, and set it up for a title, pouring oil upon the top of it.'[1] Moses was thus directed by Almighty God : 'Thou shalt make the holy oil of unction, an ointment compounded after the art of the perfumer.[2] And therewith thou shalt anoint the tabernacle of the testimony, and the ark of the testament. And the table with the vessels thereof, the candlestick and furniture thereof, the altars of incense, and of holocaust, and all the furniture that belongeth to the service of them. And thou shalt sanctify all, and they shall be most holy,'[3] a command which the Jewish lawgiver carefully complied with, as we find in the Book of Numbers, where it is recorded that 'Moses had finished the tabernacle, and set it up, and had anointed and sanctified it with all its vessels, the altar likewise and all the vessels thereof.'[4] The Church conceived

---

[1] *Genesis*, XXVIII, 17, 18.

[2] The ingredients of the unction are thus enumerated by Moses : 'Take spices, of principal and chosen myrrh five hundred sicles, and of cinnamon half so much, that is, two hundred and fifty sicles, of calamus in like manner two hundred and fifty. And of cassia five hundred sicles by the weight of the sanctuary, of oil of olives the measure hin.' *Exodus*, XXX, 23, 24.

[3] *Exodus*, XXX, 25-29.　　　　[4] *Numbers*, VII, 1.

that the anointing of her altars was an emblematical ceremony which she could appropriately borrow from the Old Law.

At what precise period the Church adopted the ceremony of anointing the altar at its consecration is uncertain. We have, however, testimonies of a date that prove its use at an early period, and it is certain that towards the commencement of the sixth century it became an ordinance enacted by more than one council. The author of the works which pass under the name of S. Dionysius the Areopagite not only observes, in a general manner, that in his time, according to a universal, and (as it would appear from his manner of speaking) a long established rule, a holy ointment was used at the consecration of every sacred thing,[1] but specifically notices, with strong emphasis, that it was a law of the most sacred mysteries that the consecration of the holy altar should be completed by pouring out upon it the hallowed ointment.[2] The Council of Agde (A.D. 506) decreed that altars should be consecrated

---

[1] Τῷ θείῳ μύρῳ χρῆται πρὸς παντὸς ἱεροῦ τελεσιουργίαν. *De Ecclesiastica Hierarchia,* cap. IV, § 10. The Church still retains this ancient practice ; for not only the altar-stone, but the chalice and paten are blessed and anointed by the bishop before they can be employed in the Eucharistic sacrifice.

[2] Καὶ τοῦτο δέ ἱεραρχικῶς ἐννόησον, ὅτι καὶ τοῦ θείου θυσιαστηρίου τὴν ἱερὰν τελείωσιν ἡ τῶν ἁγιωτάτων τελεῶν θεσμοθεσία, ταῖς τοῦ ἱερωτάτου μύρου τελετουργεῖ παναγέσιν ἐπιχύσεσιν. *De Ecclesiastica Hierarchia,* cap. IV, § 11.

not only by the unction of chrism, but also by
a sacerdotal benediction;[1] and the Council of
Epone (A.D. 517) ordained that no altars, excepting such as were made of stone, should be
consecrated with the infusion of chrism upon
them.[2]

IX.—SAINTS' RELICS ENCLOSED IN THE ALTAR-STONE.

Whenever an altar is consecrated some small
portion at least of a saint's relics is invariably
enclosed in it. This universal and established
usage has descended from a venerable antiquity.
From the earliest periods of the Church it was
usual to employ the tomb of a martyr for the
purposes of the altar. Not only did this custom
call to the remembrance of the faithful the
brethren whose souls are described by S. John as
reposing under the mystic altar of heaven,[3] but
it furnished them with an admonition of their
duty of laying down their lives like the martyrs,
if required, in the profession of the faith of Him
who was crucified for their redemption. It would
be superfluous to rehearse the observations we

---

[1] Altaria placuit non solum unctione chrismatis, sed etiam sacer-
dotali benedictione sacrari. *Con. Agathen. can.* XIV, *apud* LABBEUM,
tom. VIII, col. 327.

[2] Altaria nisi lapidea, chrismatis unctione non sacrentur. *Con.
Epaonen. can.* XXVI, *apud* LABBEUM, tom. VIII, col. 562.

[3] *Apocalypse,* VI, 9.

have made in a former chapter in illustration of this ancient practice.[1]

X.—THE ALTAR COVERED WITH LINEN CLOTHS.

Anciently, as now, the table of the altar was overspread with linen cloths. S. Optatus of Milevis notices this practice as everywhere observed in his time. 'Who,' asks that writer, 'who amongst the faithful is ignorant that when the holy mysteries are being offered up the table of the altar is covered over with a linen cloth? During the sacred rites this veil could be touched, but not the wood.'[2] According to the rubrics of S. Gelasius's Sacramentary, not only the altar but the linen cloths are directed to be blessed and consecrated, as they are to serve for enfolding the Body and the Blood of Jesus Christ. 'Deign, O Lord,' says the prayer, 'to sanctify, bless, and consecrate these linen cloths for the use of Thy altar, to cover and envelope the body and blood of Thy Son our Lord Jesus Christ.' In the

---

[1] For these proofs the reader is referred to pp. 13 to 30 of this volume. It is on account of this custom that the priest, on having ascended the steps leading to the altar, kisses that part of it which encloses the relics at the same time that he recites the prayer which may be seen at p. 9.

[2] Quis fidelium nescit, in peragendis mysteriis ipsa ligna linteamine cooperiri? Inter ipsa sacramenta velamen potuit tangi, non lignum. *De Schismate Donatistarum adv. Parmenianum*, lib. VI.

Pontifical[1] of Egbert, who was archbishop of York in 732, are contained the same prayers.[2] The ancient liturgies once used in Gaul and Spain, and at Milan, which still retains the Ambrosian rite, also contain formulas the same in substance and almost similar in expression. Throughout the Latin Church the altar is at all times covered with a cere or waxed cloth and three linen cloths, the uppermost of which should reach to the ground. Over this is laid, at the celebration of the liturgy, a second species of altar-cloth, called the Corporal, and is used for such a purpose, not only in the Western but throughout the Greek and all the Oriental Churches. The Corporal, in the Latin Church, continued for many ages of such dimensions that it completely covered the table of the altar; but the gradual curtailments through which it passed reduced it to its present size of about eighteen inches square, merely sufficient to cover the spot more immediately before the priest upon which he consecrates the Eucharist.

The Greeks also have more than one linen pall

---

[1] A volume which contains all the services in which the bishop takes the chief or a particular part. Martene, in his work *De Antiquis Ecclesiae Ritibus*, mentions a beautiful manuscript copy of Egbert's Pontifical, written in Saxon characters, about the year 950.

[2] Sanctificare, benedicere, consecrareque digneris haec linteamina in usum altaris Tui ad tegendum involvendumque Corpus et Sanguinem Filii Tui Domini nostri Iesu Christi : qui Tecum vivit et regnat Deus. I. M. Thomasius, *Codices Sacramentorum*, p. 121.

upon their altars. The first covering has at its four corners pieces of linen or silk embroidered or painted with the names of the four Evangelists. The second is denominated the flesh-cloth, because, as one of their writers remarks, since the altar may be likened at the same time to the sepulchre and to the throne of Jesus, so the linen cloths which cover it are considered to represent both the shroud that enveloped His blessed body and the mantle of His glory.[1] As a third covering, is spread out a long towel corresponding to the Corporal[2] of the Latin Church, called Εἰλητόν, which has been already noticed at p. 107 of vol i.[3]

XI. — ORNAMENTS OF THE ALTAR—CIBORIUM OR CANOPY—VEILS—THE CROSS—CANDLESTICKS—CHALICES—FLOWERS.

Ciborium.— As soon as the Christian religion had triumphed over Paganism sumptuous churches were erected at Rome, Jerusalem, and in other

---

[1] SIMEON THESSALONICEN., *Liber de Templo et Missa.*

[2] The Greeks have another linen covering for the altar, denominated Antimensia, which is an oblong piece of linen, having attached to it a small purse or bag containing saints' relics. Palls of this description are blessed by their bishops at the dedication of churches, and afterwards are carried about and spread out, before saying Mass, upon those altars that have never been consecrated. They serve, in reality, all the purposes of the portable altars in use throughout the Latin Church.'

[3] In the Constitutions promulgated by the Catholic Archbishops of Canterbury several particular mandates were issued concerning altar-cloths. Walter Reynolds (1313–1327) decreed that 'Lintea-

cities of the empire;[1] in all these the altar
became the principal object of devotion and ornament. The sacred table, which, whenever practicable, was erected over the subterranean tomb of
an apostle or martyr, was itself surmounted and
protected by a canopy of wood, stone, brass, or
silver,[2] supported by four columns, in general of
porphyry or some precious marble, planted at the
four corners of the holy altar.[3] This dome-like

---

mina, Pallae, Corporalia, et alia indumenta altaris integra sint et
mundissima' (LYNDEWODE, Provinciale, p. 235); and amongst the
articles of church furniture which Archbishop Robert Winchelsey
(1293-1313) determined to be incumbent on the parishioners in his
province to provide for their respective parish churches were 'fron-
tale ad magnum altare, cum tribus tuellis,' which Lyndewode, in
his annotations, explains to be an antependium for the high altar,
and three linen napkins—one which was to serve as a towel for
wiping the priest's fingers when he washes them at Mass (see vol. 1,
pp. 29 and 113), the remaining two as cloths to be spread under the
corporal, which, he remarks (p. 252), is denominated by this name
because it signifies the linen bands with which the Body of our
Divine Redeemer was enveloped in the sepulchre.

[1] These churches were denominated Basilicae, not only from the
circumstance of being built after the models of such edifices as bore
that name amongst the Pagan Romans, and of which not a few were
converted into churches, but also from the regal magnificence and
riches which adorned them.

[2] PAULUS SILENTIARIUS (A.D. 555), Descriptio ecclesiae S. Sophiae,
v. 738.

[3] According to the fathers of the Church who have written on
mystic theology, such materials, independently of their richness,
were selected on account of the spiritual meaning attached to them
(S. DIONYSIUS AREOPAGITA, De Caelesti Hierarchia, cap. II, § 2).
Gold was esteemed as a symbol of the celestial essence; hence
the doves and vessels containing the Eucharist were made of this
precious metal. Porphyry, by its deep glowing tinge, was regarded
as a type of divine and lively fervour (De Caelesti Hierarchia, cap.
xv). Most of the ancient altars in Rome have porphyry columns
around them.

canopy was more usually denominated *ciborium* [1]
—Κιβώριον—from its supposed resemblance to the

---

[1] There anciently prevailed a custom, as was remarked before
(vol. I, p. 266), of enclosing the Blessed Eucharist, reserved, under
the form of bread, for the communion of the dying, in a hanging
vessel of gold or silver, made in the form of a tower or of a dove,
which was suspended by a chain from the centre of the altar-canopy
or ciborium, beneath a little tent or tabernacle of silk or precious
stuff.   In process of time this custom was in many churches
changed, and the Blessed Sacrament, contained in a pyx, was
deposited within a tower that was erected on the altar, and that
was accessible only to the priest who possessed the key of its little
portal.   In France the use of the suspended dove or pyx was retained in many churches until the middle of the eighteenth century ;
in the cathedral of Amiens and a few other churches until recently.

The ancient practice of keeping the Blessed Eucharist reserved for
the communion of the sick, and to receive the perpetual adoration
of the people, in a pyx suspended above the altar was observed
in Catholic England down to the fifteenth century, and in many
churches until the schism ; the use, for a similar purpose, of a tower
fixed in the centre of the altar not having been introduced until the
middle of the fifteenth century.   Of this custom we have various
traces in our old native writers.   Roger of Hoveden, professor of
theology at Oxford in 1198, refers to it, as he notices the snapping,
on a certain occasion, of the chain which upheld this pendent
tabernacle, and says : 'Cecidit etiam super altare pyxis, cui corpus
Christi inerat, abrupto vinculo' (*Hist. Anglic.*, p. 486).   And Ger-
vase, the monk of Canterbury (A.D. 1201), in his description of a
fire which consumed part of the cathedral in that city, relates that
the pyx containing the Blessed Eucharist which used to hang over
the high altar was rescued by a certain monk from the conflagration :
'Suscepit a monacho quodam pyxidem cum Eucharistia quae desuper
maius altare pendere solebat.'   Lyndewode observes that, although
the custom followed at his time (A.D. 1422) of keeping the Body of
our Lord within a canopy suspended over the altar was commend-
able, inasmuch as it exhibited the Eucharist in a way more conspicuous to public view for adoration, yet he preferred the method
which he had lately witnessed to prevail in the Netherlands and
in Portugal, of depositing the Blessed Sacrament either under lock
and key within a niche in the wall, or in a tower of masonry
called a Sacrament-house.   For in this manner all irreverence
towards the Sacrament was prevented, by placing the sacred vessel

bowl of a reversed cup, so designated by the Greeks.[1] These ciboria were in very general use during the Middle Ages. In those churches where

---

which contained it beyond the rash and unhallowed touch of the profane, and in a place of security where the cupidity of the sacrilegious could not reach it. 'Licet enim consuetudo Anglicana ut scilicet Eucharistia in canopeo pendeat super altare—commendabilis sit illa consideratione, qua citius repraesentatur nostris aspectibus adoranda, non tamen est commendabilis eo respectu quo ponitur in loco publico, sic quod ad eam manus temerariae de facili valeant extendi. Nam licet in cupa, quae forsan clausa est, pendeat ; tamen ad illam deorsum mittendam, vel forsan cum illa cupa totaliter auferendam, manus temerariae de facili possunt apponi. Et ideo, ut mihi videtur, commendabilior est usus aliorum locorum quae vidi, viz., in Hollandia et Portugallia, in quibus ordinatur unus locus singularis honestus prope altare, in quo reponitur Eucharistia sub clavibus infra parietes vel locum bene munitum conservanda, sic quod nullus ad ipsam Eucharistiam accedere poterit nisi sacerdos loci illius clavem custodiens.' LYNDEWODE, *Provinciale*, lib. III.

In England and France the tower on the altar is now commonly called the tabernacle. In Italy, however, what we understand by 'tabernacle' is termed 'ciborio;' and the canopy (which is usually suspended over the high altar, and in general hangs from the roof of the church, though sometimes, as at Rome, it rests, as anciently, upon four columns) is called 'baldacchino.'

It should be observed that the term 'ciborium,' which properly designates the canopy over the high altar, and is now in Italy applied to signify the little temple in which the holy Eucharist is reserved, has been assigned in England to signify the covered cup itself which contains the sacred species ; while elsewhere the same vessel is generally denominated by the more appropriate appellation of pyx. In the Greek Church the Blessed Sacrament is reserved behind the altar, upon which a volume of the Gospels always rests. A lamp, kept perpetually burning, is suspended in such a manner as to hang between the altar and the place for the Blessed Sacrament, and is regarded by the Greeks as a becoming token of reverence towards the word of God inscribed within the sacred volume, and the Word made flesh, Christ Jesus dwelling amongst us, but veiled under the appearance of the sacramental species. GOAR, Εὐχολόγιον, p. 15.

[1] It is greatly to be desired that the high altar in our churches should be detached from the east wall, at least so far as to afford

there is no ciborium the high altar is required to be surmounted by a canopy of wood or of cloth.[1]

Veils.—Between these columns were suspended veils or curtains, frequently embroidered in the richest manner, and interwoven with threads of gold,[2] which were drawn around the altar until after the Communion. Where the canopy was suspended, the curtain-rods were supported by six or eight latten pillars surmounted by figures of angels holding candles. The custom of veiling the altar at any part of the holy Sacrifice has fallen into disuse in the Latin Church, but is still, though in a manner varying from the ancient practice, retained amongst the Greeks, who divide their sanctuary from the body of the church by a wainscot partition in which there are three door-ways, fitted up below with a small wicket and

---

sufficient room for the bishop with the attendant deacon and sub-deacon to walk round it without inconvenience, as the rubric of the Pontifical directs.

[1] See the *Caeremoniale Episcoporum*, lib. I, cap. XII, § 13, 14, and cap. XIII, § 3.

[2] These veils were called *Tetravela* in the Latin, and Ἀμφίθυρα or Παραπετάσματα in the Greek Church ; and the mystic signification of them, when drawn around the altar, is explained in beautiful language by Simeon of Thessalonica, in his book *On the Temple and the Liturgy*, when he says : 'By the veils of the altar is imaged the celestial tabernacle of God, wherein dwell legions of angels and the saints repose in peace.' GOAR, Εὐχολόγιον, p. 215. The *Liber pontificalis* frequently mentions the presents of these veils which were made by the Popes to the several great churches at Rome : 'Hic fecit in circuitu altaris basilicae tetravela octo, quatuor ex albis, et quatuor ex coccino.' *In Sergio.* 'Fecit et in circuitu altaris, ubi supra, alia vela alba holoserica rosata, quae pendent in arcu de ciborio numero quatuor.' *In Leone* III.

having the higher part of the interstice veiled with curtains on which is painted the figure of the archangel S. Michael, with a stern, terrific countenance, holding in his hand a flaming sword.[1]

The centre opening in this partition, which somewhat resembles the rood-screens in our old English churches, is denominated the royal gate, because it is through it that the deacon, previously to receiving the Eucharist, exhibits it to the adoration of the people, and, also, because at its threshold the laity are permitted to communicate.[2] These gates are closed and the veils spread over them when that part of the liturgy arrives which we denominate the Creed,[3] and they continue so until the elevation.[4] We have already[5] adverted to the beautiful passage in the writings of S. John Chrysostom in which he describes this ceremony. The painting on the curtains is not without its spiritual meaning amongst the Greeks, who conceive that, as the gates of Paradise were guarded by cherubim with a flaming sword,[6] the figure of the archangel brandishing his radiant arms is not inappropriately affixed, like a heavenly sentinel, at the portals of the sanctuary, the Eden where they consider Jesus Christ to have descended, and to be really and substantially present in the Eucharist.[7]

---

[1] GOAR, Εὐχολόγιον, p. 18.   [2] Ibid., p. 151.
[3] Ibid., pp. 75, 134.   [4] Ibid., pp. 84, 151.
[5] Vol. I, page 135.   [6] Genesis, III, 24.
[7] GOAR, Εὐχολόγιον, pp. 134, 135.

Cross.—When the period had arrived that no danger existed of giving scandal to the newly initiated neophyte by exhibiting the figure of the Cross before him, this holy sign was made to constitute a conspicuous ornament on the summit of the Ciborium or canopy [1] above the altar.[2] It was not until the tenth century that the Cross began to be introduced on the altar itself; the Crucifix not until much later.

Candlesticks.—Another conspicuous ornament were the gold and silver lamps and candelabra which encircled the altar, and during the celebration of the holy mysteries shed not only splendour and brilliancy, but fragrance around it, fed as they were sometimes with the most costly aromatic balsams, or supplied by perfumed wax, that diffused odours while they burned.[3]

Chalices.—The chalices and sacred vessels used for offering up the Eucharistic sacrifice were not unfrequently employed on great solemnities to ornament the sacred table, upon which they were arranged in rows, and intermingled with the diptychs or carved ivory tablets of which mention was made in a preceding chapter.[4] Although the

---

[1] PAULUS SILENTIARIUS, *Descriptio ecclesiae S. Sophiae*, v. 738.

[2] SOZOMEN (A.D. 440), *Hist. eccl.*, lib. II, cap. 3. Evagrius (A.D. 594) takes notice of the silver crosses presented by Chosroes to one of the churches at Constantinople to be placed upon the altar. *Hist. eccl.*, lib. VI, cap. 21.

[3] See p. 199 of this vol.

[4] That the altars erected by the early Christians in the catacombs, and those that were built, at later periods, in the side-chapels and

service to which these vessels were dedicated, and not the richness of the materials, formed the criterion of their value in the estimation of the pious Christian, still, however, from a reverence towards the tremendous Sacrifice,[1] we observe that, wherever circumstances would allow it, the most costly substances were appropriated to that purpose and chalices were made not only of glass[2]

---

oratories of large churches, were ornamented with paintings, either in fresco or on panel, is certain. In proof of this may be noticed the chapel with its altar in the catacombs given as a frontispiece to this volume, as well as the description of a cemeterial oratory and altar in the verses of Prudentius. (See pp. 11 and 21 of this vol.) It was only when the custom was introduced of saying Mass in such a manner that the celebrant stood, not with his face, but with his back towards the people, as now, that the altar-piece according to its present form was introduced. The diptychs, exhibiting their sculptures to the spectator, stood unfolded on the isolated altars that looked towards the people. When the position of the altar was changed, that of the diptychs was also, and in time these were replaced by carved or painted reredoses. Hence the origin of our present form of altar-pieces. (See pp. 285–288.)

[1] Not only the altar, but the chalices, patens, and every utensil employed in offering up the Eucharistic sacrifice, were regarded with much religious reverence. They were consigned to the jealous custody of the deacons, who deposited them in a particular recess near the altar, called Scenophylacium, whither they were conveyed, in general, immediately after Mass. Not only the laity, but sub-deacons and every other order of inferior clergy were forbidden to handle them (*Concil. Laodicenum*, cap. XXI, apud LABBEUM, *Concil. Gen.*, tom. II, col. 568 ; *Concilium Agathense*, cap. LXVI, *ibid.*, tom. VIII, col. 336), and it was reputed a sacrilege of the deepest profanation to use them for any other purpose than the celebration of the holy Sacrifice, excepting in the season of distress, when it was considered an act of laudable charity to apply even the sacred vessels of the sanctuary in alleviating the distresses of the poor.

[2] That the chalice used by the impostor Mark was of glass or crystal may be inferred from the manner in which S. Irenaeus notices one of the proceedings of that heresiarch. This Mark, who

and of silver, but sometimes of crystal, onyx, sardonyx, and of the purest gold. Like the altar, they were anciently, as they are now, consecrated and anointed before being used in the service of religion throughout all the Church, whether Latin or Oriental.[1]

Flowers.—The innocent and expressive, and at

---

lived in the second century, availed himself of some sleight-of-hand, or rather of the knowledge of a chemical secret, for the propagation of his errors. Over a chalice containing white wine mingled with a little water it was his custom to pronounce, in imitation of the Christian priesthood in the consecration of the Eucharist, a solemn formula of prayer. At the end of his impious invocation, which was very long, this impostor contrived, no doubt by the dexterous infusion of his chemical secret, that the mixed wine and water in his transparent chalice should be seen to change colour and become purple red, and thus the surrounding gazers were persuaded to believe that through his words the visible transmutation of the wine had been accomplished by the great Charis causing her own blood to flow into the cup for them to drink. 'Pro calice vino misto fingens se gratias agere, et in multum extendens sermonem invocationis, purpureum et rubicundum apparere facit, ut putetur ea Gratia ab iis, quae sunt super omnia, suum sanguinem stillare in illius calicem, per invocationem eius.' Unless the Church then taught, and the faithful believed in, the doctrine of Transubstantiation, the impostor Mark would never have pretended to possess a power similar to that publicly recognised in the priesthood, of changing, by virtue of the words of consecration, wine into the blood of Christ at the Eucharistic sacrifice. Seroux d'Agincourt has given three chalices of glass, one of which is coloured and highly ornamented, tom. VI, pp. 30, 31 ; tom. XII.

[1] See RENAUDOT, *Liturgiarum Orientalium Collectio*, tom. I, p. 323. From the ancient custom of the Church of consecrating by prayers and unctions, not only chalices, but every other vessel and utensil destined for holding the Eucharist, joined to her solicitude in depositing them in places secure from the touch of any but the ministers of religion, and preserving them from the remotest danger of being employed in profane uses, may be collected a powerful argument in favour of the general and ancient belief in the real presence of Jesus Christ in the sacrament of the altar.

the same time beautiful, ornament of flowers was not forgotten by the ancient Christians in the decoration of their churches, but especially of the canopies of the altars. S. Augustine particularly mentions this custom as he notices the renunciation of Paganism for Christianity made by the expiring Martial, whose son-in-law, after praying with much fervour for his conversion at the foot of S. Stephen's altar, approached as he was going away, and carried off from it some of the flowers that were placed there,[1] and conveyed them to the couch of his dying relative.

S. Jerome particularly panegyrizes his friend Nepotian for his devotional assiduity in adorning the walls of the church with a variety of flowers and the boughs of trees;[2] and S. Paulinus of Nola refers to the same practice as he describes the manner of celebrating the annual festival of his patron saint, S. Felix, in the following verses:

Ferte Deo, pueri, laudem, pia solvite vota,
spargite flore solum, praetexite limina sertis:
purpureum ver spiret hiems, sit floreus annus
ante diem, sancto cedat natura diei.
De S. Felice Natalitium, carmen III, v. 108 *et seq.*

---

[1] Deinde abscedens, aliquid de altari florum, quod occurrit, tulit. *De Civitate Dei*, lib. XXII, cap. 8. Flowers should never be placed on the table of the altar; this custom, first introduced in the community chapels of women, whose piety is often not in accordance with reason, has in the present century gradually become common.

[2] Basilicas Ecclesiae et martyrum conciliabula diversis floribus, et arborum comis vitiumque pampinis adumbravit. *Epistola LX, ad Heliodorum.*

Hymn praise to God, ye youths; discharge your vows;
strew flowers around; the threshold wreathe with boughs:
let hoary winter sigh like purple spring,
and the young year his earliest garlands bring
before their season; thus shall nature pay
a fitting homage to this hallow'd day.[1]

XII.—THE RESPECT PAID TO ALTARS.—ASYLUM.

That the ancient fathers of the Church, whether Greek or Latin, were unanimous in exhibiting much religious reverence towards the altar, and in requiring the faithful to regard it with similar respect, is evident from those unequivocal epithets, indicative of honour and of sanctity, under which they designate it in their writings and discourses. The sacred—the divine table; the holy—the most holy altar; the altar of Christ; the table of the Lord, are the common appellations under which they mention it.[2] Nor did this reverence consist in words alone; it was unceasingly manifested by other proofs of homage.

On entering a church, Latins, Greeks, and Orientals have, from time immemorial, been ac-

---

[1] The custom of ornamenting the church with flowers, of strewing leaves upon the pavement and hanging wreaths of evergreens at the doors, is still kept up in Italy. The beautiful flower-carpet, called the *Infiorata*, which is annually designed and strewed along one of the principal streets at Gensano, a town near Rome, for the procession of Corpus Christi, excites the admiration of every traveller by its elegance and ingenuity.

[2] Demonstrative proofs of this may be abundantly collected from the several extracts from their writings which have been noticed in this chapter.

customed to bow towards the altar;[1] we still continue to show this token of our homage to the
sacred table.[2] That not only the threshold and
door-posts of the church were reverenced by the
prostrations and embraces of the pious,[3] but that
similar honours were also paid to the altar, is
evident from the testimony of ancient writers.
S. Ambrose particularly mentions the joy which
animated the soldiers as they entered his church
at Milan and crowded round the altar, which they
devoutly kissed, as they published the news that
the emperor had revoked his edict for surrender-
ing the churches in that city to the Arians;[4] and
S. Athanasius bears witness to the devotion of
many whom he beheld going to the holy altar,
embracing it with fear mingled with joy.[5]

---

[1] See the Liturgies of S. Chrysostom and S. Basil.

[2] The Jews, on entering the Temple, bowed towards the mercy-seat.

[3] Triumphalibus Apostolorum liminibus affusus, etc. SIDONIUS APOLLINARIS, *Epistolae*, lib. I, ep. 5.

Sternitur ante fores et postibus oscula figit.
S. PAULINUS, *De S. Felice Natalitium carmen VI*, v. 250.

Dum postibus haeret in ipsis,
Felicis sancti, lambensque per oscula tergit.
ID., *Carmen in S. Felicem*, v. 191.

See also PRUDENTIUS, Περὶ Στεφάνων *liber*, Hymnus 2 ; S. CHRYSOS-TOMUS, *Hom.* 30 *in Epist.* 2 *ad Corinthios*.

[4] Certatim hoc nuntiare milites, irruentes in altaria, osculis signi-ficare pacis insigne. *Epistola XX*.

[5] Alvarez, in his account of the Ethiopian Christians, informs us that whenever their emperor takes the field four priests accompany him, conveying on their shoulders a case, covered over with cloth of gold, containing the consecrated altar-stone ; four other priests follow to relieve their brethren in carrying the holy burden ; and two minor

Asylum.—The religious respect for the altar is attested by another usage of antiquity, by which the most inviolable protection was afforded to those who fled to the holy table, and thus obtained for themselves, against the oppression of the powerful, the vengeance of an insulted neighbour, or the power of the outraged laws, that security which is denominated 'Asylum.' The antiquity of this usage is attested by the writings of many of the holy fathers. S. Gregory Nazianzen instances the courage of S. Basil in affording protection to a widow who had sought refuge at the altar of his church from the importunity and persecutions which she had to suffer from the Governor of Pontus;[1] and in Synesius, as well as in other ancient writers, the altar is frequently denominated the Ἀσύλου τράπεζα, or table of asylum, from which it was unlawful to force anyone away.[2]

XIII.—RECAPITULATION.

In perusing the foregoing paragraphs, the most superficial observer must have noticed the similarity in the language which is employed and

---

clergy go on before, one of whom bears a cross and a thurible, while the other carries a little bell, at the sound of which everyone whom they meet upon the road stops ; and those who happen to be on horseback dismount, to exhibit a becoming respect to the altar as it passes.

[1] *Oratio XLIII in laudem Basilii Magni,* § LVI.

[2] SYNESIUS, *Epist. LVIII.*

the uniformity of ideas exhibited by all antiquity
with reference to the altar. It is a matter of fact
that forces itself upon everyone's attention, that
from the apostolic era down to the present moment
the pastors of the Church have invariably spoken
of the sacred table, however incidentally they
may have happened to refer to it, as the altar of
the living God—the holy, the sacred, the tremendous altar upon which there is offered up a true,
a real sacrifice. The victim for this sacrifice they
have unanimously proclaimed to be the Son of
God, Christ Jesus, whose same Body and whose
same Blood, once immolated in a bloody manner
on the Cross, are now daily, nay hourly, sacrificed
in an unbloody manner on our altars, and afterwards partaken of both by the sacrificing priest
and the attendant people. Not only do we hear
this doctrine insisted on as a necessary and
universally accredited article of faith, and that,
too, in expressions free from the faintest shade of
ambiguity, and by the teachers of the Christian
religion dwelling in regions widely separated from
each other and flourishing in every age; not
only do we witness the entire body of the faithful assenting to this tenet, and echoing it back,
but we everywhere behold the profound and well-
defined impression with which this belief has
stamped the entire Church of Christ, pastors as
well as laymen, and how it has, from the birth
of Christianity, not only extended its influence

to the arrangement of every liturgy and the construction of the house of God, determining the distribution of its parts and style of ornament, but has also insinuated itself into the civil institutions of so many nations. If we take the trouble to peruse and collate the ancient liturgies, we shall immediately discover that each of their respective authors had no other object in view, while arranging them, than to draw up a rite or ceremony for offering up sacrifice; for in all these venerable documents of primitive belief, without one solitary exception, the correlative terms of victim, sacrifice, priest, and altar are invariably found. If we search amongst the earliest monuments of Christianity in every nation, whether these monuments consist of edifices dedicated to the worship of the Deity and are now standing,[1]

---

[1] During a thousand years, so indissolubly associated in the minds of the inhabitants of these islands were the ideas of altar and of sacrifice, that, on the breaking out of the great heresy at the commencement of the sixteenth century, the patrons of the new belief soon began to encounter the difficulty of eradicating the old doctrine of the Eucharistic sacrifice of the Mass as long as the sacred table upon which it used to be offered was permitted to continue standing. Their innovating zeal was, therefore, immediately employed in overturning every altar which could be discovered, in cathedral, parish church, or private oratory; and such was the searching diligence with which they perpetrated the annihilation of the altars of the Most High God, that scarcely one of the many thousands that once stood in England can now be pointed out to satisfy the cravings of the antiquarian scholar or the architect. How much the turbulence of the religious innovators in the sixteenth century resembled the outrages committed in the fourth by the Donatists and Arians, who burned and overturned the altars of the Catholics! (See p. 301 of this vol.)

or whether they be descriptions of splendid temples now dwindled into dust, and only known by an enumeration of their beauties and magnificence recorded in the writings of the ancients, everywhere we shall find an altar for sacrifice, occupying the principal and most conspicuous situation, and regarded by all as an object of peculiar respect, the immediate boundary of which was considered so hallowed, on account of the sacrifice of Christ Jesus there, that to desecrate it was a heinous crime; and not only the demon-sisters, Hatred and Revenge and Persecution, but Justice herself, glowing with lawful indignation, would arrest her footsteps at the threshold of the sanctuary, nor dare to go forward and drag the object of her pursuit from the horns of that altar which he was embracing. We shall see, too, that it was profound devotion towards the Victim there offered that stimulated the piety of the faithful to spread the richest carpets round the altar; to hang the most gorgeous veils on every side of it; to canopy it with domes of porphyry or silver; to pile gold and precious stones upon it; to render it, in fine, as glorious as possible. Having ascertained the sense of the Church of Christ upon this article of doctrine through such a multitude and variety of testimonies, the sincere Christian will recognise the Mass to be a true and real sacrifice.

CHAPTER XVII.

ON INCENSE.

I.—INCENSE USED UNDER THE OLD LAW.

OF the several rites which the Catholic Church employs for the celebration of her liturgy, and in performing the other functions of Divine worship, the burning of incense is not the least conspicuous. Hence a separate chapter has been dedicated to investigate by whom this ceremony was originally employed in the service of religion, to ascertain its general observance throughout the East and West, and to enumerate some amongst those monuments of antiquity that testify to its adoption in the earliest ages of the Christian faith.

It was thus that Moses received particular injunctions from God to employ incense in the service of the tabernacle : 'Thou shalt make an altar to burn incense, of setim-wood, . . . and thou shalt overlay it with the purest gold, . . . and thou shalt make to it a crown of gold round about, . . . and Aaron shall burn sweet-smelling incense upon it in the morning.'[1] 'Take unto

---

[1] *Exodus,* XXX, 1, 3, 7.

thee spices, stacte, and onycha, galbanum of sweet savour, and the clearest frankincense, all shall be of equal weight, and thou shalt make incense compounded by the work of the perfumer, well tempered together, and pure, and most worthy of sanctification. And when thou hast beaten all into very small powder, thou shalt set of it before the tabernacle of the testimony, in the place where I will appear to thee. Most holy shall this incense be unto you. You shall not make such a composition for your own uses, because it is holy to the Lord.'[1] Directing how the high-priest was to enter into the sanctuary, the Lord commanded that, taking the censer, which he had filled with the burning coals of the altar, and taking up with his hand the compounded perfume for incense, he should go in within the veil into the holy place, that when the perfumes were put upon the fire, the cloud and vapour thereof might cover the oracle.'[2] Amongst the vessels which Solomon provided for the service of the house of the Lord are particularly enumerated the censers, which he caused to be made of the most pure gold.[3]

II.—NOTICED IN THE NEW TESTAMENT.

It was from this religious custom of employing incense in the ancient temple that the royal

[1] *Exodus*, XXX, 34-37.   [2] *Leviticus*, XVI, 12, 13.
[3] 3 *Kings*, VII, 50.

prophet drew that beautiful simile of his when he petitioned that his prayers might ascend before the Lord like incense. It was while all the multitude of the people was praying without, at the hour of incense, that 'there appeared to Zachary an angel of the Lord, standing on the right side of the altar of incense.'[1] That the Oriental nations attached a meaning not only of personal reverence, but also of religious homage,[2] to an offering of incense is demonstrable from the instance of the Magi, who, having fallen down to adore the new-born Jesus and recognise His Divinity, presented Him with gold, frankincense, and myrrh.[3] That he might be more intelligible to those who read his book of the Apocalypse, it is very probable that S. John adapted his language to the ceremonial of the liturgy then followed by the Christians in celebrating the Eucharistic sacrifice, at the period the evangelist committed to writing his mysterious revelations. In depicting, therefore, the scene which took place in the sanctuary of heaven, where he was given to behold in vision the mystic sacrifice of the Lamb, we are warranted to suppose that he borrowed his imagery and selected several of his expressions from the ritual then actually in use, and has, in consequence, bequeathed to us an outline of the

---

[1] *S. Luke*, I, 11.　　　[2] CALMET, *Dissert. in C. II. S. Mark.*
[3] *S. Matthew*, II, 11.

ceremonial which the Church employed in the apostolic ages for offering up the unbloody sacrifice of the same Divine Lamb of God, Christ Jesus, in her sanctuaries upon earth. Now, S. John particularly notices how the 'Angel came, and stood before the altar, having a golden censer; and there was given to him much incense, that he should offer of the prayers of all saints upon the golden altar, which is before the throne of God; and the smoke of the incense of the prayers of the saints ascended up before God from the hand of the Angel.'[1]

III.—ADOPTED BY THE PRIMITIVE CHURCH.

The primitive Christians imitated the example of the Jews,[2] and adopted the use of incense at the celebration of the Liturgy.[3] By the third of the apostolical canons we find it enacted that amongst the very few things which might be offered at the altar whilst the Eucharistic sacrifice was celebrating were oil for the lights and incense.[4] To demonstrate, in his refutation of Daillé, that the use of incense in the Church

---

[1] *Apocalypse*, VIII, 3, 4.

[2] CASALIUS, *De Sacris Christianorum Ritibus*, p. 229.

[3] BONA, *Rerum Liturg.*, lib. I, cap. XXV, § 9.

[4] Μὴ ἐξὸν δὲ ἔστω προσάγεσθαί τι ἕτερον εἰς τὸ θυσιαστήριον, ἢ ἔλαιον εἰς τὴν λυχνίαν καὶ θυμίαμα τῷ καιρῷ τῆς ἁγίας προσφορᾶς.

In answer to the words of Tertullian, who says, 'Thura plane non emimus. Si Arabiae queruntur, scient Sabaei pluris et carioris suas merces Christianis sepeliendis profligari, quam diis fumigandis'

service was coëval with the apostolic age, the learned Protestant Bishop Beveridge adduces an apposite passage from the writings of S. Hippolytus Portuensis, who evidently establishes the fact of its being employed in the ceremonies of the Church in his days by the prophetic remark, that at the consummation of the world the Churches would be overwhelmed with profound grief as they witnessed the cessation of sacrifice and incense.[1] The testimony of S. Ambrose concerning the use of incense at the altar is lucid. 'Oh,' exclaims the illustrious bishop, 'Oh that with us, while incensing the altar and offering up sacrifice, an angel would assist—nay, would render himself visible!'[2] S. Ephrem, a father of the Syriac Church (d. c. 373), directed in his will that no aromatic perfumes should be bestowed upon him at his funeral, but that the spices should

---

(*Apologeticus,* cap. XLII), the Protestant Bishop Beveridge replies that the only legitimate consequence that can be adduced from them is, that perhaps in Tertullian's time the Church of Africa did not use incense, but it by no means follows that incense was not employed elsewhere. *Codex Canonum Ecclesiae primitivae vindicatus,* p. 171.

[1] Πενθοῦσι δὲ αἱ ἐκκλησίαι πένθος μέγα, διοτι οὔτε προσφορὰ, οὔτε θυμίαμα ἐκτελεῖται. *Lib. de Consummatione Mundi.* In an excavation near S. Laurence's outside the walls at Rome, A.D. 1551, was discovered a marble statue of this learned and venerable martyr, who is represented as sitting in an episcopal chair, on the sides of which are engraved his celebrated Paschal cycle and the titles of several works of his composition. This statue is now deposited in the Vatican library.

[2] 'Utinam nobis quoque adolentibus altaria, sacrificium deferentibus assistat angelus, immo praebeat se videndum.' *Expositio Evangelii sec. Lucam,* I, 11.

rather be given to the sanctuary, the aromatics offered to the Almighty, and the incense burned in the house of God.[1]

IV.—INCENSE PRESCRIBED IN ALL THE LITURGIES.

The use of incense in all the Oriental churches is perpetual and almost daily, nor do any of them ever celebrate their Liturgy without it, unless compelled by necessity.[2] The Coptic as well as the other Eastern Christians observe the same ceremonial as the Latin Church in incensing the altar, the sacred vessels, and ecclesiastical personages.[3]

The most ancient of the three Greek Liturgies is that of S. James, from whom it is esteemed by the Greeks and Syrian Christians of Jerusalem to have been originally derived.[4] This liturgy commences with burning incense, which the celebrant puts into the thurible after he has approached to the altar. Immediately afterwards he incenses the Eucharistic bread, the smaller veil with which

---

[1] 'Ne cum aromatibus me sepeliatis ; non enim hic mihi honor prodest: neque mecum suaves odores ponatis ; non enim decet me gloria. Sed thura date in sanctuario ; me autem orationibus vestris comitamini. Aromata offerte Deo, et Psalmis me prosequimini. Pro odoribus et aromatibus, mei memoriam in deprecationibus vestris peragite. Quid enim mortuo proderit suavis odor, iam sensu carenti ? Incensa adolete in domo Dei, ut qui illam ingrediuntur, suavi odore perfundantur.'

[2] RENAUDOT, *Liturgiarum Orientalium Collectio*, tom. I, p. 200.

[3] *Ibid.*   [4] *Ibid.*, tom. II, pp. 2, 3.

he covers the chalice, and the larger one which he spreads over the disc and chalice. He then incenses all the altar around, as well as those who are assisting there. Meanwhile all recite the following prayer as the officiating priest passes: 'Through the grace of Thy benignity, receive the pure incense which the sons of the faithful Church have offered to Thee to propitiate Thy divinity. Have mercy on the penitent, and as Abraham's oblation on the mountain's top was received, and as the odour of the incense of Aaron the priest was sweet to Thee, so may the odour of our incense be grateful unto Thee, and mayest Thou be appeased by it, O God of much mercy.'[1]

Amongst the munificent and truly imperial donations of Constantine the Great to the churches of Rome, the *Liber pontificalis* mentions two thuribles formed of the purest gold presented by that emperor to the Lateran basilica, and a third, likewise of the purest gold and ornamented with a profusion of gems and precious stones, given by him to the baptistery of the same church.[2]

The use of the thurible for burning incense during the solemnization of Mass amongst the Anglo-Saxons was not passed over without an

---

[1] RENAUDOT, *Liturgiarum Orientalium Collectio*, tom. II, p. 4.

[2] Thimiamateria duo ex auro purissimo pens. libras triginta. . . . Thimiamaterium aureum cum gemmis prasinis et hyacinthinis xlii. pens. libras decem. *Liber pontificalis, in vita S. Silvestri.*

especial notice by our countryman, the celebrated
Alcuin, who has left a poetical description of this
rite.[1]

V.—SPIRITUAL MEANING OF INCENSE.

If we come to inquire, we shall find that it
would be difficult to select anything which could
be a more appropriate symbol of prayer.

1. The burning of incense at the altar indicates
that the place is holy and consecrated to the
worship of Almighty God, in whose service every
creature ought to be employed, and, if necessary,
consumed, to exhibit a proper homage and to
proclaim His glory.

2. A venerable antiquity informs us that the
incense burnt around the altar, whence, as from
a fountain of delicious fragrance, it emanates and
perfumes the temple of God, has ever been regarded as a type of that good odour of Jesus
Christ which should exhale from the soul of
every true disciple.

3. Incense has invariably been considered as
beautifully figurative of the sincere Christian's
prayers. In fact, it would be impossible to select
any symbol better calculated to signify to us

---

[1] Hic quoque Thuribulum capitellis undique cinctum,
   pendit de summo fumosa foramina pandens
   de quibus ambrosia spirabunt thura Sabaea
   quando sacerdotes Missas offerre iubentur.

                ALCUINUS, *Poema* III.

what our prayers should be. The incense cannot ascend on high unless it be first enkindled; so our prayers, which are, in reality, the desires of the heart, cannot mount before the throne of Heaven unless that heart be glowing with the fire of God's holy love. Nothing arises of the incense but what is of a grateful odour; we should, therefore, ask of God that He would prepare our hearts in a manner that such petitions may be breathed from them as have a holy fragrance; we should exclaim with the Psalmist: 'Let my prayer, O Lord, be directed as incense in Thy sight.'[1] The whole of the incense is consumed, and every particle of it ascends in odorous vapours; so, also, all our aspirations should tend upwards towards our God, nor ought any of them to hover on the earth.

4. This spiritual perfume, to which all the ancient liturgies refer, is not only symbolical of our petitions, but especially typifies the prayers of the saints, which are so often described in Holy Scripture to be an odour of sweetness before Heaven. 'The four-and-twenty ancients,' says S. John, 'fell down before the Lamb, having every one of them harps, and golden vials full of odours, which are the prayers of saints.'[2]

---

[1] *Psalm*, CXL, 2.   [2] *Apocalypse*, v, 8.

CONCLUSION.

We have now brought to a conclusion the remarks which were considered expedient to illustrate those several points of doctrine and ritual observance comprehended in the Liturgy or holy Sacrifice of the Mass. The reader, in his perusal of them, must have observed the perpetual and, in numerous instances, exclusive reference which was made to the testimony of the sacred volumes, and it is presumed, in the opinion of the unbiassed reader, with such success as to warrant the assertion that those articles of Catholic doctrine here elucidated, far from being in any wise opposed to the spirit or contradicted by the letter of the Holy Scriptures, are triumphantly confirmed by them on every occasion.

Not only will the celebration of the holy Sacrifice exhibit to him who is separated from the Catholic Church in religious credence, a form of public worship which alone accurately realizes the prophetic declaration of Malachias;[1] not only will it point out to his pious notice that clean oblation offered up to Heaven amid every nation of the Gentiles, from the rising to the setting of the sun; but the Scripture proofs on which it is based must vindicate the truth of its being instituted by Jesus Christ Himself.

---

[1] *Malachias*, I, II.

In the illustration of the ceremonies and usages which accompany the solemnization of Mass, however superficial in his observations, every stranger to our Liturgy must have had his attention at once arrested by the venerable and apostolic antiquity of this service. In its rites he witnesses a ceremonial, in its language he hears a voice, in the vestments which array its ministers he perceives so many testimonials which alone are sufficient to substantiate the ancient origin of the Mass and refer its introduction to an epoch which beheld the birth of Christianity.

A doctrine which was promulgated by the lips of Truth itself, Christ Jesus, and invariably delivered as a portion of His Gospel to those people who were initiated in its mysteries—a ceremonial which was instituted by the Apostles and regulated by those who more immediately succeeded them, assuredly demand, and should obtain from each sincere follower of Christ, the recognition of their several claims upon his reverence. Such is the Eucharistic Sacrifice of the New Law, called the Mass, an elucidation of the doctrines and an explanation of the ceremonies of which have constituted the object of the present volumes.

APPENDIX.

APPENDIX I.

Referred to at p. 225, and exhibiting extracts from the Ancient Liturgies, in proof that the doctrine of the Real Presence must have been taught in all the Churches which the Apostles or their immediate disciples founded.

THE late venerable Bishop Poynter, from whose work entitled 'Christianity ; or, The Evidences and Characters of the Christian Religion. London, 1827,' the following extracts were made, observes : 'The substance of the ancient Liturgies was derived from the Apostles, and communicated by them to the Churches where they preached and established the religion of Christ. The first Liturgy was that which was formed and used by the Apostles in the Church of Jerusalem. . . . Then other Liturgies were introduced into the other Patriarchate Churches in the East, viz., of Alexandria, Antioch, and Constantinople.

'The names or titles affixed to the Liturgies are of little signification. Some of them, indeed, refer to the apostle who introduced the form of Christian worship in the churches where these Liturgies were used. But what is of the highest consequence is, that the Liturgies contain the common form and order of public worship observed in those churches, and, consequently, that they contain a public profession of the faith of all the clergy and people attached to them in the ages in which these Liturgies were in use.

'The most sacred part of the form of Divine worship, the *Canon* (called the *Anaphora* in the Oriental Liturgies), during the first two or three centuries was only committed to memory and retained by the bishops and priests, as the Apostles' Creed was learnt and retained by the faithful. The *Canon* was not written till about the beginning of the fifth age, when the danger of exposing all that was most sacred in the mysteries of religion to the derision and blasphemy of infidels was not so great as it was in the first two or three centuries. But when the *Canon* was generally committed to writing, it was found to be the same, in substance, in all Christian countries. This showed the unity of its origin, in the unity of that faith which was everywhere taught by the Apostles, and which was the spirit of the body and language of the Liturgies.

'Amongst the Oriental Liturgies, those of the Greek schismatical Church, and particularly those of the Nestorians and Eutychians, are very deserving of notice. These Churches have received no rite of religion, no tradition, no doctrine, from the Church of Rome since the time of their separation from its faith or communion. The Greek schismatical Church separated about the year 890, the Eutychians about 451, and the Nestorians about 431. The doctrinal language of the Liturgies of these Churches was not borrowed from the Church of Rome after the period of their separation; nor can any reasonable suspicion be entertained that it was worded with any design of favouring the doctrine of the Roman Catholic Church.

'The Liturgies of the Nestorians and Eutychians were not originally composed by the founders of those sects; they were the Liturgies of the Churches in which Nestorius and Eutyches were instructed in the Christian faith. A few insertions were afterwards introduced into them, expressing the peculiar doctrines of these heretical teachers, which were as much in opposition to each other as they were to the common doctrine of all other Christian Churches. But on all the other points of Christian doctrine and worship, on the Trinity, on the Sacrifice of the Mass, on the Real Presence, on Transubstantiation, on the Invocation of Saints, on Prayers for the Dead, etc., the Liturgies of the Nestorians and Eutychians are perfectly conformable to all other ancient Liturgies. This circumstance affords strong evidence that the doctrines and religious rites of all Christian Churches were the same previously to the period of the separation of Nestorius and Eutyches from the faith of the Catholic Church. Their errors were against two articles of the mystery of the Incarnation. Nestorius denied the unity of person in Christ, and Eutyches denied the distinction of two natures in Christ.'

From the Liturgy of S. James.[1]—RENAUDOT, tom. II.

'*Priest.* Have mercy on us, God the Father Almighty, and send Thy Holy Spirit, the Lord and Giver of life, equal in dominion to Thee and to Thy Son, consubstantial and co-eternal, . . . that coming, He may make this bread the life-giving body, the saving body, the heavenly body, the body giving health to souls and bodies, THE BODY OF OUR LORD GOD AND SAVIOUR JESUS CHRIST; for the remission of sins, and eternal life to those who receive it.

'*People.* Amen.

'*Priest.* And may make what is mixed in this chalice the blood of the New Testament, the saving blood, the life-giving blood, the heavenly blood, the blood giving health to souls and bodies, THE BLOOD OF OUR LORD GOD AND SAVIOUR JESUS CHRIST; for the remission of sins and eternal life to those who receive it.

'*People.* Amen.'—*Page* 33.

'*The Priest from the larger part of the Eucharistic bread breaks off a smaller part, which he dips in the chalice, and with it signs the rest, in the form of a cross, saying:* The blood of our Lord is sprinkled on His body, in the name of the Father ✠, and of the Son ✠, and of the Holy Ghost ✠.'— *Page* 41.

'*The Priest takes the body of Christ, saying:* Grant, O Lord,

---

[1] This Liturgy was used in the Church of Jerusalem, and is usually denominated the Liturgy of S. James, as the substance of it was delivered by that apostle. Of all the Liturgies it is the most venerable for its antiquity, and has been commonly employed throughout Syria. The most celebrated critics consider it as the Liturgy expounded by S. Cyril of Jerusalem in his lectures to the catechumens delivered in Lent, and to the newly baptized during Paschal time, probably in the year 347.

that our bodies may be sanctified by Thy holy body, and that our souls may be purified by Thy propitiatory blood,' etc.

'*Then he distributes the Eucharist to the priests, deacons, and laity, saying:* The body and blood of our Lord Jesus Christ is given to thee, for the pardon of offences, and the remission of sins, in this world, and in the next.'—*Pages* 41, 42.

From the Liturgy of S. Mark.[1]—RENAUDOT, tom. I.

'*Priest.* To Thee, O Lord our God, from Thy own gifts we have offered before Thee what is Thine: . . . send down upon us, and upon this bread and chalice, Thy Holy Spirit, that He may sanctify and consecrate them, as God Almighty, and may make the bread indeed the body.

'*People.* Amen.

'*Priest, raising his voice.* And the chalice, the blood of the New Testament, of the very Lord, and God, and Saviour, and our sovereign king, Jesus Christ.'—*Page* 157.

'*Priest.* Supreme Lord, God Almighty, . . . we beseech Thee to expel the darkness of sin from our minds, and to exhilarate them with the splendour of Thy Holy Spirit, that, filled with a lively sense of Thee, we may worthily partake of the good things that are given unto us, THE IMMACULATE BODY AND PRECIOUS BLOOD OF THY ONLY BEGOTTEN SON, our Lord and God, and Saviour, Jesus Christ,' etc.

'*The Priest, when he gives the communion to the clergy, says:* The holy body; *and at the chalice he says:* The precious blood of our Lord and God, and Saviour.

'*The Priest says the prayer of thanksgiving:* We pray and beseech Thee, O good Lord, lover of mankind, that the communion of the holy body and precious blood of Thy only begotten Son may be to us . . . a viaticum of eternal life,' etc.—*Page* 163.

---

[1] This Liturgy was used in the Church of Alexandria, and is generally denominated the Liturgy of S. Mark. It exhibits the ancient rite of the Church of Alexandria, and was constantly employed amongst the Melchites or orthodox Christians of Egypt, till they were compelled to adopt the Liturgy of Constantinople.

'*Priest.* Thou hast given us, O Lord, sanctification, in the participation of the most holy body and precious blood of Thine only begotten Son.'—*Page* 165.

From the Liturgy of S. Chrysostom.[1]—GOAR.

'*The Deacon goes to the Priest, and both adore thrice before the holy table, and they pray secretly:* O God, be propitious to me a sinner.

'*The Deacon, bending his head, shows the holy bread on the stole, and says secretly:* Bless, O Lord, the holy bread. *And the Priest, standing erect, signs the holy mysteries thrice with a cross, and says secretly:* Make indeed this bread the precious body of Thy Christ.

'*The Deacon.* Amen. *And again the Deacon:* Bless, O Lord, the holy chalice; *and the Priest, blessing it, says:* And what is in this chalice, the precious blood of Thy Christ.

'*The Deacon.* Amen.

'*The Priest prays in secret:* Look down on us, O Lord Jesus Christ our God, from Thy holy dwelling, and from the throne of the glory of Thy kingdom, and come to sanctify us, Thou who sittest together with the Father in the highest heavens, and art here invisibly present with us; and vouchsafe, with Thy powerful hand, to impart to us Thy immaculate body and Thy precious blood, and by us to all the people.

'*Priest.* Holy things for holy persons.

'*The Priest, with attention and devotion, dividing the holy bread into four parts, says:* The Lamb of God is broken and divided, the Son of the Father; He is broken, but is not diminished; He is always eaten, but is not consumed; but He sanctifies those who are made partakers.'—*Page* 81.

'*The Priest, holding the holy bread, presents it to the Deacon; and the Deacon, kissing the hand presenting it, receives the holy*

---

[1] This Liturgy is followed by all the Greek Christians of the Oriental and the Western Churches, as well as by the Georgians, Mingrelians, Bulgarians, Russians, etc.

bread, saying: Give me, O Lord, the precious and holy body of our Lord God and Saviour Jesus Christ. *The Priest says:* I give to thee the precious and holy and pure body of our Lord and God and Saviour Jesus Christ, for the remission of sins unto life everlasting.

'*In like manner the Priest receives the holy bread, and bowing down his head before the holy table, prays in this sort:* I believe, O Lord, and I confess, that Thou art the Christ the Son of the living God,' etc.—*Page 82.*

'*Holding the chalice, he calls the Deacon, saying:* Deacon, approach; *and the Deacon approaches, and adores once, saying:* Behold, I come to the immortal King, *and* I believe, O Lord, and confess,' etc.

'*And the Priest says:* 'Servant of God, Deacon N., thou dost communicate of the precious and holy body and blood of our Lord and Saviour Jesus Christ, for the remission of thy sins, and everlasting life.'—*Page 83.*

From the Syriac Liturgy of S. Basil, one of the most ancient in use among the Syrians.—RENAUDOT, tom. II.

'*The Priest.* May Thy Holy Spirit come down upon us and upon these gifts which we have presented, and may He sanctify them, . . . and make this bread, the glorious body of our Lord Jesus Christ, the heavenly body, the life-giving body, the precious body for the expiation of faults and the remission of sins, and eternal life, to those who receive it.

'*The People.* Amen.

'*The Priest.* And this chalice, the precious blood of Jesus Christ, the Lord God, who has dominion over all things, the redeeming blood, the life-giving blood, the expiating blood, which was poured forth for the redemption and life of the world, for the expiation of faults, and the remission of sins, and eternal life to those who receive it.

'*The People.* Amen.'—*Page 554.*

From the Liturgy used by the Nestorians, called the Liturgy of the Holy Apostles.[1]—RENAUDOT, tom. II.

'*The Priest breaks the Host, which he holds in his hands, into two parts; places that which is in his left hand on the paten, and with the other, which he holds in his right hand, he makes a sign over the chalice, saying:* The precious blood is signed with the holy body of our Lord Jesus Christ. In the name of the Father, and of the Son, and of the Holy Ghost. Amen.

'*Then he dips it to the middle of the chalice, and with it signs the body, which is on the paten, saying:* The holy body is signed with the propitiatory blood of our Lord Jesus Christ. In the name of the Father, and of the Son, and of the Holy Ghost. Amen.

.   .   .   .

'*The Priest.* Christ our God, Lord, King, Saviour and giver of life, has graciously made us worthy to receive His body and His precious and sanctifying blood,' etc.—*Page* 596.

From the Liturgy of Nestorius.—RENAUDOT, tom. II.

'May the grace of the Holy Ghost come, and dwell, and rest on this oblation which we are offering before Thee; may He sanctify it, *i.e.*, this bread and chalice, the body and blood of our Lord Jesus Christ, Thou transmuting them, and sanctifying them, by the operation of the Holy Ghost; that the receiving of these holy mysteries may avail all who receive them, unto eternal life, and resurrection from the dead, and expiation of bodies and souls, enlightening of knowledge, confidence before Thee, and everlasting salvation, etc. May we be worthy with a pure conscience to partake of the body and blood of Thy Christ,' etc.—*Pages* 633, 634.

---

[1] The Liturgy of the Holy Apostles is the ancient Liturgy of the churches of Syria before Nestorius. In the Liturgy of Nestorius, which was the old Liturgy of the Church of Constantinople, that heresiarch has inserted his error in the Preface.

After Communion.

'Since we have externally received Thy body, may Thy virtue internally dwell in us. . . . Grant that Thy living body, O Lord, which we have ate, and Thy pure blood which we have drunk, may not turn to our detriment, but to the expiation of our crimes, and the remission of our sins, O Lord of all,' etc.—*Page* 634.

From the Coptic Liturgy, used by the Jacobites (or Eutychians), called the Liturgy of S. Basil.[1]—RENAUDOT, tom. I.

'*The Priest shall say the invocation:*
'We beseech Thee, O Christ our God, . . . that Thy Holy Spirit may come down upon us, and upon these gifts and offerings, and may sanctify them, and may make them Thy holy of holies.

'*People.* Amen.

'*The Priest raising his voice:* And may He make indeed this bread (*he shall make the sign of the Cross thrice over the bread*) the holy body of the same Lord our God and Saviour Jesus Christ, which is given for the remission of sins, and eternal life, to him who shall partake of it.

'*People.* Amen.

'*The Priest shall make the sign of the Cross thrice over the chalice, and shall say:* And this chalice, the precious blood of Thy New Testament, of the same Lord our God and Saviour Jesus Christ, which is given for the remission of sins and life everlasting to those who shall partake of it.

'*People.* Amen.—*Page* 16.

'*Priest.* We pray (God the Father) to make us worthy of the communion and participation of His divine and immortal mysteries, the holy body and precious blood of His Christ.

---

[1] The Liturgies of S. Basil, of S. Gregory, and of S. Cyril were in common use among the Jacobites in Egypt, so called from James the Syrian (who died in 557), one of the Eutychian leaders who rejected the Council of Chalcedon and taught that there is only one nature in Christ.

'*People.* Amen.

'*The Priest elevates the Despoticon (or larger part of the consecrated Host), bows down, and says with a loud voice:* Holy things for holy persons. *All the people prostrate themselves with their faces to the ground. The Priest, holding his right hand elevated with three parts of the consecrated Host in it, says:* The holy body and precious, pure, true blood of Jesus Christ the Son, our God. Amen. The body and blood of Emanuel, our God, this is in real truth. Amen. I believe, I believe, I believe and confess, to the last breath of my life, that this is the life-giving body of Thine only begotten Son, our Lord God and Saviour Jesus Christ. He received it from the Lady of us all, the Mother of God, the sacred and holy Mary.'—*Page 23.*

From the Alexandrian Liturgy of S. Basil.—RENAUDOT, tom. I.

'*After elevating the larger part of the consecrated Host, and saying,* Τὰ ἅγια τοῖς ἁγίοις, *the Priest says the Confession of Faith:* The holy body and precious blood of Jesus Christ the Son of God. Amen.

'*People.* Amen.

'The holy, precious body and true blood of Jesus Christ, the Son of God. Amen.

'*People.* Amen.

'I believe, I believe, I believe and confess, till my last breath, that it is the very life-giving flesh of Thy only begotten Son, our Lord God and Saviour Jesus Christ. He took it of our holy Lady, Mother of God, and ever Virgin Mary,' etc.—*Page 83.*

APPENDIX II.

*Extracts from the Liturgies referred to at p. 335 of vol. 1,
showing the unanimity of all the Oriental Liturgies in
the invocation of the saints departed.*

From the Liturgy of S. James.—RENAUDOT, tom. II.

'*Deacon. The Memorial of Saints.* Again and again we
commemorate the truly happy, and praised by all the generations of the earth, the holy, blessed, ever Virgin Mary,
the Mother of God; and at the same time we celebrate
the memory of the prophets, apostles, evangelists, preachers,
martyrs, and confessors, etc.

.   .   .   .

'*The Priest, raising his voice, says:* Place us by Thy grace
amongst Thy elect, who are written in heaven. Wherefore
we celebrate their memory, that whilst they are standing
before Thy throne they may be mindful of our poverty and
weakness, and may, together with us, offer to Thee this tremendous and unbloody sacrifice, for the protection of the
living, for the consolation of the weak and unworthy, such
as we are, for the repose and good name of those who have
already departed in the true faith, our fathers, our brothers,
and our masters, through the grace and mercy,' etc.

'*People.* Amen.'

From the Liturgy of S. Chrysostom.—GOAR, Εὐχολόγιον
sive Rituale Graecorum.

'*Priest.* By the intercession of the most holy, immaculate,
blessed above all, our glorious Lady, Mother of God, and ever
Virgin Mary, by the virtue of the glorious and vivifying Cross,
and of all the saints, may Christ, our true God, have mercy
on us, as a God of goodness and clemency.

'*Choir.* Amen.'—*Page* 63.

'*Priest.* We also offer to Thee this rational service, for the sake of those who repose in Christ . . . the prophets, apostles, martyrs. . . . *Raising his voice.* Particularly the most holy, pure, blessed above all, our glorious Queen, the Mother of God, and ever Virgin Mary.

'*The Choir sings:* It is truly meet to praise thee, Mother of God, who art always to be blessed, and art free from all sin, who art the Mother of our God, to be venerated above the cherubim, and incomparably more glorious than the seraphim, who in all purity didst bring forth God the Word; we magnify thee, who art truly the Mother of God. Protect us, O God, by the prayers of S. John the Prophet, Precursor and Baptist, of Saint N., whose memory we celebrate, and of all the saints; and be mindful of all who have slept before us in the hope of the resurrection to eternal life.'

*From the Liturgy used by the Nestorians, called the Liturgy of the Holy Apostles.—*RENAUDOT, tom. II.

'*The Priest says this prayer in secret:* Mother of our Lord Jesus Christ, pray for me to the only begotten Son, who was born of thee, that He may forgive me my offences and my sins, and may receive from my weak and sinful hands this sacrifice, which in my weakness I offer on this altar, through thy intercession for me, O holy Mother.'—*Page* 588.

*From the Liturgy of Nestorius.—*RENAUDOT, tom. II.

'*Priest giving the blessing.* May He (the King of kings and Lord of lords) bless this congregation, and preserve us; may He heal our wounds, and cleanse our consciences; may He instil the dew of His grace and mercy on our souls; may He establish tranquillity and peace amongst us; may we be sealed up and guarded by the living sign of the Cross, against all evils, by the prayer of our Lady, the blessed Mary, and by the prayer of all the saints of our Lord, who have pleased Him, and who please Him now and for ever.'—*Page* 635.

'*Prayer on Festivals:* May Saint D. N., who is glorious in the assembly of the saints, preserve you from ill fortune, from devils and wicked men. May he pray for this weak, poor, and unworthy congregation of those who are still his disciples, that they may be preserved from all trouble.'—*Page* 637.

From the Coptic Liturgy, used by the Jacobites (or Eutychians), called the Liturgy of S. Gregory.—RENAUDOT, tom. I.

'*Priest.* Vouchsafe, O Lord, to be mindful of all the saints who have pleased Thee from the beginning, of our holy fathers, . . . and of all the spirits of the just, who being made perfect, are departed in the faith; but principally, of the holy, glorious, ever Virgin Mother of God, holy Mary, and of S. John, . . . and of the whole choir of Thy saints, by whose prayers and intercessions, have mercy on us all, for the sake of Thy holy name which is invoked upon us.'—*Pages* 33, 34.

From the Coptic Liturgy used by the Jacobites (or Eutychians), called the Liturgy of S. Cyril.—RENAUDOT, tom. I.

'*Priest.* We, O Lord, are not worthy to offer prayers for these blessed souls; but, whereas they are standing before the throne of Thine only begotten Son, may they intercede for us, poor and infirm as we are. Forgive our iniquities, for the sake of their prayers, and for the sake of Thy blessed name, which is invoked upon us.'—*Pages* 41, 42.

APPENDIX III.

VINDICATION OF THE CATHOLIC CANON OF SCRIPTURE.

As some amongst those books which are erroneously enumerated as apocryphal by Protestants have in the preceding pages been quoted with equal reverence as those other portions of the sacred volume which are recognised by all to be the genuine word of God, it may perhaps be useful to offer to the reader's consideration the following remarks on the Catholic Canon of the Holy Scriptures.

Protestants object that the book of Tobias, the first and second books of Macchabees, with several other portions of Scripture, are apocryphal, and that the Church of England 'doth read them for example of life and instruction of manners, but yet doth not apply them to establish any doctrine.'[1] To this the Catholic will reply, in the words of the 20th of the 39 Articles, that the 'Church hath authority in controversies of Faith,' and has decided, by the assistance of the Holy Ghost, that all these books are Divinely inspired, Canonical Scripture, and that, consequently, they may be employed, as well as any other portion of the Bible, 'to establish any doctrine.' Moreover, the Catholic will pass some observations on that article of the Church of England by which she declares that, 'In the name of the Holy Scripture, we do understand those canonical books of the Old and New Testament of whose authority was *never any doubt in the Church.*' Against this Protestant rule for determining what is and what is not sacred Scripture the Catholic will advance the following objections. He will observe, in the first place, that this rule is fallacious and erroneous. In the second place, he

---

[1] See the 6th of the 39 Articles.   [2] 6th of the 39 Articles.

will prove that the Church of England has, in a variety of instances, most notoriously abandoned the very rule which she so solemnly and formally insists upon. 1. That this rule is fallacious and erroneous is evident. The bloody persecutions inflicted on the Church during the first three centuries prevented free communication between her numerous and widely separated members, and thus rendered unavoidable doubts being entertained by a portion of the Church in Gaul or Spain, for instance, concerning an epistle of Scripture written in Greece or Asia, or any book of the Old Testament venerated as the word of God in the Churches there. It was only when peace had been given to the faithful that the pastors of the Church could congregate from every corner of the earth, and, gathering together in a general council, compare, with one another, the Gospel which they had preached to their respective flocks. Then, and not till then, were they able to investigate minutely step by step the tradition which handed down any controverted book as being Divinely inspired, and pronounce with certitude, under the guidance of the Holy Ghost, as to the value of such tradition. Hence it will appear that, though the book had been doubtful, and had not, in consequence, been inserted in the Scripture Canon, immediately such doubts had been removed by an authoritative decision, it could be securely enrolled amongst the sacred books, and without the slightest fear or hesitation be considered as the genuine and Divinely inspired word of God. We may well conceive that a variety of circumstances could have combined to prevent the apostolical tradition relating to any particular book from being widely or generally diffused. If those, therefore, who could not possibly know the reasons which established its inspiration should, through such ignorance, doubt as to its canonicity, it is impossible to imagine why such a doubt should, after it had been sufficiently dissipated, prevent the book from being recognised as Scripture. The book of the Apocalypse is an instance in point. The Council of Laodicea, held about the year 363, would not inscribe the Apocalypse in its Canon; but as soon as the tradition in its favour became more minutely ascertained, the third Council of Carthage, celebrated in 397, acknowledged it to be genuine Scripture. The Councils subsequently held at Rome, at Florence, and at Trent have reiterated the recognition; yet this book should, according to the principles laid down in the 6th Article of the Protestant Church of England, be unhesitatingly rejected, since doubts *have been entertained in the Church* concerning its canonicity. This rule, therefore, is fallacious and absurd.

2. The Church of England has, in various instances, most flagrantly violated this rule which she herself promulgated for determining what is the genuine word of God; for she has recognised as Scripture many entire books, and parts of others, whose genuineness has been long and seriously debated in the Church. The historian Eusebius,[1] S. Athanasius,[2] and S. Gregory Nazianzen [3] not merely express their doubts of such portions of the book of Esther which the Anglicans admit, but have cancelled the whole of that history from their catalogues. With regard to the New Testament, it is a fact of common notoriety that, of the epistles, the second of S. Peter's, a part of the first and all the second and third of S. John's, the whole of S. James's and of S. Jude's, the Epistle of S. Paul to the Hebrews, and the Apocalypse, together with the last chapter of S. Mark, the history of the bloody sweat in the twenty-second chapter of S. Luke, and the story of the woman taken in adultery, noticed in the eighth chapter of S. John, have been repeatedly doubted of in the Church; still, the Church of England admits every one of them to be Divinely inspired Scripture. With this well-authenticated fact before her eyes, she nevertheless asserts in her Articles that 'By Scripture is to be understood those canonical books of the Old and New Testament, of whose authority *was never any doubt in the Church.*' The truth is, in determining what should be accounted by her followers as Holy Scripture, the Protestant Church established in England consulted her own caprice, or rather the most expedient way of upholding her

---

[1] *Hist. Eccl.*, lib. IV, cap. 26.   [2] *Fest. Epist. XXXIX.*
[3] *Carm. XXXIII.*

novelties in doctrine, instead of either interrogating ecclesiastical history or appealing to the decisions of the early Church ; for she cannot direct us to one single ancient authority, much less point out one solitary Council, with which she agrees in every respect concerning her Canon of the Scriptures. The books which the Catholic Church at the present day admits are precisely those which were declared canonical by the third Council of Carthage fifteen hundred years ago.

OBJECTIONS ANSWERED.

Against the book of Tobias, which was quoted to establish the invocation of angels ; and against those of the Macchabees, the second of which is produced as an authority for praying for the dead ; and, indeed, against all the others of the Old Testament improperly called Apocrypha, Protestants advance the following objections :

1st. That they were not inserted in the Hebrew Canon. It is not ascertained at what precise period the Jewish Canon of Scripture was drawn up, though, by almost universal consent, Esdras is admitted to have been its author. That Esdras did not, could not, enumerate the books which Protestants consider as apocryphal is evident, since it is certain that some, and highly probable that all, of them were not written until after the death of that zealous Israelite. But, abstracting from this fact, undoubtedly the Apostles, delegated by Jesus Christ to teach all nations all truths, were invested with quite as much authority as Esdras and the Synagogue ; assuredly the Church of Christ exhibits many more titles to our confidence and possesses a higher claim to our obedience than the Church of Moses and the Jewish Councils. We may, therefore, justly remark with Origen : 'Though the Church of the Jews place those books among the Apocrypha, the Church of Christ teaches them and honours them as Divine.' Protestants affect to despise tradition, and yet they tenaciously adhere to the Jewish tradition concerning the Canon of Scripture, arranged by Esdras in such a way that the number of books should amount to twenty-two—the number of letters in the Jewish alphabet—and that each book should be designated by its numerical letter, as we gather from S. Jerome. Protestants admit tradition as a sufficient authority to determine what books are the Divinely inspired word of God; but though they suffer tradition to be the arbiter in deciding on a portion of their faith, a moment after they refuse to listen to this same tradition, when it declares that there are other books which are Divinely inspired. Catholics do not entangle themselves in such a difficulty. While they assert Divine tradition[1] to be imperative, they

---

[1] As tradition on the unwritten word of God constitutes one of the questions that are continually agitated between Catholics and Protestants, it will not be impertinent to the present subject if a passing view be taken of it.

The term 'Tradition' is employed to signify the word of God not written in the Canon of Scripture, though it may be read in the Canons of Councils and works of the holy fathers. The most ancient ecclesiastical writers made this distinction. S. Irenaeus (*Contra haereses*, lib. III, cap. 2, § 2) in the second century, while upbraiding certain heretics of those days, remarks that they agree neither with Scripture nor Tradition. Tertullian (*Lib. de corona militis*, cap. IV) observes: 'If you seek to find a law for this, you will find no Scripture, but tradition is the authority which presents itself to you;' and S. Cyprian says (*Epist. LXIII, Ad Caecilium de Sacramento Dominici Calicis*): 'You should know that we have been admonished how, in offering the chalice of the Lord, the tradition of the Lord is to be observed, so that the chalice which we offer in commemoration of Him should be offered mixed with wine;' that is, wine and water mingled should be used at the Eucharistic Sacrifice of the Mass. It would be easy though useless, to accumulate a thousand other testimonies.

Tradition is denominated the word of God, or a doctrine not written; not because it has never been committed to any kind of writing, but because it was not penned by its first author or promulgator. Infant baptism is an apposite example. The doctrine which allows the baptism of infants is called an apostolic tradition, and unwritten, because no vestige of it can be traced in any of the apostolic writings, although it is discernible in almost every book that claims one of the ancient fathers for its author.

Tradition is divided into Divine, apostolical, and ecclesiastical. Those are esteemed as Divine which have been received from the lips of Christ Himself while teaching His apostles, and are nowhere found recorded in the sacred pages. Of this description are those traditions which regard the matter and the form of the Seven Sacraments, as well as the septenary number of the sacraments themselves. On these points we read very

refuse to recognise in what is purely human any other power of demanding their assent than what belongs to it as such; but they listen with confident docility to Jesus Christ and His apostles, who, as they are convinced by the unvaried and unanimous declarations and the authoritative decisions of an infallible Church, delivered to them as the genuine word of God, those very books which Protestants denominate apocryphal.

---

little in the Scriptures, and yet it is certain that no one but Christ Himself could have either elevated a ceremony to the dignity of a sacrament or could have severally defined what should be the essence of each particular one of them. Hence the Apostle observes to the Corinthians (1 *Corinthians*, XI, 23): 'For I have received of the Lord that which also I delivered unto you.'

Apostolical traditions, accurately speaking, are those which were instituted by the Apostles; not, however, without the inspiration and especial assistance of the Holy Ghost, though, indeed, we do not find them mentioned in any of their epistles. Of this class are the fast of Lent, infant baptism, baptism by aspersion (for the genuine meaning of the word 'baptize' is to immerse or dip), the change in the observance of the Sabbath, the inspiration and canon of the Scriptures, etc., all of which we must attribute to the Apostles if we follow the rule laid down by S. Augustine (*De Baptismo contra Donatistas*, lib. IV, cap. 24): 'That which the Church observes, and what is not decreed by Councils, but always retained, is of apostolic origin.'

By a kind of interchange in language, it not unfrequently happens that Divine are called apostolical, and apostolical Divine traditions. Divine traditions are denominated apostolical, not because they deduce their origin from the Apostles, but because the Church became acquainted with and received such traditions, first of all, through them to whom they had been immediately delivered by Christ Himself; and apostolical traditions are termed Divine, not because ordained by them, but because the Apostles had been moved by the Holy Spirit to promulgate them. In this manner all the epistles of the Apostles are included under the denomination of Divine and apostolical writing. Though certain precepts and injunctions insisted on in these epistles are properly Divine, certain others are properly apostolical, as is evident from S. Paul (1 *Corinthians*, VII, 10): 'To them that are married, not I, but the Lord commandeth;' and just after (12): 'To the rest I speak, not the Lord.'

Ecclesiastical traditions are those ancient ordinances and usages which were originally introduced by the pastors of the Church or commenced amongst the people, and being gradually brought into universal practice, have acquired the authority of law, by the tacit approbation of the Christian world.

2nd. Protestants endeavour to elicit internal evidence against some of those books, and allege imaginary contradictions or the nature of some moral principles, which they erroneously suppose they have detected in them. Such was the precise line followed by the Manichæans. Those heretics objected that many portions of the Bible afforded unbecoming notions of the Deity, who was represented there as a corporeal being, subject to the same emotions of anger, jealousy, and revenge that agitate the bosom of created man. They also observed that the law, which in reality existed in nature anterior to the promulgation of the Decalogue by Moses, was disfigured by threats and temporal and earthly promises, highly unbecoming a God of love and a spiritual and celestial ruler. They animadverted on the scandalous conduct and the pernicious example which some amongst the patriarchs exhibited in their actions. They stigmatised the Jewish ceremonial prescribed in the Old Testament as gross and loaded with absurdity, and animadverted on one religious rite observed amongst the Hebrew nation as highly indecorous. That such exceptions of those heretics were nothing more than idle cavils is evident, and they have been as ably answered by Protestants themselves as by Catholic vindicators of the holy volume.

The same observations, however, which Protestants have corroborated, with so much force of language and weight of argument, in defence of the Scriptures, while refuting the obloquy of the heretic and infidel, may be rebutted with triple energy by the Catholic against those objections which the Protestant turns about and raises concerning those portions of the Bible which the Catholic receives as the Divinely inspired word of God, but which the English Establishment enumerates in her Canon as apocryphal. The Protestant would say to the Manichæan: 'If the Scriptures mention any moral turpitude, it is not to applaud, but merely to relate it as a fact of history.' The Catholic, in like manner, replies to the objection of the Protestant—who argues that the book of Macchabees cannot be inspired, since it seems to approve of self-destruction—that the inspired author of that book did not wish to laud the deed of Razias, who fell upon his sword, and then precipitated himself from the wall of his house, and afterwards tore out his own bowels, lest he should fall into the hands of the wicked and suffer abuses unbecoming his noble birth, but intended only to recount the fact as it happened, and to notice the opinion of those who were witnesses of this transaction, and considered, in their way of thinking, that this patriotic Israelite had conducted himself with manly courage and devoted heroism. In the second place, no objection against that portion of Scripture miscalled Apocrypha, as in this instance of the book of Macchabees, because it seems to countenance a violation of moral or religious conduct, can ever be put forward, except with the most glaring inconsistency, by Protestants; since, as they explicitly affirm in the 6th of their 39 Articles: 'The Church doth read them (the Apocrypha and the second book of Macchabees, among the rest) for example of life and instruction of manners.'

APPENDIX IV.

THE CATACOMBS.

THOSE subterranean chambers and corridors that are now usually denominated Catacombs, and in which the early Christians were accustomed to seek refuge in the times of persecution,[1] have been so repeatedly referred to in various parts of this work that it cannot be deemed out of place to offer some short notice of them, at least to such as take interest in the study of ecclesiastical antiquities.

To the Italian traveller, and to those especially who have examined the ruins of ancient Rome or visited the shores of Naples and its enchanting environs, the fame of the ancient

---

[1] There were twelve general persecutions of the Church.

cement, made from a ferruginous sand of volcanic production, called pozzolana, must be well known. Not only the site of Rome itself, but the whole circumjacent campagna abounds in pozzolana, and in a light, hard substance, called by the Italians 'tufo.' To procure these materials on the spot, or at the least possible distance, for the construction of their gigantic edifices, and, at the same time, not to break up and spoil the surface of the ground, but to reserve it for building or for ornamental cultivation, the Romans opened excavations in a way very much resembling our mode of working coal-mines in England. They sank shafts of some depth, whence they extracted the pozzolana and the tufo.[1] Many of these shafts still remain unclosed, and visible in various parts of the ground, in the more immediate neighbourhood of Rome; nor have they escaped the notice of ancient writers.[2] The ancients selected and exhausted the most copious strata of the sand, which they wrought in such a manner that the excavation, by the number of its wide and narrow galleries and passages which sometimes diverged from and at other times intersected one another, very much resembled a subterranean city with its streets and alleys, and still recalls to our remembrance what ancient authors have written, and modern travellers have verified, concerning the appearance of the Cretan and other classic labyrinths. That these subterranean corridors were commenced by the ancient Romans, and the greater part of them the work of that people, anterior to the preaching of the Gospel, is certain; though it is equally well attested that

---

[1] To us this may seem a difficult and tedious process for procuring stone and mortar; but it should be borne in mind that the Romans, by reason of the number of their slaves, could accomplish with despatch and facility many operations which, in a nation amongst whom slavery is not tolerated, would be beset with insurmountable difficulties and trouble.

[2] Prudentius notices them in the description which he gives of the entrance into the cemeteries:

Inde, ubi progressu facili nigrescere visa est
   nox obscura, loci per specus ambigium,
occurrunt celsis immensa foramina tectis,
   quae iaciunt claros antra super radios.

      Περὶ Στεφάνων *liber*, Hymnus XI, v. 159.

they were arranged, enlarged, and rendered available for the several purposes of sepulture, of religious worship, and of occasional residence by the persecuted Christians.

The term Catacomb, however, is their Christian, not their classic appellation. We find no traces of this name before the fourth century. At first it was applied merely to the subterranean tombs immediately about the basilica of S. Sebastian on the Appian Way; but as the other cemeteries became less frequented, with the exception of that the entrance to which was from this church, the name of Catacomb was gradually extended to all the cemeteries about Rome, and, eventually, to every similar excavation in other parts of Europe.[1] By pagan writers they are denominated *Arenariae cryptae*, or simply *Arenaria*. The notice which Cicero takes of the assassination of one Asinius in these Arenaria[2] not only establishes the fact of their having been excavated during the times of the Republic, but also of their being lonely and unfrequented places. It was to these dark recesses that Nero was recommended to fly for refuge when pursued by the soldiers of Galba, who sought his life. But, according to Suetonius, the emperor replied to his adviser Phaon, that, as long as he was alive, he would never go under ground.[3] By the early Christian writers they are called *Areae*, *Areae sepulturarum*, *Cryptae*, *Concilia martyrum*, and *Coemiteria*.[4]

---

[1] The word Catacomb is compounded of a Greek preposition and substantive—κατά and κύμβη. Κύμβη has the same signification as crypt or hollow; *Cata cumbas*, or *ad cumbas*, would therefore mean the same thing as 'at the crypts or subterranean tombs.'

[2] Asinius autem brevi illo tempore, quasi in hortulos iret, in Arenarias quasdam extra portam Esquilinam perductus, occiditur. CICERO, *Oratio pro Cluentio*, cap. 13.

[3] Ibi hortante eodem Phaonte, ut interim in specum egestae arenae concederet, negavit se vivum sub terram iturum. SUETONIUS, *Nero Claudius Cæsar*, cap. 48.

[4] Cemetery is derived from the Greek, and means a dormitory or sleeping-room. Such an appellation was appropriately given by the early Christians to their places of sepulture, in conformity with their belief in the resurrection of the flesh; whence they regarded the tomb but as a place of temporary sleep, from out of which the body would rise again. S. IOANNES CHRYSOSTOMUS, *Homilia de Coemeterio et de Cruce*.

No place could be better calculated to answer all the purposes of the primitive and persecuted Christians than these subterranean caverns. Here they might consign to the sepulchre the mortal remains of their brethren in the faith, without fear of commingling their dust with the ashes of their Gentile fellow-citizens. Here they might deposit with all possible respect the bodies of those amongst their venerated teachers and heroic brethren who had sealed their faith with martyrdom. Hither they could come, in compliance with the instructions of their apostolic teachers, to ask the prayers of those saints, as they knelt at the foot of the altars which were erected over their tombs, and on which the Holy Sacrifice was celebrated. Here, too, they promised themselves a grave, wherein their bones would repose, respectfully distant from the sepulchres of those martyrs, yet still within their neighbourhood, with the emblems of their belief in Jesus affixed over them, to arrest each brother in the faith and bid him pray a prayer for their departed soul. Here they could assemble on the Sunday to solemnise and partake of the holy Eucharistic sacrifice, in comparative security from the sudden intrusion of their persecutors, and unapprehensive of derision from the pagan scoffer. Here, in fine, they possessed a refuge in the day of fiery trial, and worshipped the one true God, in spirit and in truth, according to the dictates of their conscience.

It is a well-authenticated fact that the Catacombs served at the same time for three purposes : (1) as a place of sepulture for the martyrs and the rest of the faithful; (2) of assembly for the exercise of religion, and in particular for the celebration of Mass ; and (3) of refuge during the seasons of persecution.

In support of the first of these assertions, nothing can be clearer than that the Catacombs were appropriated, at some distant period or another, as a place of burial. This is demonstrated by a variety of proofs. It is incontrovertible that these Catacombs exhibit thousands of graves in which are discovered human bodies. It is equally certain that innumerable tombs, which have never been disturbed, still exist in these ancient cemeteries. Three questions now naturally present themselves for solution. 1st. To what division of the inhabitants of ancient Rome do these mortal remains that have been discovered belong—to the Christian or the Pagan portion of citizens, or to a mixture of both? 2nd. At what epoch did the Christians commence to inter their brethren, especially the martyrs, in the Catacombs? 3rd. If they must be assigned, exclusively, to the Christian part of the population, how can the grave of a martyr saint be distinguished from that of the other less holy and less heroic Christians who lie buried there?

In answer to the first of these queries, it may be replied that nothing can be more evident than that the remains of the dead discovered in the Roman Catacombs belong exclusively to the Christian citizens of ancient Rome. This is demonstrated by several arguments. In the first place, it is a well-established fact in the history of Roman manners, that as early as four centuries and a half previous to the Christian era the custom of burning the bodies of the dead prevailed at Rome;[1] and that the only exception to such a practice, which was in the Cornelian family, ceased at the death of its chief, the Dictator Sulla, who ordered his body to be burned—an example that was imitated by the rest of his tribe, who afterwards complied with the universal custom.[2] A long time, therefore, previous to the birth of our Divine Redeemer, and consequently many years before the preaching of the Gospel at Rome, the custom was established in that city of burning the bodies of the dead, rich and poor;[3] and it was not until the demise of Constantine, whose corpse, instead of being burned, in conformity with the practice which had hitherto been invariably

---

[1] There was an enactment to this effect in the laws of the twelve tables (CICERO, *de Leg.*, lib. II, 23), which were framed in the year 300 after the foundation of the city—that is, 450 years before the birth of our Redeemer.

[2] CICERO, *de Leg.*, lib. II, 22.

[3] That the remains of the poor were burned, as well as those of the rich, we collect from a variety of testimonies. The dramatic writer, Terence, has thrown the customs of his times and country into his plays. In one of

observed, was inhumed, that this custom commenced to be abandoned by the pagan subjects of the Roman empire. The exception of not burning, but burying, the bodies of infants who departed this life before they had cut their teeth,[1] and of those individuals who had been scathed by lightning,[2] proves the observance of the general rule of burning the bodies of all such dead as did not come within its limits. In the second place, it must be observed that the Christians, on the contrary, were very particular in following, on this point, the practice of the Jews, and, like them, invariably buried, and would on no account burn, the bodies of their deceased brethren. Their belief in the resurrection of the flesh, and the consequent idea that the bodies of the righteous after death were reposing, as it were, in a peaceful transitory slumber,[3] was one amongst other motives which influenced them to consign their brethren to the tomb.

---

these he introduces Chrysis in the character of a poor female, compelled by distress to abandon her country, and to relieve her misery by spinning wool.

> Parce, ac duriter
> agebat, lana ac tela victum quaeritans.
> *Andria*, Act I, Scene I.

After the death of this poverty-stricken female, he describes her being borne to the funeral pyre, and the burning of her corpse, in the following manner :

> Funus interim
> procedit : sequimur : ad sepulchrum venimus :
> in ignem posita est.   *Ibid.*

Martial observes that the corpses of the poorest people were burned ; but it was in heaps, and not singly, like those of more substantial citizens :

> Quatuor inscripti portabant vile cadaver,
> accipit infelix qualia mille rogus.
> MARTIALIS, *Epigrammatum* 75, lib. VIII.

[1] PLINY, VII, 15 ; JUVENAL, XV, 140. The place in which such children were interred was denominated 'Suggrundarium.' FULGENTIUS, *De Pres. Serm.* 7.

[2] PLINY, II, 55 ; SENECA, *De Ira*, III, 23. The spot was called 'Bidental,' because consecrated by a sacrifice of sheep. PERSIUS, II, 27.

[3] Hundreds of funeral inscriptions discovered on the graves of the martyrs in the cemeteries might be noticed. 'Dormit dulcis in Deo,' 'Requiescit in Deo dulcis,' 'In pace et in refrigerio,' 'In somno pacis,' are expressions which perpetually occur.

Such a wide departure from the universal practice did not fail to attract the notice and provoke the objurgations of the Gentiles; nor was it disavowed, but, on the contrary, unhesitatingly acknowledged and defended by Tertullian, Minucius Felix, and other Christian writers.[1]   From this historical fact, that the pagan Romans burned the bodies of their dead, poor as well as rich, while, on the contrary, Christians everywhere buried in graves the corpses of their brethren, and from this reciprocity of dislike to be entombed together, we gather that those remains of the dead which have been discovered in the Catacombs must belong, not to the Gentiles, but exclusively to true believers in the Gospel.[2]   Some Protestants have attempted, but in vain, to wrestle with this argument.[3]   They first endeavour to identify those pits which are called by the Latin classic authors *puticuli* with those subterranean corridors or cemeteries that we more generally denominate Catacombs, and hence insinuate that the bodies of the poorer classes of pagan Romans, which are recorded by ancient writers to have been thrown into these *puticuli*, are intermingled with the bodies of the ancient Christians.   The study of archæology has made, however, such advances that no one who has become but slightly acquainted with the Latin classics and the local antiquities of Rome will have the hardihood to advance such an objection at the present day.   *1st.* We know from the

---

[1] Et cremabitur ex disciplina castrensi Christianus, cui cremare non licuit, cui Christus merita ignis indulsit? TERTULLIANUS, *liber de Corona militis*, cap. XI. Minucius Felix, in his admirable dialogue, introduces the defender of paganism as alleging the following accusation against Christians: 'Inde videlicet et exsecrantur rogos, et damnant ignium sepulturas;' to which the champion of Christianity replies: 'Nec, ut creditis, ullum damnum sepulturae timemus, sed veterem et meliorem consuetudinem humandi frequentamus.' *Octavius*, cap. XI et XXXIV.

[2] How Eustace, with his knowledge of the Latin classics, could have for a moment conceived that such bodies as have been found in the Catacombs, without any inscription, mark, or indication of name or profession, may have belonged to pagans (*A Classical Tour through Italy,* vol. II, ch. 3, p. 106. *Leghorn*, 1817) is difficult to conceive. Had that gentleman lived to retouch his elegant and learned work on Italy, he would have, no doubt, corrected several inaccuracies and cancelled some passages which now deform it.

[3] BASNAGE, *L'Histoire de l'Eglise;* and BURNET, *Travels*, Letter IV.

united testimonies of two ancient writers, Varro[1] and Festus,[2] that these *puticuli* were situated outside the Esquiline gate; whereas everyone who is acquainted with the topography of Rome is aware that the cemeteries or Catacombs lie in every direction around that city. *2ndly*. From what has just been noticed, it is evident that the poorest plebeian's body was burned before his ashes were cast into these *puticuli*. *3rdly*. Granting that the bodies of some slaves were borne at night and thrown without the Esquiline gate, it is certain that to this particular place, and to no other, such bodies were brought, and that they were cast there in such a manner that beasts and birds of prey could come and feed upon them;[3] whereas the bodies of Christians are found everywhere in the Catacombs, and discovered arranged in their separate niches, in great regularity and with the most respectful care. *4thly*. The greatest horror and repugnance against having their remains commingled were felt with mutual intensity by Christian and by Gentile. The latter considered that the greatest punishment which the gods, in their wrath, could inflict upon him was to entomb him with one who was of a different country or religion; and the true believer regarded the neighbourhood of a pagan's ashes to his grave as a profanation.[4] Hence they reciprocally endeavoured to secure for themselves a separate place of burial.

In this respect, moreover, the Christians of Rome were as exclusive and as studious to avoid all communication with the Jews as they showed themselves in reference to the Gentiles. It is a fact that up to the present period neither Hebrew name nor inscription, nor anything exhibiting the slightest traces of the Hebrew style of character, has been discovered in the Christian cemeteries.[5] The Jews of ancient Rome, who

---

[1] Lib. IV.   [2] Under the word Puticuli.

[3] HORATIUS, *Epod. lib.*, Ode 5, v. 97–102.

[4] One of the serious accusations urged by S. Cyprian, A.D. 258, against Martial was, that he had been guilty of profanation, by entombing his children in a Gentile burial-place. 'Filios,' says that celebrated martyr, 'exterorum gentium more, apud profana sepulchra depositos et alienigenis consepultos.' *Epist.* LXVIII.

[5] BOLDETTI, *Osservazioni sopra i Cimiteri de' Santi Martiri*, pp. 330, 474.

inhabited and had their synagogues in that part of the city which lies beyond the Tiber, possessed a burial-place of their own near that region, out of the gate which is now called 'Porta Portese.' This Jewish cemetery was discovered by Bosio, who found in it various tombs with inscriptions. On one of these was sculptured the seven-branched candlestick, and another of them, written in Greek, displayed the word CYNAΓΩΓ, Synagogue.

II. We have now to ascertain the period at which the Christians commenced to use these subterranean galleries as a place of sepulture.

That the Catacombs had been employed as a burial-place for the martyrs and the faithful in general long before the fourth century is evident from the accidental notice which S. Jerome takes of the cemeteries, as he informs us that while he was at Rome pursuing his studies in elegant literature it was his custom to go about on Sundays with those of his own youthful age and occupation from one cemetery to another, visiting the tombs of the Apostles and martyrs in their dark corridors, the walls of both sides of which exhibited to him the tombs of the dead arranged one above the other.[2]

The inscriptions which have been discovered in these cemeteries will also furnish data to resolve the question. Many of them not only establish the fact that these Catacombs were used as burial-places for the martyrs during the several persecutions endured by the Church, but determine the precise epoch when the martyrs' remains were deposited there.

---

[1] ARINGHI, *Roma Subterranea*, vol. I, p. 396.

[2] Dum essem Romae puer, et liberalibus studiis erudirer, solebam cum caeteris eiusdem aetatis et propositi, diebus Dominicis sepulcra Apostolorum et Martyrum circuire ; crebroque cryptas ingredi, quae in terrarum profunda defossae, ex utraque parte ingredientium per parietes habent corpora sepultorum, et ita obscura sunt omnia, ut propemodum illud propheticum compleatur : Descendant ad infernum viventes ; et raro desuper lumen admissum horrorem temperet tenebrarum, ut non tam fenestram, quam foramen demissi luminis putes : rursumque pedetentim acceditur, et caeca nocte circumdatis, illud Vergilianum proponitur : Horror ubique animos, simul ipsa silentia terrent. S. HIERONYMUS, *Comment. in Ezechielem*, lib. XII, cap. 40.

PRIMITIVVS IN PACE QVI POST MVLTAS ANGVSTIAS

FORTISSIMVS MARTIR ✗ VIXIT ANNIS P. M.

XXXVIII. CONIVG. SVO PERDVLCISSIMO

BENEMERENTI FECIT.[1]

PECORI DVLCIS ANIMA BENIT IN CIMITERO VII IDVS

IVL. D. P. POSTERA DIE MARTVORV.[2]

IIIC RECONDITVM EST CORPVS ALMI LEVITAE ET MAR-

TYRIS CYRIACI A MATRONA LVCINA RECONDITVM.[3]

RVFFINVS ET CHRISTI MARTYRES

C. L. MARTYRES CHRISTI.[4]

Several of the inscriptions which have been discovered affixed to the sepulchral niches pierced in the walls of the cemeteries, and containing the body of the Christian champion, with the vial of blood placed at his head, are highly valuable. One of them informs us of the burial of the martyred soldier Marius, during the reign of the emperor Hadrian:[5]

TEMPORE ADRIANI IMPERATORIS MARIVS ADO-

LESCENS DVX MILITVM QVI SATIS VIXIT DVM

VITAM PRO CH̄O CVM SANGVINE CONSVNSIT

IN PACE TANDEM QVIEVIT BENEMERENTES CVM

LACRIMIS ET METV POSVERVNT. I. D. VI.[6]

---

[1] This inscription was found in 1643 in the Ostrian cemetery, which is on the Salarian Way. The Ostorian family, a member of which gave name to this branch of the Catacombs, was one of the most illustrious in Rome, and is frequently mentioned by Tacitus and Tertullian. Tradition points out these subterranean chambers as one of the places to which S. Peter resorted for the purpose of administering baptism to the converted Gentiles. See BOLDETTI, *Osservazioni*, p. 56, who gives this inscription, and A. MAI, *Scriptorum veterum nova Collectio*, tom. v, p. 400.

[2] From the cemetery of SS. Processus and Martinianus, on the Aurelian Way. MAI, *Script. vet. nova Collectio*, tom. v, p. 396.

[3] From the cemetery of Cyriaca.—MAI, *Ibid.*, p. 373.

[4] From the cemetery of S. Ermetes. BOLDETTI, p. 233.

[5] A.D. 117.

[6] This inscription was found in the cemetery of S. Ermetes. BOLDETTI, *Osservazioni*, p. 233; MAI, *Script. vet. nova Collectio*, p. 391.

Another refers to the consulship of Surra and Senecio, which took place in the year 107 :

N XXX SVRRA ET SENEC. COSS.[1]

and a third dates from the time of Vespasian,[2] that is, not forty years after the Crucifixion.

VCVESPASIANO IĪI COS IAN.[3]

To somewhere about this epoch may be referred another valuable inscription on which is recorded the ingratitude of Vespasian towards an architect who had rendered his reign illustrious by the erection of a theatre, but was afterwards put to death by order of that emperor on account of his belief in Christianity.[4]

SIC PREMÌA SERVAS VESPASÌANE DÌRE PREMÌATVS ES MORTE GAVDENTÌLETARE
CÌVITAS VBÌ GLORÌE TVE AVTORÌ PROMÌSÌT ÌSTE DAT KRÌSTVS OMNÌA TÌBÌ
QVÌ ALÌVM PARAVÌT TEATRV̄ ÌN CELO

These inscriptions completely overthrow the gratuitous insinuation, or rather calumny, of Burnet, who pretends to doubt whether, previous to the fourth and fifth centuries,

---

[1] This inscription was scratched in the mortar which overspread the mouth of the niche. BOLDETTI, p. 79.

[2] A.D. 69.

[3] This inscription is incrusted in the wall of the first corridor in the Vatican Museum, where it was placed by Marini.

[4] A distinguished writer in ecclesiastical antiquities, Marangoni, who was one of the literary ornaments of Rome at the commencement of the eighteenth century, conjectures, from the context of this inscription, that the theatre here made mention of is no other than the stupendous Colosseum, the architect of which was Gaudentius, who, having contributed to the glory of the capital of the world by the erection of that gigantic, though certainly not correct nor elegant, edifice, was rewarded with the martyr's crown by Vespasian. The train of reasoning and the arguments by which Marangoni labours to fortify his supposition, if they do not amount to demonstration, are at least strongly presumptive, and by no means to be despised. See G. MARANGONI, *Delle Memorie sacre e profane dell' Anfiteatro Flavio.*

This inscription was discovered in the cemetery of S. Agnes outside the walls, and is at present affixed to the walls of the subterranean oratory under the Church of S. Martina, in the Roman Forum.

Of the stroke-like accents in the place of dots over the letter I, it should

the Catacombs were employed as a burial place by the Christians.[1]

Precisely the same customs respecting the choice of sub-terranean chambers, distinct from the sepulchres of their unbelieving fellow-citizens, and the mode of depositing their dead in niches pierced in the sides of these caverns one above another, were, as far as circumstances would permit, exactly imitated by the rest of the faithful scattered through the cities of the Roman empire. At Nepi, a town in the neighbourhood of Rome, was discovered in 1540 a natural grotto which had been converted into a cemetery or catacomb, for the burial of the first inhabitants of that place who embraced the Gospel. The graves were excavated in the walls, which were of tufa, precisely as they are in the Roman cemeteries, and amounted to the number of nearly six hundred, amongst which thirty-eight were ascertained to be the tombs of as many martyrs, over one of whom was placed the following inscription :

MARCVLVS CIVIS NEPESINVS HAC DIE XXII.
IVLII MARTYRIO CORONATVS CAPITE TRVNCATVS
IACET QVEM EGO SAVINILLA IESV CHRISTI ANCIL-
LA PROPRIIS MANIBVS SEPELIVI.[2]

III. It is now time for us to pass on to the third question for solution, and ascertain how the saints' and martyrs' tombs may be distinguished from the graves of the less perfect and less heroic crowd of Christians who people these subterranean cities of the dead.

That the multitude of those heroic believers who yielded their life-blood to sign their belief in the doctrines of Jesus was almost innumerable is authenticated by a variety of testimonies. S. John the Evangelist, who lived through the

---

be observed that such a method of writing began to appear in the inscriptions of the time of Augustus, and continued in use up to the era of the Antonini, when they ceased to be employed. G. MARINI, *Atti e Monumenti de Fratelli Arvali*, p. 760.

[1] BURNET, *Travels*, Letter IV, p. 170.

[2] BOLDETTI, p. 580 ; MAI, p. 390.

persecutions raised by Nero and Domitian, would seem to bear witness to the tides of blood that had already been poured out by the disciples of his Divine Master, as he symbolises pagan Rome under the figure of a 'woman drunk with the blood of the saints, and with the blood of the martyrs of Jesus.'[1] Many years after, when the Church had smarted under additional sufferings, S. Cyprian (A.D. 248), after applauding the exuberance of courage and constancy in faith exhibited by the Christians, proclaims that the number of those who had suffered martyrdom for the faith was incalculable.[2] The multitude of these is also attested by the Roman cemeteries, in which whole galleries are often found with niches, occupied with bodies, crowded close to one another, and the passage itself filled up with the earth that was extracted from a new branch excavated to afford additional room for the martyred Christians brought in every night for sepulture. Nor are there wanting inscriptions to certify this fact. Sometimes the number of the saints entombed within is indicated merely by numeral figures surrounded by palm-branches and wreaths, the emblems of victory and martyrdom, scratched in haste upon the upright tiles and mortar on the mouths of these passages; at other times an inscription tells the fact.

XL. L. FAB. CIL. M. ANN. LIB. COS.[3]

XV. IN. P.

A A[4]

☧   TIGRINA   ☧

XXXX[5]

---

[1] *Apocalypse*, XVII, 6.

[2] Exuberante copia virtutis ac fidei, numerari non possunt martyres Christiani. *Lib. de Exhortatione Martyrii*, cap XI.

[3] This inscription was found traced on the mortar of the tomb in the cemetery of Priscilla on the Salarian Way. Fabius Cilus and Annius Libo were consuls, A.D. 204.

[4] BOLDETTI, *Osservazioni sopra i Cimiteri de' Santi Martiri*, p. 436.

[5] *Ibid.*, p. 435.

MARCELLA ET CHRISTI MARTYRES
CCCCCL.[1]

RVFFINVS ET CHRISTI MARTYRES
CL. MARTYRES CHRISTI [2]

LOC. MA. C. CL. VIII. INC.[3]

The poet Prudentius, born in 348, who visited the Roman cemeteries or Catacombs, has noted this circumstance in some verses that will furnish an appropriate illustration of the above inscriptions :—

Innumeros cineres sanctorum Romula in urbe
    vidimus, O Christi Valeriane sacer.
Incisos tumulis titulos, et singula quaeris
    nomina ? difficile est ut replicare queam.
Tantos iustorum populos furor impius hausit,
    quam coleret patrios Troia Roma deos.
Plurima litterulis signata sepulchra loquuntur
    martyris aut nomen, aut epigramma aliquod.
Sunt et muta tamen tacitas claudentia tumbas
    marmora, quae solum significant numerum.
Quanta virum iaceant congestis corpora acervis, ʼ
    nosse licet, quorum nomina nulla legas ?
Sexaginta illic, defossas mole sub una,
    relliquias memini me didicisse hominum ;
quorum solus habet comperta vocabula Christus,
    utpote quos propriae iunxit amicitiae.[4]

The surest sign by which a martyr's grave may be identified is the attestation of martyrdom by the inscription. This, however, was not always practicable in the hurry and the apprehension in which those were involved who were the objects of a violent persecution. Nor was it possible to ascertain the names of many of the individuals. To supply, therefore, the place of a regular inscription, a palm-branch or

---

[1] BOLDETTI, *Osservazioni sopra i Cimiteri de' Santi Martiri*, p. 233.
[2] *Ibid.*, p. 233.
[3] BOTTARI, *Sculture e Pitture*, tom. II, p. 173.
[4] Περὶ Στεφάνων *liber*, Hymnus XI, v. 1-16.

a laurel crown was rudely scratched or drawn in red letters on the outside of the sepulchre, and inside was deposited, near the head of the deceased, a vase, containing such portion of his blood as it had been possible to collect with sponges or handkerchiefs,[1] together with the instrument of punishment, had it been procured, or a linen cloth tinged with blood.[2] When such unequivocal proofs of martyrdom are wanting, though the inscription on the tomb may announce the Christian belief of the dead within, and though the palm-branch, or the crown, or garland may grace it, still the remains are not to be accounted as the relics of a saint, but only the mortal spoils of some early Christian.[3]

Not only did the Catacombs serve as cemeteries for the dead, but they were very often converted into a temporary

---

[1] See what has been noticed on this point at p. 8 of this vol.

[2] Many instruments which had been used by the public executioner to inflict death upon the martyrs, and which are now in the various museums of Rome, were discovered along with the bodies of the martyrs in their graves. Some of these instruments may be seen in the engraving at p. 8. Amongst them, not the least interesting are certain large orbicular polished blocks of black marble, which served as weights, and were attached to the neck, the hands, and the feet of the martyr who had been condemned to suffer death by drowning—a sentence which, it is well known, was passed and executed upon very many Christians.

> Summo pontis ab ardui
> sanctae plebis episcopus
> in praeceps fluvio datur,
> suspensum laqueo gerens
> ingentis lapidem molae.
> PRUDENTIUS, Περὶ Στεφάνων liber, Hymnus VII, v. 21.

Of the number of such martyrs we find Simplicius and Faustinus, who were precipitated into the Tiber, as appears from the inscription on the marble sarcophagus in which their bodies, at their burial in the cemetery of Generosa, were deposited :

> MARTYRES SIMPLICIVS ET FAVSTINVS
> QVI PASSI SVNT IN FLVMEN TIBERE ET POSI-
> -TI SVNT IN CIMITERIVM GENEROSES SVPER
> FILIPPI.

This inscription is given in ARINGHI, tom. I, p. 365, and MAI, Scriptorum veterum nova Collectio, tom. V, p. 405.

[3] SCACCHIUS, De Notis et Signis Sanctitatis, Sect. IX, cap. 2.

residence by the living, who retired thither from the storm of persecution whenever prudence suggested that a retreat from public notice would calm the fury of the tempest.

The saints of the new emulated the edifying constancy in faith and imitated the example exhibited by those of the old Law. Like them, 'they were racked, not accepting deliverance, that they might find a better resurrection;' 'they were stoned, they were cut asunder, they were tempted, they were put to death by the sword.' Like them, they sometimes retired, not through fear, but prudence, and 'wandered in deserts, in mountains, and in dens, and in caves of the earth.'[1]

Amongst those who retired from the sword of the persecutor may be enumerated several Roman pontiffs. S. Alexander,[2] with a crowd of his faithful flock, retreated to the Catacombs;[3] S. Urban sought and experienced a temporary concealment amongst the holy martyrs' sepulchres.[4] Of S. Stephen,[5] the first Roman pontiff of that name, it is also recorded that he went about the crypts of the martyrs celebrating Mass and holding meetings there.[6] That this Pope passed many of his days in the retirement of the Catacombs is evident from the records of his life. Hence it was that he used to despatch the companions of his retreat, the learned priest Eusebius and the deacon Marcellus, to exhort or invite to a personal conference those amongst the faithful who might particularly need his pastoral solicitude. Here it was that he used to assemble his clergy in religious conference and collect the neophytes, to instruct and afterwards baptize

---

[1] *Hebrews*, XI, 35, 37, 38.

[2] A.D. 122.

[3] Nec praeterimus in eorumdem Martyrum Actis notatum haberi, Romanum Pontificem, qui his temporibus praeerat Dei Ecclesiae, una cum multis in Catacumbis, persecutionis causa, latuisse. BARONIUS, *Annales*, tom. II, p. 106.

[4] Cum secundo esset confessor, latebat in sanctorum martyrum monumentis. *Acta S. Caecil.*, quoted by Bosio.

[5] A.D. 259.

[6] Beatus vero Stephanus repletus gratia Spiritus Sancti per cryptas Martyrum, Missas et concilia celebrabat. BARONIUS, *Annales*, tom. III, p. 72.

them. It was while in these subterranean caverns that the zealous pontiff had recourse to the ingenious expedient by which he converted and baptized not only the two interesting Gentile children, brother and sister, who were in the habit of coming secretly to bring food to their Christian uncle, Hippolytus, in his concealment in the Catacombs, but their unbelieving parents also.[1]

To strike terror into the minds of the Christians, Pope Xystus II. was put to death, on the plea that by going to the Catacombs he had been guilty of violating the edict promulgated by the emperor Valerian, who had, in an imperial rescript, prohibited the Christians from going to the cemeteries.[2]

---

[1] BARONIUS, tom. III, p. 69. Hippolytus, a Christian of Rome, had sought refuge in the Catacombs. His sister Paulina, and her husband Adrias, both pagans, were entrusted with the secret of his retreat, and humanely supplied him with the requisites of life by means of their two only children, a boy of ten and a girl of thirteen years of age, who were in the habit of stealing to their Christian uncle's hiding-place with a basket of provisions. Hippolytus often sorrowed within himself over the melancholy reflection that these lovely children and their generous and amiable parents were living on enveloped in the darkness of idolatry, and sighed for some propitious opportunity for procuring their minds to be irradiated with the light of the Gospel. S. Stephen was residing in the same quarter of the Catacombs. Hippolytus sought the venerable pontiff, and consulted with him on the subject of his painful solicitude. The advice of the sacred pastor was, that he should detain his little niece and nephew at their next visit, in the hope that the parents, on perceiving that they did not return home as usual, would hasten to the uncle in the Catacombs to seek and enquire for their children, when the opportunity of discoursing with them might be seized. Hippolytus admired and adopted the suggestion. The children came as usual, and were easily persuaded to remain. Both the parents, at the expiration of the ordinary interval, became alarmed, and hurried to the cemetery, where they found their beloved son and daughter with S. Stephen, who used all his persuasive eloquence to make them converts to the Christian faith. They retired unbelievers; but the seed was sown. They returned again, at the instance of the pontiff, and after a series of events and due instruction they and their children were baptized; and all four, as well as S. Stephen and Hippolytus, were honoured with the crown of martyrdom and buried in the Catacombs.

[2] Cum autem priori Valeriani edicto vetiti Christiani essent ingredi coemeteria; Sixtum, ceu legis transgressorem, eodem in coemeterio, ub

The annals of ecclesiastical history prove that not merely the reigning Pope and his clergy, but also multitudes of the faithful took up their abode in the cemeteries, and the incident to which a reference was just now made may be cited as an illustration of the fact. Hippolytus was not the only layman who inhabited the Catacombs, for we learn that those relatives of his, Adrias and Paulina, with their two children, whose conversion from paganism he had been so instrumental in achieving, after distributing their riches to the poor, deserted their house and came to fix their abode there along with Hippolytus.[1]

The affectionate commiseration felt by friends and relatives, and those, too, who still continued to be the followers of paganism,[2] and the charitable compassion for the brethren of the faith which animated the more wealthy, and sometimes secret, Christians, supplied the suffering inmates of these sepulchral recesses and voluntary prisons with necessary food and raiment; and the piety of those who were particularly pre-eminent in exercising such a work of mercy has been especially recorded.[3] Facilities for the performance of such charitable offices were furnished by the nature and construction of the Catacombs, which did not merely branch out in different directions beneath the gardens and the vineyards beyond the walls of Rome, but ran under several parts of the city itself. It required no great skill and very little trouble to pierce from a vault beneath a house in the interior of the capital an entrance into these subterranean passages; and the shafts[4] which descended into them, the mouths

---

visus esset in legem peccasse capite truncandum, Praefectus, ad absterrendos caeteros a coemeteriorum latebris, consulto praecepit. BARONIUS, *Annales*, tom. III, p. 93.

[1] BARONIUS, tom. III, p. 70.

[2] As was exemplified in the case of Hippolytus.

[3] Palmatius is one amongst those who have been enumerated as benefactors of the Christians who lay concealed in the Catacombs. 'Coepit Palmatius omnem facultatem suam pauperibus Christianis erogare, et perquirere cryptas si inveniret absconditos Christianos quibus de facultatibus suis victum vel tegumentum ministrabat.' *Ex. Cod. M.S. Basil. Fontis Olei Romae.*   [4] See p. 365.

of which are still discernible in many parts of the Campagna more immediately round Rome, presented a mode of easy communication for the conveyance of food and every other requisite to those who were living in them.[1] On some occasions, however, neither the darkness, nor the horror, nor the labyrinthian windings of the Catacombs could furnish an asylum secure from the molestations of the infuriated persecutors of the Christian name. This is established by the monuments and the historical facts which belong to that melancholy period. It is noticed in a very beautiful and feeling manner in the following inscription :

ALEXANDER MORTVVS NON EST SED VIVIT SVPER
ASTRA ET CORPVS IN HOC TVMVLO QVIESCIT
VITAM EXPLEVIT CVM ANTONINO IMP. QVI
VBI MVLTVM BENEFICII ANTEVENIRE PREVIDERET
PRO GRATIA ODIVM REDDIT GENVA ENIM FLE
CTENS VERO DEO SACRIFICATVRVS AD SVPPLICIA
DVCITVR. O TEMPORA INFAVSTA QVIBVS INTER
SACRA ET VOTA NE IN CAVERNIS QVIDEM SAL
VARI POSSIMVS. QVID MISERIVS VITA SED QVID
MISERIVS IN MORTE CVM AB AMICIS ET PAREN
TIBVS SEPELIRI NEQVEANT TANDEM IN CAELO
CORVSCAT. PARVM VIXIT QVI VIXIT IV. X. . . . TEM.[2]

And it was while celebrating Mass that Pope S. Stephen was discovered in the cemeteries and surrounded by a band of soldiers, who permitted him to conclude the Holy Sacrifice, when they thrust him into his pontifical chair and beheaded him.[2]

The reader has been already made acquainted with some of the many proofs which might be deduced to certify the fact that the Catacombs were resorted to by the faithful for the purposes of religious worship.

---

[1] During the author's residence in Rome an entrance into the Catacombs was discovered in a garden out of the Porta Portese. The descent into it was by a narrow flight of steps.

[2] This valuable inscription, which belongs to the time of Antoninus Pius, who commenced his reign in 138, was discovered in the cemetery of Callistus, and may be seen in ARINGHI, *Roma Sott.*, lib. I, cap. 22 ; BOLDETTI, p. 232 ; and MAI, *Script. vet. nova Collectio*, tom. V, p. 361.

[3] BARONIUS, *Annales*, tom. III, p. 76.

As was before observed, it is particularly recorded of S. Stephen that he used to offer up the Holy Sacrifice in different parts of the cemeteries.[1] It was there, too, that the same venerable pontiff frequently administered the sacrament of Baptism to crowds of neophytes.[2] It was in coming out of one of these secret oratories, where he had received and was carrying away with him the Blessed Eucharist, that the acolyte Tharsicius was apprehended, and put to death upon the spot by the soldiery for refusing to discover to them the precious treasure that had been entrusted to his custody.[3]

The cemetery of Ostrianus, on the Salarian Way, was, from the most remote period, held in particular veneration on account of being that part of the Catacombs more frequently resorted to by S. Peter for the purpose of administering baptism.[4] Such, in reality, was the assiduity of the faithful in attending to the offices of religion, which were celebrated in these subterranean chambers, that it very soon attracted the attention of the Heathen, who reviled them for being a people who avoided the light and loved hiding-places,[5] and constituted the subject of a legal enactment against them in the reign of Valerian,[6] who promulgated a decree prohibiting the Christians from visiting the Catacombs, with the denunciation of death to everyone who should be detected violating the imperial mandate.[7] But if these and other written testimonies were wanting, the deficiency would be more than amply supplied, in corroboration of this historical fact, by the

---

[1] See p. 379.

[2] BARONIUS, *Annales*, tom. III, pp. 69, 72.

[3] See vol. I, p. 264, note 2. Surely, had Tharcisius believed the Eucharist to be nothing more than a piece of bread, he would have shown the Blessed Sacrament to the soldiers, and have saved his life.

[4] BOLDETTI, p. 40.

[5] This is one of the many accusations alleged by the pagan Cœcilius, in Minucius Felix (A.D. 210), against the Christians of Rome, whom he calls : 'Latebrosa et lucifugax natio.' MINUCIUS FELIX, *Octavius*, cap. VIII.

[6] A.D. 253.

[7] Proconsul dixit : Iussum est (de Christianis scilicet) ut nulla conciliabula faciant, neque coemeteria ingrediantur ; quod qui facere comprehensus fuerit, capite plectatur. BARONIUS, *Annales*, tom. III, p. 79.

many monuments which still exist in the Catacombs, where we may, at the present moment, behold the oratories, with their frescoed walls and ceilings, the altars, and the baptisteries, erected by the first professors of our holy faith.

Independently of the religious veneration with which they must be contemplated by every fervent Christian, the Catacombs will be regarded with especial interest by the ecclesiastical antiquary, who discovers in their inscriptions, their sculptures, and their paintings numerous and powerful auxiliaries to aid him in the prosecution of his studies. Of these venerable monuments the paintings are not the least important, as they constitute an epoch in the history of the fine arts amongst the ancients, and also serve to illustrate the religious customs and belief of the early Christians. It may, therefore, be worth while to ascertain, as near as possible, the era to which they properly belong.

Prudentius, who was born A.D. 348, during a visit which he paid to Rome, inspected the Catacombs, and has left us a description of the altars and the oratories which he found in the subterranean city. From his hymn in honour of S. Hippolytus, it would seem that the poet's attention was arrested by the painting which adorned the crypto-chapel in which the martyr's body was deposited.[1] The testimony of Prudentius proves the existence of pictures in the cemeteries of Rome at the close of the fourth century; we have evidence that ascends up to a much earlier period.

That many of these paintings were executed prior at least to the era of the last persecution, which was raised by Diocletian, is certain; for the circumstance that the walls in several chapels have been pierced with niches to receive the bodies of the martyrs, notwithstanding the injury thus inflicted on the paintings which already adorned them, proves the fact. Moreover, the paintings of the Roman Catacombs bear internal evidence of their own antiquity, which demonstrates them to have been, in many instances, the production of artists who lived in the second century of the Christian era. This opinion comes recommended to us by one of the most learned critical

---

[1] The description is quoted at length in a note on p. 11 of this volume.

and competent judges who have ever investigated this depart-
ment of the fine arts, accompanied by a weight of arguments
and of deductions which is irresistible. Seroux d'Agincourt,
by his love for the study of antiquities, was attracted to Rome,
where he purposed to pass only one winter. He was, however,
induced to spend the remainder of his life, a space of thirty
years, within the walls of that city. During this lengthened
period he visited, he meditated on, he read of all its monuments, profane as well as sacred. He descended into the
Catacombs, which he thoroughly explored and excavated in
various directions, and procured plans of their oratories and
copies of their paintings to be taken by able artists. He made
occasional visits to all the interesting cities of Italy; but
Rome was the centre of his work, for here it was that he
could leisurely look down the many vistas of antiquity, some
of which passed through a space of more than two thousand
years, and sketch accurate views and institute correct com-
parisons between the most prominent objects in architecture,
sculpture, and mosaic-work that appeared at various ages in
Pagan and in Christian Rome, in illustration of his 'History
of the Arts, from their Decline up to the Sixteenth Century,'
a work which engrossed the undivided attention of its author
during the better portion of a long and studious life. It
cannot, therefore, be denied that, if anyone be competent to
deliver an authoritative opinion on this question, it must be
such a judge as he, who had so entirely and so leisurely investigated, and was so intimately conversant with this subject.
Now, he unhesitatingly pronounces many of these paintings
to be the productions of the second century; some he conceived to have been executed in the first. He had the paintings of Pompeii, which was overwhelmed by the eruption of
Vesuvius, A.D. 79; the paintings in the Baths of Titus, A.D.
80; the paintings in the tomb of the Nasoni family, erected
and ornamented in the second century; and various fresco-
paintings of the time of Constantine. After diligently comparing the cemeterial chapels in the Catacombs with the
sepulchral chamber at the tomb of the Nasoni, and discovering in both a perfect identity of manner in distributing the

departments and arranging the necessary ornaments, and a close correspondence in the style of drawing the human figure, united with a remarkable similarity in treating their respective subjects, as far as the mythological nature of the pagan sepulchre and the scriptural one of the Christian cemeteries could admit, he pronounced many of the latter to be coëval with the former, and in consequence the production of the second century. A few, he is of opinion, belong to the era of the first persecution,[1] A.D. 56. The testimony of our own illustrious Flaxman on any subject connected with the arts is highly valuable. His opinion on the paintings of the Catacombs corroborates the judgement of Seroux d'Agincourt.[2]

Not only the Christians of Rome, but also those of Jerusalem, were careful to ornament their burial-places in crypts and Catacombs with paintings of religious subjects. Dr. Clarke tells us that near the holy city there is a place still shown as Aceldama, or the field of blood, which was purchased by the chief priest for the burial-place of strangers, and now belongs to the Armenians. It is still, as it ever was, a place of sepulture, and its appearance maintains the truth of the tradition which points it out as the Aceldama of Scripture. In it there are many sepulchres excavated in the side of the mountain. In some of these sepulchres were ancient paintings executed after the manner of those found upon the walls of Herculaneum and Pompeii, except that the figures were those of the Apostles, the Blessed Virgin, etc., with circular lines, as symbols of glory, round their heads. These paintings appeared upon the sides and upon the roof of each sepulchral

---

[1] SEROUX D'AGINCOURT, *Histoire de l'Art*, tom. IV, pp. 62, 63, 69, 70; tom. VI, pp. 12, 13, 14, 15, and pl. V, VI.

[2] See Flaxman's observations upon them at p. 151 of this volume. On some occasions it is difficult to determine whether to smile at or compassionate the dogmatic presumption of some authors whose flippancy is only commensurate with their profound ignorance of a greater part of the subject on which they are occupied, and whose horror is so great for anything which tends, though in an indirect manner, to prove the antiquity of the belief and practices of their ancestors, which they have the politeness to nickname Popery. Some of those writers, with a magnanimous contempt of all authority, have insisted that the paintings in the Roman Catacombs are the works of the monks during the Middle Ages!!!

chamber, preserving a wonderful freshness of colour, although much injured by Arabs and Turks, whose endeavours to deface them were visibly displayed in many instances. 'The sepulchres themselves are, from these documents, evidently of Christian origin,' observes this traveller, who sneers at and calumniates the Catholic religion whenever he lights upon an opportunity; and, after having asked the question of the antiquity of these interesting memorials, and attempted its solution, admits that, if his conjectures be true, 'these paintings may be considered as exhibiting specimens of the art belonging to the second century.'[1]

The Christian who feels a pious interest in beholding the spot in which his holy religion was cradled in her infancy in Europe will find his devotion amply repaid by a visit to the Roman Catacombs. In these subterranean recesses he will tread the very ground that was hallowed by the footsteps of the Apostles and their immediate successors; he will stand within the walls that, eighteen centuries ago, echoed back the heart-stirring eloquence of a Peter and a Paul, of a Xystus and a Stephen, and the sighs and sobs and protestations uttered by hundreds of their faithful audience, that they would allow the Gentile to thrust his hand upon their hearts and wring the very life-blood from them rather than deny Christ Jesus. He will view the ground that was bedewed with the tears of a crowd of recently converted Gentiles prostrate at the feet of the Prince of the Apostles, by whom they were about to be guided to the regenerating waters of baptism. He will behold the plain and modest altar around which multitudes of primitive believers used to kneel while the Apostle, or some succeeding pontiff, alone stood up, pre-eminent and venerable, bending over it as he offered up the holy Eucharistic Sacrifice, and he will in fancy hear the echo of the fervent prayers and hymns and Alleluias here poured forth, like the song of the three children in the fiery furnace, by many a confessor of Christ. In these cemeterial oratories, frequented by the primitive Christians, he will, in fine, not only observe the prototypes of those splendid edifices that

---

[1] CLARKE, *Travels.* London, 1817, vol. IV, pp. 343, 345, 347

arose in the fourth and succeeding ages, but he will detect in them documents that proclaim the similarity of discipline and identity of doctrine which by a unity of faith incorporate the Catholics of the nineteenth century with the Apostles and their disciples and immediate successors in one spiritual body. The altar, by its very form and name, demonstrates that the Sacrifice of the Mass was a portion of the creed delivered to the world by the Apostles. The tomb of the martyr, which was used as the sacred table; the care with which his mangled body, each drop of blood, the vial that contained it, the linen on which it had been sprinkled, the instrument of his torture and death, were carefully collected and deposited apart, with the emblems of victory inscribed upon the sepulchre, prove the respect which was exhibited to relics by the primitive Christians. The funeral tile or marble slab, ceiling up the mouth of the sepulchre, and inscribed with a request to a departed servant of Heaven for his prayers, speaks a contradiction to the asseverations of those who pretend that the invocation of saints is a novelty, a thing unknown to the first believers; while the petition for peace and refreshment to the soul of him who sleeps within, so feelingly expressed and traced over the tomb by the piety of surviving friends and relations, immediately attests the ancient existence of the belief in a middle state, where the soul of the faithful, though not perfectly spotless, Christian might be suffering some temporary punishment, and could experience the efficacy of supplications put up from earth in its behalf. Moreover, he will conclude that if the earliest professors of the faith, all glowing as they were with primitive fervour, could derive assistance from the aid of pictures, to fix their wandering thoughts or enkindle their devotion when present in the house of God, by looking on the representations of holy subjects depicted on their walls, the same auxiliaries may be as innocently employed, and will produce the same desirable results, in the nineteenth as in the first century.

INDEX.

ABLUTION, spiritual meaning of, i. 114; how performed, 115.

Ablutions, the, i. 54.

Acolytes, i. 72; form of ordination, 73; their offices, 73, 98; how anciently employed, 145; those of Constantinople forbidden to ask fees for their torches at funerals, ii. 191.

Address, modes of, to God and angels or saints, i. 81.

Adoration of the Blessed Sacrament, i. 154.

Agnus Dei, the, i. 49.

Alb, the, ii. 214; its form and colour, 215; its various names amongst the Oriental Christians, 216; figurative meaning of, 217.

Alleluia, meaning of, i. 95.

Altar, the, kissing of, i. 82, 86, 126; bowing down before, 86; prayer recited while incensing, 112; use of, in the Old and New Testaments, ii. 290; from the times of the Apostles to the present day, 292; derivation of the term, 293; in what sense the Christians had none, 298; noticed in all the liturgies, 299; of what material and in what form constructed, 300; isolated in ancient churches, 302; an appropriate form of, suggested, 302; placed to look towards the east, 305; the dedication of, 308;

anointed, 310; saints' relics enclosed in the altar-stone, 313; covered with linen cloths, 314; ornaments of: ciborium or canopy, 316; veils, 320; cross, 322; candlesticks, 322; chalices, 322; flowers, 324; the respect paid to, 326; respect of the Ethiopian Christians for, 327; asylum, 328; idea of, associated with the doctrine of sacrifice, 329.

Altar-cloths, ii. 314; mandates of the Catholic archbishops of Canterbury regarding, 316.

Altar-pieces, modern, derived from the diptychs, ii. 287.

Altar-screens, in Greek and Oriental churches, i. 294, 295.

Altar-stone, the, saints' relics enclosed in, ii. 313.

Altar-veils, i. 295; ii. 320.

Alternation in chanting Psalms and hymns, i. 74.

Amen, derivation and meaning of the word, i. 92.

Amenti, the Egyptian middle state of souls, ii. 50.

Amice, the, ii. 212; its form, 213; figurative meaning of, 213; why so called, 214.

Ἀμφίθυρα. *See* ALTAR-VEILS.

Angelic hymn, the, i. 84.

Angels and saints. *See* INVOCATION.

Anglo-Saxons, Latin used in their

THE END.

BALLANTYNE PRESS
PRINTED BY BALLANTYNE, HANSON AND CO.
EDINBURGH AND LONDON

Printed in the United States
955500003B